MW01001944

"A work of a mature thinker, this boo̶[...]
It is a comprehensive theological re̶s̶[...]
evil exists even assuming the omnipotent and omnibenevolent God of Christian faith, and is all the more compelling given its biblical, philosophical and scientifically informed tapestry—no mean feat! The faithful across all Christian traditions will be encouraged to live a life of love even as skeptics will be invited to think again and again."

Amos Yong, professor of theology and mission, Fuller Theological Seminary

"Can I believe in the providence of God without making God responsible for evil? Open and relational theology answers yes, combining biblical and philosophical resources. Here Thomas Oord, the leading open and relational theologian, makes a powerful case for miracles and the providential care of the self-emptying God. His remarkably clear book offers readers a compelling theodicy and a welcome gift to personal faith."

Philip Clayton, author, *The Predicament of Belief*

"A much-discussed option on the contemporary theological scene is so-called open theology. Working within the framework of open theology, and with some truly horrendous examples of evil constantly in mind, Thomas Oord develops a fresh and original doctrine of providence, the central thesis of which is that it belongs to God's nature to offer to creatures non-controlling, other-empowering love. Anyone who subsequently writes about providence will have to engage Oord's cogently argued and lucidly presented account."

Nicholas Wolterstorff, Noah Porter Professor Emeritus of Philosophical Theology, Yale University, senior research fellow, Institute for Advanced Studies in Culture, University of Virginia

"Can we reconcile a biblical understanding of divine love and creativity with the universe of human experience and scientific understanding? Not a new question, of course, but one that requires fresh faith and intellectual subtlety. Tom Oord's new book offers both. And it is written with a clarity and passion that should appeal to a wide range readers."

John F. Haught, distinguished research professor, Georgetown University, author of *Resting on the Future*

"This is a scholarly and readable book arguing that God is essentially a God of self-giving love, and that this provides a way of seeing how evil can exist in a world created by God. It is an important theological work, and continues Oord's project of constructing a fully Christian 'open and relational' theology."

Keith Ward, FBA, Regius Professor Emeritus of Divinity, University of Oxford

"Written in his characteristically winsome style, Oord's account of *The Uncontrolling Love of God* is a highly accessible yet richly sophisticated affirmation of God's providential engagement with creation that takes seriously the insistence on randomness and novelty in recent science. Oord sprinkles throughout pastorally wise advice on how Christians might think about and engage the undeniable evil and ugliness in life by probing the implications of our fundamental commitment to the self-emptying love of God as manifest in Jesus Christ. Highly recommended!"

Randy L. Maddox, Duke Divinity School

The
Uncontrolling
Love *of* God

AN OPEN AND RELATIONAL
ACCOUNT OF PROVIDENCE

THOMAS JAY OORD

IVP Academic
An imprint of InterVarsity Press
Downers Grove, Illinois

InterVarsity Press
P.O. Box 1400, Downers Grove, IL 60515-1426
ivpress.com
email@ivpress.com

InterVarsity Press® is the book-publishing division of InterVarsity Christian Fellowship/USA®, a movement of students and faculty active on campus at hundreds of universities, colleges and schools of nursing in the United States of America, and a member movement of the International Fellowship of Evangelical Students. For information about local and regional activities, visit intervarsity.org.

Scripture quotations, unless otherwise noted, are from the New Revised Standard Version of the Bible, copyright 1989 by the Division of Christian Education of the National Council of the Churches of Christ in the USA. Used by permission. All rights reserved.

While any stories in this book are true, some names and identifying information may have been changed to protect the privacy of individuals.

Cover design: Cindy Kiple
Interior design: Beth McGill
Images: lightning over city: © jerbarber/iStockphoto
*   blue sky/white clouds: © janniwet/iStockphoto*

ISBN 978-0-8308-4084-7 (print)
ISBN 978-0-8308-9901-2 (digital)

Printed in the United States of America ∞

Library of Congress Cataloging-in-Publication Data
Oord, Thomas Jay, author.
The uncontrolling love of God : an open and relational account of providence / Thomas Jay Oord.
*   pages cm*
Includes bibliographical references and index.
ISBN 978-0-8308-4084-7 (print : alk. paper) -- ISBN 978-0-8308-9901-2 (digital)
1. Providence and government of God--Christianity.   I. Title.
BT135.O57 2015
231'.5--dc23

2015033924

P	24	23	22	21	20	19	18	17	16	15	14	13	12	11	10	9	8	7	6	5	4
Y	35	34	33	32	31	30	29	28	27	26	25	24	23	22	21	20	19	18			

For my daughter, Alexa:

a Christian, a scholar,

a leader

and so much more

Contents

Acknowledgments

An eclectic set of ideas is present in this book. Many of these ideas emerged from conversations with good and wise people, some of whom I list below. Having written or edited more than twenty books, I know authors never succeed alone. It takes a proverbial village to make a book, even when one person does the writing.

In addition to the people I will mention, two experiences undoubtedly influenced me as I wrote this book. The first involved frequent hiking excursions into the wilderness and open country of Idaho, Oregon, Wyoming and California. A few weeklong treks, some weekend excursions, and numerous daylong or afternoon walks helped me decompress, meditate, focus and pray. Often I photographed the beauty of the natural world on these walks. I'm grateful to my wife, daughters, friends and others who not only allowed me to take these walks but also encouraged me to take them.

The second exercise involved negotiating pain in my professorial life. I endured difficult days as I laid out the ideas in this book. Through that trying time, I felt strongly supported by university colleagues, scholars around the world, former students, pastors and leaders, friends from many arenas of life, and especially family. I am sure this trying experience shaped and deepened my views of providence, especially my view that God guides us on a lively adventure and calls us to live lives of love.

As a multidisciplinary scholar, I work with a wide range of research.

I read widely and engage scholars from various fields. I also contribute to these conversations through publications of scholarship in theology, philosophy and science. Much of what I write portrays my creative synthesis of scholarship in various disciplines. Integrating this material and offering it in understandable language is an art and ministry I strive to practice. As the book progresses to the middle and final chapters, more of my original ideas emerge. In fact, I offer numerous original ideas in the book because I think we need creative originality to better understand God's providence.

As I came to the end of my writing, I realized that this book fits nicely alongside two others I have written in the last five years. In *Defining Love: A Philosophical, Scientific, and Theological Investigation*, I addressed love from philosophical and scientific perspectives. As the title suggests, I offer a definition of love in light of various disciplines and visions of reality. Much of *Defining Love* explores love's forms and expressions in the social, biological and cosmological sciences. Only in the final chapter do I address theology and, briefly, essential kenosis.

In *The Nature of Love: A Theology*, my focus is mostly on theological issues pertaining to love, although biblical and philosophical themes emerge too. After talking about the need to place love at the center of formal theology and after defining love, I explore the biblically informed theology of Anders Nygren, the philosophically informed theology of Augustine, and the open theology of Clark Pinnock. In the final chapter, I make an argument for essential kenosis starting with Christology. I conclude by presenting essential kenosis in relation to other doctrinal issues.

Philosophy, science, Scripture and theology come together in the present book in a more balanced way. This allows me to address issues of providence—especially evil and randomness—in a sustained manner. I also develop and explain essential kenosis more fully than I have previously. My overall goal is to make sense of randomness and evil in light of my conviction that a loving and powerful God exists and acts providentially.

As I said earlier, I am a firm believer that books emerge out of relationships, communities and networks. Although I cannot mention all who have influenced my writing, I do want to acknowledge some.

The book project was supported by a grant from the Randomness and Divine Providence project, directed by Jim Bradley and funded by the John Templeton Foundation. I especially thank Jim for believing in the importance of exploring the kinds of questions I address.

Several organizations, groups and societies have shaped my thinking, and I mention them alphabetically in appreciation: BioLogos Foundation, Christian Theological Research Fellowship, the University of Edinburgh (especially David Fergusson), the Faraday Institute for Science and Religion, the Ian Ramsey Centre for Science and Religion (especially the Special Divine Action conference), the International Society for Science and Religion, Nazarene Theological College—Manchester, the Open and Relational Theologies group of the American Academy of Religion, the School of Theology and Christian Ministries at Northwest Nazarene University, the Wesleyan Philosophical Society, the Wesleyan Theological Society, WesleyNexus and Word Made Fresh.

I thank Burton Webb, Mark Maddix and Paula Kellerer for granting me a sabbatical at Northwest Nazarene University. During that time, I wrote a large portion of this book. Students in my graduate theological online-education classes at Northwest Nazarene University offered their evaluations; these students included Anita AlbertWatson, David Allen, Michelle Borbe, Sarah Brubaker, Amy Byerley, Barry Carney, Nicholas Carpenter, James Cendrowski, Joe Crosby, Sarah Dupray, Buford Edwards, Rodney Ellis, Thomas Evans, Cezarina Glendening, Jennifer Glover, Anthony Kayser, Angela Lerena, Aneel Mall, Rosanne McMath, Aaron Mednansky, Philip Michaels, Francis Mwansa, Jason Newman, Christopher Nikkel, Leslie Oden, Michael O'Neill, Raquel Pereira, Donald Smith, Topher Taylor, Brad Thompson, Jonathan Thompson, Brian Troxell, Margaret Tyler, Tara West and Cassandra Wynn.

Many people read portions of the book and offered encouragement, correction or critique. Others influenced my thinking through conversation. I especially thank Craig Adams, Jay Akkerman, Dik Allan, Paul Allen, Denis Alexander, Ben Arbour, Ken Archer, J. J. Asson, Vaughn Baker, Wes Baldassare, Jeremy Bangs, Joseph Bankard, Ian Barbour, John Bechtold, Keith Besherse, Craig A. Boyd, Gregory Boyd, David Brown, Rachel Bryant, Anna Case-Winters, Charles Christian, Jeff Clarke, Philip Clayton, John Cobb, Ron Cole-Turner, Monica Coleman, Robin Collins, C. S. Cowles, John Culp, Scott Daniels, Celia Deane-Drummond, Hans Deventer, Brent Dirks, Chris Donato, Craig Drurey, Ben Duarte, Ray Dunning, Bo Eberle, George Ellis, Bruce Epperly, Michael Faber, Darrel Falk, David Fergusson, Terry Fretheim, Rob Fringer, Tripp Fuller, Karl Giberson, Jim Goetz, Joe Gorman, Nathan Greeley, David Griffin, Erik Groeneveld, Joe Groessl, Doug Hardy, Mark Harris, William Hasker, Jack Haught, Todd Holden, John Daniel Holloway, Curtis Holtzen, Nancy Howell, Jeremy Hugus, Jacob Hunt, Bob Hunter, Randy Isaac, Werner Jeanrond, Tyler John, Kurt Johnson, David Larson, Jacob Lett, Michael Lodahl, Kevin Lowery, Bob Luhn, Butch Karns, Catherine Keller, Jeffery Keuss, Megan Krebs, Diane Leclerc, Frank Macchia, Mark Maddix, Randy Maddox, Eric Manchester, Dave Mann, Mark Mann, Dan Martin, Steve McCormick, Jay McDaniel, Alister McGrath, Chad Meister, Marty Michelson, Bev Mitchell, Paul Montague, Brint Montgomery, Maynard Moore, T. C. Moore, Aaron Moschitto, Rocky Munoz, Les Muray, Tom Nees, Tim O'Connor, Roger Olson, Bryan Overbaugh, Alan Padgett, Dong-Sik Park, Larry Parsons, Brent Peterson, Tom Phillips, Andrew Pinsent, John Polkinghorne, Stephen Post, Rob Prince, Jon Privett, Cliff Purcell, Eleanor Puttock, David Rainey, Joshua Rasmussen, Josh Reichard, Caleb Reynolds, Alan Rhoda, Richard Rice, Stephen Riley, John Sanders, Jeff Schloss, Andrew Schwartz, Lea Schweitz, Tony Scialdone, Graeme Sharrock, LeRon Shults, Ignacio Silva, Chad Simmons, Russ Slater, Bethany Sollereder, Rob Staples, Eric Stark, Jim Stump, Libby Tedder-Hugus, Sam Tenizo, Richard Thompson, Don Thorsen, Kevin Timpe, Ekaputra Tupamahu, Eric Vail, Keith Ward, Dale Wayman, Burton

Webb, Jordan Wessling, Kurt Willems, Mark Wilson, Karen Winslow, Mark Winslow, Celia Wolff, Nick Wolterstorff, Joseph Wood, David Woodruff and Amos Yong.

My wife, Cheryl, and my daughters, Sydnee, Alexa and Andee, and son-in-law, Logan, have in their own ways influenced me positively. I thank each of them, especially my wife.

I dedicate this book to Alexa, my daughter and a Harvard philosophy student. As my assistant during the summer of 2014, she read chapters as a preliminary editor, ran down references and quotes, did substantive research, made helpful suggestions, and played a significant role in making this book as good as it could be. She is a budding scholar with a bright future.

Thanks, Lexi!

1

Tragedy Needs Explanation

We all want to make sense of life.

Most of the time, we ask immediate questions to make sense of what's happening in our world: Why did she look at me that way? Why is it cold? Why can't my team win a championship? Why do I feel hungry? Why can't I relax? Why do I see so many advertisements?

Most of us ask big questions of life too. These questions and their answers are at the heart of the world's religions, the impetus for scientific endeavors and the domain of philosophy. Theology, science and philosophy explore both the minutiae and the big picture to make sense of reality. Big questions and our attempts to answer them are a big deal.

Those who believe in God—and I am a believer—typically think fully adequate answers to big questions include God. Science, philosophy, humanities, arts or other disciplines contribute to our quest to answer life's questions. Everyday experiences matter too. Comprehensive answers draw from all these domains.

Reflection on God—theology—should not be the trump card in efforts to understand reality. Phrases like "God only knows" or "it must be God's will" sometimes end conversations rather than shed light on how things might work or how things are. Theology doesn't have all of the answers.

But if God's presence and influence have the far-reaching effects most believers think, theology cannot be set aside during discussions of existence. It must be included. In fact, theology should play a central role when seeking adequate answers to the most important questions of life.

And what an amazing life it is!

Existence abounds in feelings, facts, information, values, action, desires and unanswered questions. We experience love, joy and happiness, along with evil, pain and sadness. We act purposefully and intentionally. We also encounter randomness, chance and luck—good and bad. We seem to act freely. But circumstances, our bodies and the environment limit what we freely do. We decide, feel, relate and ponder.

In one moment, goodness and beauty delight us. In the next, we cringe in response to horror and ugliness. At times we're happy, and at other times we're not. Most of the time our lives consist of the mundane, usual and routine. And on it goes. We live.

Making sense of life—in light of such diversity—is a daunting endeavor. But we inevitably take up the task. In more or less sophisticated ways, we try to figure out how things work and what makes sense. We are all metaphysicians, in this sense, because metaphysics seeks the fundamental explanations of reality.

This book explores the big picture with a special emphasis upon explaining randomness and evil in light of God's providence. By *providence,* I mean the ways God acts to promote our well-being and the well-being of the whole.

In this exploration, I will not ignore purpose, beauty, goodness and love. But the positive aspects of life are fairly easy to reconcile with belief in God. Randomness and evil are far more challenging. Unfortunately, some believers dismiss the challenging aspects of life as inconsequential or unreal. By contrast, I think we must take seriously these aspects, so seriously that many believers will need to rethink their views of God. We may need deconstruction so reconstruction can occur.

By the end of this book, I will offer answers to some of the most significant questions of life. I take seriously randomness and purpose, evil and good, freedom and necessity, love and hate—and God. I'll be offering a novel proposal for overcoming obstacles that have traditionally prevented believers from finding satisfactory solutions to the big problems of life. My solutions may even prompt unbelievers to reconsider their belief that God does not exist.

For millennia, many people have asked, "If a loving and powerful God exists, why doesn't this God prevent genuinely evil events?" Thanks especially to recent developments in philosophy and science, a related question has also gained prominence: "How can a loving and powerful God be providential if random and chance events occur?"

In this book, I propose answers to both questions. At the heart of these answers is a particular understanding of God's power and love. Theology, science, philosophy and Scripture inform this understanding. When appealing to these sources, I aim to account for the cruel and unpredictable realities of life, in their wide-ranging diversity. But I also account for purpose, freedom and love. I draw upon research in various disciplines to proffer a model of divine providence that I find both credible and livable.

To get at the heart of my proposals, it seems appropriate to begin with accounts of real life situations involving randomness and evil.

It's Utter Pandemonium

On April 15, 2013, Mark Wolfe finished the Boston Marathon. Not long thereafter, Wolfe witnessed the massive destruction of terrorist-devised bomb blasts near the finish line. "It's utter pandemonium," he said, describing the chaos. "Everybody's just in disbelief and sadness."[1]

While Wolfe and others observed the devastation firsthand, people around the nation and world turned to the media for details of the tragedy. The explosions caused more than chaos and damage to nearby structures. At least 250 bystanders and runners were injured. Fourteen required amputations. Three died.

---

[1]M. Alex Johnson, "'Pandemonium': Witness Accounts of the Boston Marathon Bombing," *NBC Nightly News*, April 15, 2013, http://usnews.nbcnews.com/_news/2013/04/15/17765308-pande monium-witness-accounts-of-the-boston-marathon-bombing?lite.

The stories of the injured, maimed and deceased captured hearts around the world. Reports of heroic helpers at the bombing scene soon emerged. Police officers, firefighters, nurses, physicians and ordinary citizens were good Samaritans in a time of dire need. While the public lauded the helpers, grief and shock prevailed. Making sense of things proved difficult.

A few days later, FBI agents identified Dzhokhar and Tamerlan Tsarnaev as the disaster's masterminds. The brothers placed nails, ball bearings and other metals in pressure cookers and detonated the homemade explosives with remote devices. After police had found the two, a chase ensued and authorities killed one. Authorities eventually captured the second, and he admitted to their crime. Religious beliefs motivated them, Mr. Tsarnaev said. This calamity seemed another in a long list of evils perpetrated in the name of God, Allah or some other religious ultimate.

The Boston Marathon bombing is not unique of course. Terror-motivated bombings occur throughout the world, although in the United States they occur less frequently. Some blasts are more deadly and more damaging. Any terrorist bombing—no matter where it occurs—is one too many.

Believers in God explain events like the Boston Marathon bombing in various ways. Writing as a guest columnist in the *Orlando Sentinel*, Josh Castleman affirmed his belief in God despite the Boston horror. "I realize that many people will see this tragic event as evidence against God's existence," wrote Castleman in the newspaper. "But the reality is that in order for thousands of people to feel relief and joy, some had to feel unspeakable pain and heartache."

Castleman concluded his piece with a rhetorical question: "Where was God during the bombing?" He answers: "I think he was right in front of us, and he was hoping we wouldn't just focus on the brief moment of evil, but instead, recognize him in the hours and days that followed."[2]

[2]Josh Castleman, "Where Was God During the Boston Marathon Bombings?," *Orlando Sentinel*, April 21, 2013, http://articles.orlandosentinel.com/2013-04-21/news/os-ed-god-boston-bombings-042113-20130419_1_god-tragedy-animal-instincts.

Some believers make sense of life by saying we need evil to appreciate the goodness of God and that God consoles those who suffer. Castleman seems to think evil is necessary for this purpose when he says that "in order for . . . people to feel relief and joy, some had to feel unspeakable pain and heartache." Without evil, we would not know good, says this argument. To know firsthand the God of all consolation, we need reasons to be consoled.

We must go through hell to appreciate heaven.

The belief that God is present with those who suffer is increasingly common. "God suffers with us," many say. God experienced pain and death in the crucifixion of Jesus Christ, say Christians, and as a Fellow Sufferer, God now suffers with those in the throes of pain. In the midst of our greatest difficulty, God is present and empathetic. Many believers say they worship a suffering God. But must we endure evil to appreciate good? And can we best account for evil by saying God is present to and suffers with victims?

Most believers think God can do anything. God could control people or situations and stop any evil event, they say. If this is true, God must voluntarily allow evil just to suffer alongside victims. God permits evil in order to feel our agony. God could stop such evil, says this view, but God allows it so that we can feel supported in the midst of our pain.

Does this view make God a masochist? And do we want to emulate masochists? Do *we* always allow loved ones to suffer so we can suffer with them? Do we think it more loving to suffer with others than to prevent evil, if we were able, in the first place?

I think we should doubt that evil is a prerequisite for good, especially the vast amount of evil in our world. The amount of evil far outweighs whatever we might need to appreciate good. Besides, most Christians believe in an afterlife of eternal bliss. If we follow the logic of "good requires evil," heaven must include pain and evil so saints can appreciate the heavenly hereafter. Not only does this way of thinking make evil necessary, but it causes one to wonder if the saints could experience perfect bliss knowing that evil makes their bliss possible.

Presumably, the Tsarnaev brothers used their free will to construct and detonate the Boston bombs. Yet their victims were apparently random: runners and bystanders just happened to be where bombs exploded. The brothers freely wreaked deadly havoc, yet their victims unknowingly came near the blast.

This may prompt believers to ask different questions: Was the Boston Marathon bombing part of God's providence? Although the victims seemed random, did God pick them to be injured or killed as part of a divine master plan? Are free will and randomness ultimately unreal because they actually manifest God's all-controlling hand?

Should we say evil is required, God-intended or even God-allowed?

IT'S AN ACT OF GOD

It was a typical fall day, on a typical Canadian road, with a typical Calgary family. The clan had vacationed in British Columbia, and they were driving south of Fairmont Hot Springs. A news report describes what happened around noon. "The family was in a northbound Subaru Legacy and was approaching a southbound semi with an unloaded low-bed trailer," reads the report. "A rock measuring 30 by 13 centimetres crashed through the front windshield and hit the mother of two in the head, killing her."

In an instant, a stone penetrated a windshield. It crushed a woman's skull and killed her without warning. A life ended tragically.

Investigators of the accident stopped the semi driver whose trailer pitched the rock. After analyzing the truck, its tires, the victim's car and the accident scene, investigators determined the stone must have been lodged between the trailer's dual tires. It shot out from the tires, smashed through the car's windshield and killed the victim.

Those investigating said the truck driver was not blameworthy. "'There's no intent on the driver to stick a rock between his tires and launch it in the air,' said Cpl. Tom Brannigan. 'It's an act of God.'"[3] An act of God?

---

[3]Stephane Massinon, "Police Call Highway Accident That Killed Calgary Woman 'an Act of God,'" *Calgary Herald,* October 8, 2012, www.calgaryherald.com/Police+call+highway+accident+that +killed+Calgary+woman+with+video/7363376/story.html.

This accident is not the first time, of course, that an unintended event caused death and destruction. It's not the first time an unexplained accident has been called "an act of God." We're more likely to hear the phrase "act of God" to describe hurricanes, tornadoes or floods. But perhaps this woman's death is also a natural disaster: an unplanned event with dreadful consequences.

Many believers recoil in disgust when God gets blamed for accidents, tragedies and natural disasters. Yet many also think that God totally controls life, or at least that God controls the natural world and its inanimate objects. These people must think such events—including rocks kicked up by semitrailer wheels—are part of God's providence. After all, they say, an omnipotent God could stop those accidents. Therefore, God must permit them. Yet, for many others, God's causing or permitting evil conflicts with their belief that God loves perfectly.

Can we believe that random events or events resulting from chance or luck do occur in the world—especially those with negative consequences—and also believe in divine providence? If God has a plan, how does randomness figure in? Is this a divine blueprint, in which all details are predetermined or foreknown? If God can control people and nature, why recoil in disapproval when some people say the accidents of life are acts of God?

It Was Just Meant to Be

Hank Lerner and his wife gave birth to their second daughter six weeks early. An emergency C-section brought Eliana Tova—a name meaning, "God answered with good"—into the world. Even before doctors delivered Eliana Tova, they knew she'd need heart surgery. And at two days old the tiny infant underwent a major procedure to address her life-threatening condition. This was not how her parents imagined life would begin for their child!

A month later, Eliana Tova's kidneys began to shut down. Her health deteriorated. Hank and his wife were faced with a decision, as he puts it, "either to put her on dialysis for the next two years or so in the hopes of getting her to the point where they can do a transplant, or just let her go quietly." Sometimes death is preferable to the grim struggle for life.

When Hank and his wife met their rabbi, the cleric asked, "Are you angry with God?" Hank certainly was! "Every time I heard someone say something like 'it's all part of His plan,' or 'it was just meant to be,'" he said, "I growled a little bit inside."

Further tests revealed that little Eliana Tova had a rare condition diagnosed only 250 times in the last fifty years. By the time Hank blogged about Eliana Tova's condition later that year, she had undergone five operations. More surgeries would be required, in addition to hospital visits for related health problems. Her life, were she to survive, was destined for enormous adversity.

"I'm more than a little peeved that my child's life depends on hooking her to machines 12 hours a day, every day, until she can grow large enough for a transplant," Hank said. This doesn't include infections and possible health complications Eliana Tova will likely endure as she moves through life. There's plenty to infuriate Hank!

"At the end of the day," says Hank, "it doesn't matter whether I'm angry at God. What matters is that we—Mom, Dad, and Big Sister—stop thinking about the past and worrying about the future so we can concentrate on kicking down doors and moving Eliana forward just a little bit every day."[4]

Eliana Tova, of course, is not the only infant born with debilitating conditions, disease, defective body parts or severe deformities. Millions of infants are so burdened annually. Some survive but endure a lifetime of surgeries and suffering. Others survive for a short time before succumbing to whatever ails them. Still others are stillborn, not capable of living beyond the womb.

Parents with severely debilitated children encounter the "rationalizations" given Hank: "it was meant to be" or "it's God's plan." Other

---

[4]Hank Lerner, "Getting Angry with God over My Daughter's Rare Disease," *Kveller* (blog), October 28, 2013, www.kveller.com/blog/parenting/getting-angry-with-god-over-my-daughters-rare-disease/.

parents stop believing in God, or at least stop believing that God makes any difference. They become practical atheists. Along the way, many people rely more on sheer determination than on any reassurance that God providentially directs their lives. "God doesn't seem to be helping," they say. "So we'll have to work this out ourselves."

If it's to be, it's up to me.

When children with severe debilities like Eliana Tova are born—or, for that matter, when anyone suffers from diseases caused by random genetic or prenatal malfunctions—we wonder if perhaps God mis-dialed the controls. If God is responsible for the dialing, are health problems divinely allotted? Are genetic and physical mutations truly random, or are they divinely planned?

While some believers give up believing that God makes any dif-ference, others turn their anger toward God. In fact, a number of biblical passages report the laments of ancient believers venting their ire. Expressing anger can prove cathartic. But as natural as anger may be, one wonders if God deserves blame when evils occur. Is it really God's fault? Is God culpable?

Some say God should *not* be the object of our anger—in the sense of being blamed for causing or allowing evil. God only does what is good. But if we should not blame God when things go badly, should we praise God when things go well?

Does God have a hands-off approach to our lives?

I Don't Know If My Heart Will Ever Heal

Zamuda Sikujuwa pushed apart her thighs in grimaced pain, demon-strating, in a lewd-looking gesture, what they'd done. Militiamen shoved an automatic rifle inside her body during the rape.

Associated Press reporter Michelle Faul wrote of Zamuda's story from Doshu, Congo. "The brutish act tore apart her insides after seven of the men had taken turns raping her," Faul reported. "She lost consciousness and wishes now her life also had ended on that day."

The story is horrific. Rebels from a Tutsi tribe came to Zamuda's village demanding money. When her husband had nothing to give, they put a gun to his head and pulled the trigger. Her two children cried at their father's murder, so rebels shot them too. Then they attacked Zamuda, raping her and leaving her for dead.

After two operations, Zamuda still has difficulty walking. "It's hard, hard, hard," she says. "I'm alone in this world. My body is partly mended. But I don't know if my heart will ever heal. . . . I want this violence to stop."[5]

Genocide and rape both have extensive and harrowing histories on planet earth. In nearly every society, a frighteningly high percentage of women are raped. In some cultures, raped women constitute the majority. Sexual assault has a ghastly history.

Some believers think God allows evil to test us and through testing build our characters. According to them, God could prevent pain and suffering but allows it so we might grow. God most wants to strengthen our souls, says this explanation of evil.[6] And permitting suffering is God's way of leading us toward moral maturity.

What doesn't kill you makes you stronger.

Is this true? Are Zamuda and hundreds of millions of raped women better off because of their ordeals? Are they stronger? Do they now have better character? Is the world, overall, a better place? Does an omnipotent God allow every evil—including rape and genocide—as part of some elaborate plan to toughen us up?

Of course we sometimes must endure suffering for some greater good. We sometimes allow children to endure hardship to build their characters, for instance. But does God cause or allow *every* evil, whether intended or random, to make us better? If so, how is that working for Zamuda's husband and children? Is the "lesson" they learned in death worth the evil they suffered? Can dead people mature?

---

[5]Michelle Faul, "Congo Women Fight Back, Speak About Rape," Associated Press, NBCNews, March 16, 2009, www.nbcnews.com/id/29719277/ns/world_news-africa/#.UvVm11CpUfU.

[6]The most influential form of this argument in contemporary scholarship comes from John Hick, *Evil and the God of Love*, 2nd ed. (San Francisco: HarperSanFrancisco, 1977). One of the best scholarly criticisms of this view comes from C. Robert Mesle, *John Hick's Theodicy: A Process Humanist Critique* (London: Palgrave Macmillan, 1991).

Some evils are character destroying rather than character building. Many people have lives that are made far worse because of intense pain. They grow bitter, vengeful and tyrannical, making life hellish for others and themselves. The alleged divine strategy of improving personal character is often counterproductive.

For some people, witnessing evil fails to build their characters and convinces them God does not exist. When Elie Wiesel was forced to watch a young boy hanged in a Nazi concentration camp, Wiesel stopped believing in God. God dies in the belief systems of many who cannot make sense of evil. The problem of evil is the primary reason most atheists say they cannot believe in God.

Is God the grand disciplinarian?

CONCLUSION

How can we make sense of these true stories? What do they tell us about life and God? There is much goodness, purpose, and beauty in life, and we must acknowledge it. But in doing so, we must not take evil lightly. Pain, suffering, and evil are difficult matters for those who believe in a loving and providential God.

Each story points to the influence that free will and randomness have in life. Sometimes random events (e.g., rocks accidentally killing people; random genetic mutations causing deformities) cause suffering and death. Sometimes humans use freedom wrongly, and this leads to tragedy (e.g., making bombs, raping and murdering). But humans can also use free will to deal positively with suffering and misfortune (e.g., choosing surgery or helping victims). Free will and randomness seem capable of both abuse and constructive use.

If we want a plausible explanation for how God acts providentially amid randomness and freedom, we should clearly define what we mean by these terms. Without clarity, we won't make much progress in understanding life. In the following chapter, I look carefully at the randomness and regularities of life. This examination should help in seeking adequate answers to life's most difficult questions.

2

The Randomness and Regularities of Life

To a greater or lesser degree, we all want to make sense of life. Yet doing so proves difficult, even for those of us who believe in God. Although we witness beauty, purpose and goodness all around, we also witness random accidents, pain and evil. Simplistic responses to life's difficult questions—"I just trust God"—leave many of us unsatisfied. We need better answers. Believers want to reconcile randomness and evil with the idea that God acts providentially.

This task is not merely theoretical. True stories in the previous chapter remind us that the stakes are high. Making sense of life, given our diverse experiences, involves seeking answers to big and perplexing questions. The answers we give incline us to act in particular ways, become certain kinds of people, organize ourselves in various societies and imagine how the future might be. The answers we give to fundamental questions have an impact upon every area of life.

For believers, making sense of the stories from the previous chapter requires belief in God. But the answers that most give to the question of God's relation to randomness and evil leave me unconvinced and discontented. They don't make sense. Believers need better responses than the usual fare.

To make progress in thinking well about God's providence, we need to clarify what we mean by randomness, the regularities of life, free will, evil, goodness and more. Scholars like me write entire books on these subjects. But brief explanations of each should facilitate progress toward the answers we seek.

In this chapter, I offer accessible explanations for randomness and regularities. I draw from research in various disciplines, but especially philosophy and science. Getting a handle on randomness and regularity proves crucial in the effort to formulate a plausible model of providence in later chapters.

RANDOMNESS REJECTED?

Scholars define chance and randomness in various ways. In essence, these definitions point to the idea that an event or set of circumstances had no intended purpose, was not part of someone's plan, did not follow a pattern or may not have occurred as it did. In the real-life scenarios we examined above, some randomness was present.

At least it appears so.

Perhaps we too quickly think these occurrences had random aspects. Perhaps events we believe random—with good consequences or bad—are not random at all. Some people reject randomness altogether, so let's explore the possibility that randomness, chance and accident are illusions. In our exploration, I will use *randomness, chance, accident* and similar words interchangeably. Although I am aware that one can distinguish among them, these distinctions do not affect my overall argument.

The word *random* may just be our way of saying, "we don't know why." Chance may be fiction. What we think happened randomly may actually have been a foregone conclusion, necessary outcome or planned event. Someone covertly intended what we perceive as unintentional, or natural causes fully determined what we think was chance.

We call some events random, some say, because we cannot know their causes. If we could know all prior happenings, we would know with certainty why some event occurred and what will happen in the future. Because we are finite creatures incapable of identifying all prior causes, they say, what we think random is not random at all.

Historians often cite Pierre Simon de Laplace as the philosopher-scientist endorsing this view. "Given for one instant an intelligence which could comprehend all the forces by which nature is animated and the respective positions of the beings which compose it," says Laplace, and given that "this intelligence were vast enough to submit these data to analysis . . . to it nothing would be uncertain. The future as the past would be present to its eyes."[1]

In the minds of many believers, an intelligence exists with these omniscient capacities: God. Not surprisingly, those who believe God controls all things think chance and randomness are merely words expressing our limited knowledge. These believers think an omni-causal or omniscient Intelligence presently knows with absolute certainty all things that occurred in the past, that are occurring in the present and that will occur in the future. God knows all this, they say, because God determines all things or stands outside time seeing all history as if it were one moment.

This seems to be Rick Warren's view. In his bestselling book, *The Purpose Driven Life*, Warren says, "Because God is sovereignly in control, accidents are just incidents in God's good plan for you."[2] Warren seems to be saying "accidents" are not truly accidental from the divine perspective because they were predetermined as part of a divine blueprint. From a timeless divine perspective, it's all a part of a master plan.

The biblical witness can be interpreted as supporting this view because some passages seem to deny chance. Some passages suggest that God "pulls the strings" to control seemingly chance events. For instance, Israelites shared with other peoples the belief that casting lots enabled them to discern God's will (e.g., Num 26:52-65; Lev 16:9; Josh 18:6; Judg 20:28; 1 Sam 10:21; Jon 1:7). And early Christians would sometimes cast lots when making decisions (Acts 1:26). They apparently believed, as the Proverb puts it,

The lot is cast into the lap,
  but the decision is the LORD's alone. (Prov 16:33)

---

[1]Pierre de Laplace, *A Philosophical Essay on Probabilities*, trans. F. W. Truscott and F. L. Emory (New York: Dover, 1951), p. 4.
[2]Rick Warren, *The Purpose Driven Life* (Grand Rapids: Zondervan, 2002), p. 195.

Yet in other passages of Scripture, chance is affirmed. Jesus referred to a chance event to make the point that no one is necessarily exempt from injurious accidents. "Or those eighteen who were killed when the tower of Siloam fell on them—do you think that they were worse offenders than all the others living in Jerusalem?" asks Jesus rhetorically. People suffer and even die because of random events, such as towers falling upon blameless bystanders (Lk 13:2-5).

Jesus also says chance can explain a person's misfortune irrespective of anyone's decisions. The disciples bring to Jesus a man blind from birth and ask, "Why was this man born blind? Was it because he or his parents sinned?" Jesus says the blindness was not an issue of moral indiscretion or any decision at all. But given this unintended misfortune, God can squeeze some good out of it: "Because of his blindness, you will see God work a miracle for him" (Jn 9:2-3 CEV).

Many Christians have ignored biblical passages that speak of chance. Like Rick Warren, they have believed that accidents are just incidents in God's predetermined story. For them, randomness and chance are ultimately unreal. The Heidelberg Catechism, a Christian document dating from the sixteenth century, teaches this. It asks, "What do you understand by the providence of God?" It offers an answer: Divine providence is "the almighty and ever-present power of God whereby he still upholds, as it were by his own hand, heaven and earth together with all creatures, and rules in such a way that . . . everything comes to us not by chance but by his fatherly hand."[3]

We can find passages in the writings of Augustine that deny randomness. "Nothing in our lives happens haphazardly," he says. "Everything that takes place against our will can only come from God's will, his Providence, the order he has created, the permission he gives, and the laws he has established."[4] John Calvin argues the same: "We

---

[3]*The Heidelberg Catechism*, trans. Allen O. Miller and M. Eugene Osterhaven (Philadelphia: United Church Press, 1962) as reprinted in *Confessions and Catechisms of the Reformation*, ed. Mark Noll (Grand Rapids: Baker, 1991), pp. 141-42.

[4]Augustine, *Enarrationes in Psalmos*, Ps 118, v. 12, quoted in Wilfried Stinnisen, *Into Your Hands, Father: Abandoning Ourselves to the God Who Loves Us* (San Francisco: Ignatius Press, 2011), p. 17. See also *Enchiridion*, chap. 95, trans. J. F. Shaw, in *A Select Library of Nicene and Post-Nicene*

must know that God's providence, as it is taught in scripture, is opposed to fortune and fortuitous happenings."[5] Contemporary theologian R. C. Sproul rejects randomness and chance with these dramatic comments: "The mere existence of chance is enough to rip God from his cosmic throne. . . . If chance exists in its frailest possible form, God is finished."[6]

Not only do some theologians reject chance, but some unbelievers also think what we call randomness merely represents our ignorance; they believe life is absolutely determined. Stephen Hawking and Leonard Mlodinow seem to believe this: "Biological processes are governed by the laws of physics and chemistry and therefore are as determined as the orbits of the planets . . . so it seems we are no more than biological machines."[7]

Albert Einstein can speak as if chance is an illusion: "Everything is determined, the beginning as well as the end, by forces over which we have no control. It is determined for the insect as well as the star."[8] It's hard to think Einstein could affirm genuine randomness given this statement.

When we look carefully at the claims of these scientists, however, we often find references to both randomness and determinism. This adds confusion rather than clarity. Frequently, scientists use *random* to deny planned events, intentions or specific purpose. Science has no room for purpose, they say.

In sum, it could be that genuine chance does not exist. Randomness simply describes our ignorance. Accidents are inevitable outcomes in some predetermined blueprint or mechanistic system. All is fate; the

Fathers of the Christian Church, ed. Philip Schaff (Grand Rapids: Eerdmans, 1978), 3:267.
[5]John Calvin, *Institutes of the Christian Religion*, ed. John T. McNeill, trans. Ford Lewis Battles (Philadelphia: Westminster, 1960), 1.16.2, 1:198. See also John Calvin, *The Secret Providence of God*, ed. Paul Helm, trans. Keith Goad (Wheaton, IL: Crossway, 2010).
[6]R. C. Sproul, *Not a Chance: The Myth of Chance in Modern Science and Cosmology* (Grand Rapids: Baker Books, 1994), p. 3.
[7]Stephen W. Hawking and Leonard Mlodinow, *The Grand Design* (New York: Bantam, 2010), p. 32.
[8]Quoted in G. S. Vierick, "What Life Means to Einstein," *The Saturday Evening Post*, October 26, 1929, p. 117.

past, present and future are set, and nothing can be done about it. According to the skeptics of genuine randomness, either God above or the atoms and genes below entirely determine our world.

RANDOMNESS ACCEPTED

A growing number of scholars think randomness, accidents and chance reliably describe the character of at least some events in life. In other words, these people—and I'm one of them—believe randomness characterizes existence at least sometimes or to some extent. The view that randomness merely describes our ignorance is likely mistaken.

Neither prior events nor a predestining God entirely determines life.

Most of us are aware of our intuitions. Those intuitions and our life experiences tell us something true about the way the world works. Most of us are realists, in one sense or another.[9] And the way we act presupposes our belief in the reality of genuine randomness.

Our intuitions of randomness affect how we think about standards of accountability. As members of society, we know accidents happen. For this reason, we take into account the intentions of those who cause pain when we decide whether to be harsh or lenient in our responses. We judge our children, siblings or strangers based, in part, upon whether we think they intentionally or unintentionally act.

For instance, arsonists purposely start fires so we hold them morally accountable for this. But we don't hold morally accountable the person who accidentally sets a fire; that person has made a mistake. Our courts of law deal differently with people who cause intentional harm than with those who cause harm unintentionally.

We often presuppose genuine randomness when we play games. Each year, for instance, the National Football League's premier

---

[9]For introductions to theories of realism, see Hilary Putnam, *Realism with a Human Face* (Cambridge, MA: Harvard University Press, 1992); and Joe Frank Jones III, *A Modest Realism: Preserving Common Rationality in Philosophy* (Lanham, MD: University Press of America, 2001). See also John Polkinghorne's emphasis upon what he calls "critical realism" (*The Polkinghorne Reader: Science, Faith, and the Search for Meaning*, ed. Thomas Jay Oord [Philadelphia: Templeton Press, 2011], part 1).

game, the Super Bowl, begins with a flip of a coin. In fact, just about every football game in America begins with a coin toss. All involved think this chance-based event is a fair way to decide which team gets the ball first. Few think God above or the atoms below determine coin flips.

Other games require genuine chance. In fact, we wouldn't find many games interesting if randomness were not real. Some require dice, which we roll to produce random results. Few of us consider it predetermined by God or prior events when a person rolls double sixes, for instance. We are not fatalists. And we don't regard a person morally superior for having rolled sixes. We think the gamer got lucky.

The boulder that slips down an alpine mountain crushing a car below is a random event. The woman who wins the million-dollar lottery is lucky; her win was not predetermined. The man struck by lightning is unfortunately at the wrong place at the wrong time. The girl who finds a crumpled one-hundred-dollar bill on the street has caught a lucky break. The golfer whose ball is caught in a sudden gust is a victim of misfortune. Most of us think one or all of these events are examples of genuine randomness.

Although many random events occur "out of the blue," we can purposefully use randomness to our benefit. For instance, sociologists take random surveys of a small set of people. Based on surveys with randomly selected participants, sociologists gauge with great accuracy the views of the whole. Statisticians think random polls have a better chance of being unbiased than most information-gathering endeavors. Polling the randomly selected few also saves time and money.

An artist may challenge her creative capacities by randomly selecting six colors with which to paint. This selection plays a role in the beautiful art that results as she purposefully uses her random selections. Chance and purpose play a part in producing splendor and wonder.

A business may conduct a random drawing and give a prize based on it as a ploy to lure in customers. The results of the drawing are not predetermined, but the drawing itself was planned. The lucky winner happily takes her prize. The sponsoring business benefits by using random selection to increase its customer base. Randomization can be useful.[10]

Our natural reactions to unintended events, coincidental circumstances, deliberate randomizations or chance-based outcomes suggest we don't believe life is entirely predetermined. We actually believe neither prior events nor God foreordains all outcomes. Our basic intuitions tell us that sometimes people get lucky. We can set up beneficial scenarios that rely upon chance. And sometimes, through no one's fault, painful accidents happen.

If we are to make sense of life, we need to take everyday experiences of randomness seriously. We should believe our intuitions regarding randomness tell us something true about reality.

The Science and Philosophy of Randomness

For some time, scientists have wrestled with issues of randomness and predetermination. Physicists have often been at the fore of this work. Many work as both scientists and philosophers as they probe the fundamental levels of existence, observe the stars and galaxies, and design mathematical models to understand reality at its smallest and grandest levels.

Until the twentieth century, most physicists and philosophers assumed that the basic levels of existence hummed along as a closed causal chain. All events were completely determined by previous events. This idea was part of a worldview shaped by Newtonian physics. Theology reinforced it with a view of divine sovereignty that says God orders, controls and therefore foreknows all things.

Physicists and theologians in earlier eras compared the world to a well-run clock whose parts were governed by other parts. We live in a "clock-like universe," the saying went, and God is the clockmaker. Scholars such as Francis Bacon, Robert Boyle, René Descartes,

---

[10]See also David J. Bartholomew's discussion of this category of chance events in *God, Chance and Purpose: Can God Have It Both Ways?* (Cambridge: Cambridge University Press, 2008), chap. 10.

Thomas Hobbes, Johannes Kepler, Isaac Newton and William Paley advocated the view.[11] Kepler put it succinctly: "The Celestial machine is to be likened not to a divine organism but rather to clockwork."[12]

In the twentieth century, however, quantum theory overturned the clockwork view. Quantum theory rejects the notion that the fundamental units of reality are entirely determined parts of a machine. Indeterminacy—not predeterminacy—occurs at the most basic levels of existence. And the past does not determine the present or future entirely.[13] The universe is an open system, not a determined machine.

The story of quantum theory is well documented, and I will not relate the details here. For our purposes it is most important to note that quantum theory reveals something that is shocking to many: what happens at the basic levels of existence—in atomic and subatomic particles—cannot be predicted. Fundamental indeterminacy of measurements leads physicists to believe we have only probable knowledge of what goes on at elemental levels. At issue is what physicists call the collapse of the wave function. Scientists cannot predict accurately at what instant a particular atom will change.[14]

Historians of science often associate Werner Heisenberg's name with the uncertainty principle describing the unpredictability of quantum events. Heisenberg said that the more precisely we know the position of some particle, the less precisely we know its momentum, and vice versa. It is fundamentally impossible to know the full causal explanation of any event at the quantum level. "We

---

[11]For a summary of the scientific, philosophical and theological considerations of mechanism, see John Hedley Brooke, *Science and Religion: Some Historical Perspectives* (Cambridge: Cambridge University Press, 1991), chaps. 2–4.

[12]See Robert S. Westman, "Magical Reform and Astronomical Reform: The Yates Thesis Reconsidered," in *Hermeticism and the Scientific Revolution*, by Robert S. Westman and J. E. McGuire (Los Angeles: William Andrews Clark Memorial Library, University of California, 1977), p. 41.

[13]See John C. Polkinghorne, *Quantum Theory: A Very Short Introduction* (New York: Oxford University Press, 2002).

[14]Two interpretations of wave function collapse dominate. In the Copenhagen interpretation, the collapse is what it appears to be: nondeterministic. This interpretation is most common among physicists. In the Bohmian interpretation, however, physicists view the collapse as deterministic.

cannot in principle know the present in all determined parts," says Heisenberg.[15] Uncertainty reigns.

Quantum theory still affirms causation, however. Things partially determine other things. Previous moments causally link to subsequent moments. Things influence other things. But the past never entirely determines the present, which means the fundamental laws of microphysics are at best probabilistic.[16]

The behavior of more complex entities and organisms is also unpredictable. Physicists often appeal to chaos theory when exploring more complex and highly organized levels of existence. Chaos theory says that slight changes in initial conditions have unexpected and wide-ranging effects in the wider environment. In fact, the ramifications of slight changes are, in principle, unpredictable. We cannot know how life will play out.

Perhaps the most famous example of chaos theory is what Edward Lorenz calls "the butterfly effect." A butterfly fluttering in one location may set off a causal chain affecting weather elsewhere in the world. While the butterfly example may be extreme, many physicists affirm the general principle that a small change in one location—under the right conditions—may be amplified in a cascade of causal interactions. And we cannot predict with certainty how this cascade will tumble.

Complex dynamic systems present vast possibilities for how events in our world may develop. Like a choose-your-own-ending storybook, life is full of possibilities and possible endings. How things unfold is yet to be determined. Physicist John Polkinghorne puts this succinctly: "The degree of randomness . . . arises from the labyrinth of possibilities open to an inherently undetermined complex system."[17]

---

[15] Werner Heisenberg, "Über den anschaulichen Inhalt der quantentheoretischen Kenematik und Mechanik," *Zeitschrift für Physik* 43 (1927): 197.

[16] The notion that indeterminacy is not merely an epistemic issue but an ontological reality is often called "the Copenhagen interpretation" of quantum mechanics. Niels Bohr and Werner Heisenberg are its chief representatives. Summaries of this are present throughout the literature. For one of the better ones, see Philip Clayton, *God and Contemporary Science* (Grand Rapids: Eerdmans, 1997).

[17] John C. Polkinghorne, *Science and Providence: God's Interaction with the World* (West Conshohocken, PA: Templeton Press, 2005), p. 37.

A growing number of physicists—apparently the majority—think the unpredictability of the basic levels of existence tells us something true about the indeterminateness of those levels and their impact in the wider environment. Complete determinism is unlikely. The philosopher might say epistemology tells us something true about ontology. The problem of unpredictability is not faulty observation, say many physicists, because randomness describes a fundamental aspect of our world.

Physicists are not the only scientists who think randomness at least partly describes reality. Randomness also plays a significant role in contemporary biology. The unifying theory in biology—evolution—involves randomness at various levels. Those like me who believe God creates through evolution also believe we must account for this randomness.

The story biologists tell about randomness usually begins with genetics. Thanks to Gregor Mendel and discoveries made by others, biologists believe random genetic mutations occur often in the reproductive processes of life.[18] Sometimes genetic mutations affect only one individual and do not pass on. Other times mutations pass to offspring and subsequent generations.

As far as biologists can tell, most genetic mutations occur randomly. No one can detect prior factors or environmental conditions that entirely explain them. Genetic changes have no set code or design. Mutations are not entirely determined or intended by creatures.

Random genetic mutations are a main factor in the emergence of new species over long periods of time. In fact, the time scale of evolution suggests that randomness played a key role in the slow emergence of complex life. Random changes in the information of the DNA and RNA sequences led to countless changes within species and between them. Sometimes mutations are advantageous to the creature or species, sometimes disadvantageous and sometimes inconsequential. In fact, millions of species have come

---

[18]See Heather Hassan, *Mendel and the Laws of Genetics* (New York: Rosen, 2005). See also Anthony J. F. Griffiths, *Introduction to Genetic Analysis*, vol. 10 (New York: Macmillan, 2008).

and gone as new species emerged and others died out.

Random genetic mutations are not the whole story of evolutionary theory. The environment in which a creature lives, for instance, places particular conditions on whether that creature thrives, barely survives or dies. Evolutionary theory calls the influence of these conditions "natural selection." Creatures whose genetic coding and behavior afford them an advantage in a particular environment are "selected." They are "fit."

Natural selection does not mean creatures themselves do the selecting. In most cases, it makes little sense to say creatures choose their environments at all.[19] Creatures are born into settings not of their choosing. Fungi, butterflies, beetles, rats and most other creatures do not likely contemplate whether to pack up residence for a change of scenery. Some creatures migrate, but we doubt they engage in careful deliberation before journeying.

Natural selection in biology does not seem driven by any master plan. "The overall process of evolution," says biologist Francisco Ayala, "cannot be said to be teleological in the sense of proceeding towards certain specified goals, preconceived or not."[20] While various patterns and increased complexity emerge over time, biologists do not speak of evolution itself as having predetermined purposes.[21] Life is an open-ended adventure, not an already settled script.

Biology influences humans, of course. Random genetic mutations and natural selection played roles in the emergence of humans

[19]For instance, the Baldwin effect says that initiatives taken by organisms can be factors in the establishment of random genetic changes and thereby affect the direction of evolutionary change. Others can imitate the behavior of thriving organisms, and this behavior can be transmitted socially for long enough that random genetic mutations support beneficial behavior. On this, see James Mark Baldwin, *Development and Evolution* (New York: Macmillan, 1902); Ian G. Barbour, *Nature, Human Nature, and God* (Minneapolis: Fortress, 2002), pp. 33-34; and Bruce Weber and David Depew, *Evolution and Learning: The Baldwin Effect Reconsidered* (Cambridge, MA: MIT Press, 2003).

[20]Francisco Ayala, "Teleological Explanations in Evolutionary Biology," in *Nature's Purposes: Analyses of Function and Design in Biology*, ed. Colin Allen, Marc Bekoff and George Lauder (Cambridge, MA: MIT Press, 1998), p. 42.

[21]A process with predetermined purpose, often with an agent directing it, is considered *teleological*. By contrast, a process that progresses according to the programming of the process itself is considered *teleonomic*. Most biologists consider evolution teleonomic, not teleological.

as a species, although other factors also played roles. Scholars debate the extent of randomness in human evolution, however. The research of Stephen Jay Gould and Simon Conway Morris plays a central role in the current debate on the range of randomness in the history of evolution.

Gould argues that evolution's range of randomness is immense. It was enormously improbable that humans would have emerged as a species. If the process were to start over a thousand times, each evolutionary outcome would be radically different.[22] Evolutionary history is wildly random.

Morris, on the other hand, argues that various constraints exist in evolutionary history. These constraints guide evolution to the near inevitability that humans would emerge as a species. We might call these constraints "pathways" of evolution because they exclude wild tangents while relying upon genuine chance. In other words, Morris believes the range of randomness is narrower than Gould envisions. If the evolutionary process were to start over a thousand times, says Morris, outcomes would be similar though not identical.[23] Evolution is mildly random.

Whoever is right in this debate about evolution, both Gould and Morris affirm the reality of randomness in biology. Both agree that chance played a key role in human evolutionary history. Humans have emerged, in part, thanks to random mutations and variables in natural selection.[24]

If randomness occurs at quantum, genetic and environmental levels of existence, it makes sense that simple organisms and complex creatures live lives characterized by some randomness. We noted everyday examples of chance affecting human experience. This quick exploration

---

[22]Stephen Jay Gould, *Wonderful Life: The Burgess Shale and the Nature of History* (New York: W. W. Norton, 1989).

[23]Simon Conway Morris, *Life's Solution: Inevitable Humans in a Lonely Universe* (Cambridge: Cambridge University Press, 2003).

[24]One of the better books exploring the various factors that may be involved in evolution is a collection of essays edited by John B. Cobb Jr., *Back to Darwin: A Richer Account of Evolution* (Grand Rapids: Eerdmans, 2008).

of life's microphysical and biological levels should help us realize that random events in everyday experience are part of the larger story.

Randomness seems at play—to some degree—from top to bottom.

On its own, science cannot judge whether chance is merely our lack of knowledge.[25] Scientists rely upon philosophical assumptions. But a good number of contemporary philosophers also argue that chance occurs in our lives. These philosophers explore the issues of chance in relation to probability theory, induction and abduction. Many believe randomness is not just epistemic but also ontological.[26]

A century ago, C. S. Peirce proved the most insightful among philosophers when it comes to understanding chance. Peirce had the advantage of having a job that required him to measure objects carefully. Although a world-class philosopher, he worked for the government as a technician. His assignment was to measure things and improve measuring devices. In this capacity—especially as he found errors in observation—Peirce realized that chance is common.[27]

Peirce's inability to measure reality with absolute precision led him to conclude that a measure of spontaneity exists in the world. The world is not a determined machine; the spontaneity inherent in existence generates chance. Chance is irreducible, in fact, because randomness is a fundamental fact of life.[28]

Although Peirce worked more than a century ago, his conclusions about the role of randomness ring true today. We live in, as Gerda

---

[25]See John C. Polkinghorne's discussion of the relationship between scientific unpredictability and philosophical adjudication on the epistemic and ontological levels in *One World: The Interaction of Science and Theology* (Philadelphia: Templeton Press, 2007), pp. 47-49.

[26]For a book laying out nicely the issues of randomness and God's activity, see Bartholomew's *God, Chance and Purpose*. James Bradley offers a concise article laying out various aspects of the God and randomness issues in "Randomness and God's Nature," *Perspectives on Science and Christian Faith* 64, no. 2 (2012): 75-89.

[27]For a concise summary of Peirce's understanding of chance and its implications, see Ian Hacking, *The Taming of Chance* (Cambridge: Cambridge University Press, 1990), chap. 23. For the fruitfulness of Peirce's thinking on divine action, see Amos Yong, *The Spirit of Creation: Modern Science and Divine Action in the Pentecostal-Charismatic Imagination* (Grand Rapids: Eerdmans, 2011), chap. 4.

[28]Although C. S. Peirce emphasized the pervasiveness of chance, he also thought that making sense of the world required us to affirm life's regularities. Existence follows a particular priority, thought Peirce: "Chance is first, Law is second, the tendency to take habits is third." C. S. Peirce, "The Architecture of Theories," *The Monist* 1 (1891): 175.

Reith puts it, the "Age of Chance."[29] Chance, randomness, unpredictability and imprecision characterize existence, although philosophers debate how best to speak of each.[30] In this debate, philosophers often use *random* to describe the product of a series of events and *chance* to describe a single instance.[31]

If dominant views in science and philosophy are correct in their affirmation of randomness and chance, theologians such as Augustine, Calvin and Sproul are wrong. God does not control all things; randomness is real. Contemporary theologies in conversation with science, philosophy and other disciplines must propose new models for understanding how God acts providentially.[32]

We cannot make progress in understanding our world if we ignore randomness.

LAWS AND REGULARITIES

Randomness is only part of the story. To make sense of existence, we must account for the regularities in life too. In fact, if not for regularity, we would not call some events random. Regularities arise from the repetition of numerous events over vast periods of time.

Life's regularities are so pervasive that we take them for granted. Examples abound. I am typing these words on my computer, so let's take my computer as an example of something that relies on regularities.

If quantum theory is correct, the most fundamental elements forming my computer have an aspect of randomness. Yet my computer functions with amazing efficiency. Individual randomness operates among the smallest entities within my computer. But, as a whole, it functions in a highly regular way.

---

[29]Gerda Reith, *The Age of Chance: Gambling in Western Culture* (New York: Routledge, 2005).
[30]For introductions to issues in this field, see Ian Hacking, *An Introduction to Probability and Inductive Logic* (Cambridge: Cambridge University Press, 2001); and idem, *Taming of Chance*.
[31]For a technical philosophical overview of the arguments, see *Stanford Encyclopedia of Philosophy*, s.v. "Chance Versus Randomness," by Antony Eagle, last modified February 9, 2012, http://plato.stanford.edu/entries/chance-randomness/. See also David Lewis, *Counterfactuals* (Oxford: Blackwell, 1973); and Patrick Suppes, *Probabilistic Metaphysics* (Oxford: Blackwell, 1984).
[32]For an admirable attempt at precisely this, see Rob A. Fringer and Jeff K. Lane, *A Theology of Luck: Fate, Chaos, and Faith* (Kansas City, MO: Beacon Hill, 2015).

The aggregate of random events at simple levels generates highly predictable patterns at higher levels. The behavior of large numbers of events is so statistically consistent we are prone to describe them as all but entirely determined. Therefore, despite randomness at the quantum level of my computer, stability is the overall result. My computer functions consistently—most of the time.

We see evidence of regularities in statistical consistencies. For instance, if we flip a coin a thousand times, each side will land facing up about five hundred times. The result of each flip is random, but the statistical average of a thousand coin flips is uniform. The law of large numbers says that when we take into account a large number of events, the whole displays regularity. In fact, we can predict with near certainty the aggregate outcome of large collections of random events.

Computers provide just one example demonstrating the regularities of existence. In fact, no chair could continue standing, no building remain upright and no composite object remain intact if a huge number of regularities were not at play. Aggregate structures of various types—inanimate objects—are possible because of the highly consistent behavior of their constitutive parts.

Regularity is rampant.

Without regularities, the universe would fly into utter chaos. Chemistry would not exist, plants could not grow and animals could not live. Humans would not have evolved. Societies would crumble, and morality would be a sham. Relationships would deteriorate. In short, the regularities of life are as important as randomness, and these regularities exist, to some degree, at every level of the universe.

Although some people know that evolutionary theory requires randomness, they forget evolution also requires lawlike regularity. Evolution presupposes that organisms exist with inherent capacities, such as basic structures, genes, self-organization and reproductive capacities. Randomness at play in genetic mutation and accidental aspects of natural selection occur within environments—modes of regularity. Massive numbers of random genetic mutations generate regularities at higher levels of populations and ecosystems.

Realizing that evolution relies upon regularities should calm religious believers wary of evolutionary theory. If evolution requires regularities, absolute randomness is a myth. Any design we encounter—and we encounter design often—comes from randomness, regularity and other forces, including God. Because of this, arguments pitting evolutionary randomness against design and organization are usually misguided.[33]

If randomness reigned entirely, all forms, structures, organisms and societies would disappear. Chaos would ensue. We could not even think about the universe because it would not be an object of rational inquiry. However, if rigid regularity reigned entirely, nothing new would emerge. Repetition would eliminate innovation, and death would follow. The right combination of randomness and regularity makes the universe capable of existing, evolving and developing novel forms of life.[34]

Believers are wise to say that God creates in and with the randomness and regularities of existence.

LAWS OF NATURE?

Some regularities of nature are so wide-ranging and consistent that scholars in various disciplines call them "laws of nature" or "natural laws." We find instances of so-called natural laws in disciplines such

---

[33]For helpful discussions of evolutionary randomness and design, see Jimmy H. Davis and Harry L. Poe, *Chance or Dance? An Evaluation of Design*, rev. ed. (West Conshohocken, PA: Templeton Press, 2008). A number of authors argue that God creates through evolution rather than intelligent design. See, for instance, Denis Alexander, *Creation or Evolution: Do We Have to Choose?* (Grand Rapids: Kregel, 2008); Denis Edwards, *The God of Evolution: A Trinitarian Theology* (New York: Paulist Press, 1999); Darrel R. Falk, *Coming to Peace with Science: Bridging the Worlds Between Faith and Biology* (Downers Grove, IL: InterVarsity Press, 2004); Karl Giberson, *Saving Darwin: How to Be a Christian and Believe in Evolution* (New York: HarperOne, 2008); Philip Hefner, *The Human Factor: Evolution, Culture, and Religion* (Minneapolis: Fortress, 1993); Denis O. Lamoureux, *I Love Jesus and I Accept Evolution* (Eugene, OR: Wipf & Stock, 2009); Ted Peters and Martinez Hewlitt, *Evolution from Creation to New Creation: Conflict, Conversation and Convergence* (Nashville: Abingdon, 2003); and J. Wentzel Van Huyssteen, *Alone in the World: Human Uniqueness in Science and Theology* (Grand Rapids: Eerdmans, 2006).
[34]For a similar argument, see Arthur Peacocke, *Theology for a Scientific Age: Being and Becoming—Natural, Divine, and Human* (Minneapolis: Fortress, 1993).

as cosmology, physics, chemistry, mathematics, economics, social sciences, political sciences, logic and ethics.

Isaac Newton's law of gravity is a good example of widespread and persistent regularity. This law says that any two things attract each other with a force directly proportional to the product of their masses and inversely proportional to the square of the distance between them. Newton discovered this natural law by observing the world and accepting the principle of induction.

Newton speculated that this natural law, based on his observation, was universally true. In other words, the principles of gravity affect not only the apple falling from a tree. They apply throughout the universe. Consequently, we call gravity a law and not an isolated phenomenon or human-created ordinance. Although general and special relativity theories have subsequently qualified Newton's law of gravity, most describe the regularities we observe in the universe as "laws of nature."[35]

Philosophers are especially interested in the lawlike regularity of our world. Philosophers of science often speak of the natural world as an interconnected and interdependent system of systems. The entities, structures, patterns and processes all influence one another in diverse but largely uniform ways.

Lawlike regularity persists throughout the cosmos.

Contemporary philosophers of science ponder the ultimate basis of life's natural laws and regularities.[36] They wonder, Do the regularities of life conform to universal and eternal laws of nature? Or do we merely call these regularities laws based on their repetition?

Some philosophers think the regularities of life do not point to fundamental laws of nature. I will call them *regularists*.[37] Regularists

---

[35]See Isaac Newton, *Principia*, vol. 2, *The System of the World*, trans. Andrew Motte, rev. Florian Cajori (Berkeley: University of California Press, 1934).

[36]On this philosophical debate, see D. M. Armstrong, *What Is a Law of Nature?* (Cambridge: Cambridge University Press, 1993); Lewis, *Counterfactuals*; Thomas Maudlin, *The Metaphysics Within Physics* (New York: Oxford University Press, 2007); Elliott Sober, "Confirmation and Lawlikeness," *Philosophical Review* 97 (1988): 93-98; and Bas C. Van Fraassen, *Laws and Symmetry* (Oxford: Clarendon, 1989).

[37]For a clear explanation of regularism and necessitarianism, see *Internet Encyclopedia of Phi-*

admit that regularities of life are genuine, and they acknowledge the mathematical consistency and probabilities of these regularities. But they think the consistencies of existence are simply brute facts, not reflections of eternal laws. Regularities are merely our descriptions of consistent patterns among entities, organisms, creatures and planets. Regularists argue that no ultimate or transcendent explanation for this consistency needs to be given.

I use the designation *necessitarians* to describe philosophers who think the regularities of life derive from eternal laws. The repetition we observe in the world, say necessitarians, are the necessary expressions of laws governing the universe. In this sense, the laws of nature regulate existence even though chance (and perhaps free will) is also real. Necessitarians may think God put these natural laws in place. Or they may think the laws conform to Platonic forms.[38]

Theologians have a particular interest in how best to think about regularities or natural laws. Many theologians sympathize more with necessitarian arguments, especially arguments in which God plays an explanatory role. If God created everything, many say, God must have created the laws governing life's regularities. The orderliness of the universe points to God as the author of order.

Some theologians, in fact, think the laws of nature are merely God's way of controlling all things. Natural laws are simply the necessary extensions of God's all-determining will. Others affirm the force of natural laws while reserving a role for chance and creaturely freedom. For them, the regularities that the laws of nature express may or may not reveal God's will. And these regularities do not eliminate chance or free will.

The question of whether God created laws of nature mirrors an ancient question about God's relation to morality.[39] Philosophers

---

losophy, s.v. "Laws of Nature," by Norman Swartz, accessed April 10, 2015, www.iep.utm.edu/lawofnat/. See also Robin Collins, "God and the Laws of Nature," *Philo* 20, no. 2 (2009): 142-71.

[38]See William Welton, ed., *Plato's Forms: Varieties of Interpretations* (Lanham, MD: Lexington, 2002). Perhaps the best collection of Plato's primary writings is Plato, *The Works of Plato*, trans. Benjamin Jowett (New York: Tudor, 1937).

[39]For a discussion of this, see Hugh Rice, *God and Goodness* (Oxford: Oxford University Press, 2000).

commonly call the morality question Euthyphro's dilemma in honor of a conversation between Socrates and Euthyphro. The question takes many forms, but it essentially asks this: Are some deeds good simply because God declares them so? Or does God declare them good because they fundamentally are good?

To many, some deeds are good because God says so. God created all things, after all, and that would include creating standards of right and wrong, good and evil. God must have created moral laws, say these theologians, so what God declares as good is what God freely decides to be good.

But if some deeds are good simply because God says so, this means God decides the standards of good and evil arbitrarily. God could have decided murder was always good, for instance. If God arbitrarily decides right and wrong, genocide may be evil for humans but perfectly acceptable for God. And if God freely decides what is good, God's own goodness is simply whatever God decides it to be.[40] All of this seems odd.

When responding to Old Testament stories in which God commands or does what seems unloving (e.g., genocide, war, murder), biblical scholar Tremper Longman III endorses the view that God alone decides good and evil. Apparent evils are morally acceptable, says Longman, because "God defines morality—what is right and what is wrong." Longman admits that he "may struggle with this," but whatever "is initiated and directed by God . . . is moral."[41] Right is right because God says so.

Others respond to Euthyphro's dilemma by saying deeds are not good simply because God says so. God does not arbitrarily decide good or evil, right and wrong. Actions are good independent of whether God might say so, and even God answers to moral standards God did not create. Right is right, and not even God can decide otherwise.

---

[40]John Daniel Holloway explores this issue in "What God Cannot Do," *Disputatious Interpretation* (blog), September 3, 2014, http://jdhollowayiii.blogspot.com/2014/09/what-god-cannot-do.html.
[41]William L. Lyons, *A History of Modern Scholarship on the Biblical Word* Herem (Lewiston, NY: Edwin Mellen, 2010), pp. 153-54.

This answer implies that standards of morality transcend or exist outside God. And this may prompt us to wonder if God actually creates everything. It seems difficult to imagine God the source of all goodness while good exists independent of or transcends God. This may also mean that we don't need God to know what is right and wrong, good and evil. But this seems odd too.

Theists Joshua Hoffman and Gary S. Rosenkrantz opt for this answer to Euthyphro's dilemma. For them, "right and wrong, good and bad, are in a sense independent of what *anyone* believes, wants, or prefers."[42] In addition, atheists who affirm the objective reality of morality believe that, in some sense, moral standards are independent of God.[43]

When we think about the laws of nature, we ask a question similar to Euthyphro's dilemma: Do the regularities and laws of nature exist because of God's arbitrary decision to create them? Or do they exist necessarily, not due to divine decree?

Some believers think God voluntarily created the laws of nature. When creating the world from nothingness billions of years ago, God freely decided which laws to install and subsequently uphold. God could have created a different kind of world with entirely different laws. And God can supersede or negate natural laws from time to time if God decides to do so. Because God freely created natural laws at the beginning, God can withdraw, override or fail to uphold those laws at any time. Richard Swinburne puts it this way: "God is not limited by the laws of nature; he makes them and he can change or suspend them—if he chooses."[44]

Just as those who think God created moral standards face problems, those who think God created natural laws also face problems. We

---

[42]Joshua Hoffman and Gary S. Rosenkrantz, *The Divine Attributes* (Oxford: Wiley-Blackwell, 2002), p. 145.

[43]Philosophers and philosophical theologians explore these issues using the categories intellectualism (nature) and voluntarism (will). See, for instance, Robert Adams, *Finite and Infinite Goods: A Framework for Ethics* (Oxford: Oxford University Press, 1999); and Jerome B. Schneewind, *The Invention of Autonomy: A History of Modern Moral Philosophy* (Cambridge: Cambridge University Press, 1997).

[44]Richard Swinburne, *Is There a God?* (New York: Oxford University Press, 2010), p. 7.

might wonder why God decided to create these particular laws instead of others, for instance. Or we may wonder why God does not withdraw, override or fail to uphold laws of nature from time to time to prevent evil. We may think a loving God should interrupt natural laws, at least sometimes, to prevent atrocities like those we encountered in the previous chapter.

Others say God did not create the laws of nature. Instead, they simply are somehow, and they exert influence in the world. Because God didn't create them, God cannot supersede them. The laws and regularities of nature cannot be broken, even by God. Stephen Hawking puts it this way in his discussion of God and natural laws: "A scientific law is not a scientific law if it holds only when some supernatural being decides not to intervene."[45]

This way of thinking about natural laws also raises issues. According to it, the laws of nature transcend or are independent of God, which means God is not their source. If this is true, there is an advantage: we should not blame God for failing to override these laws to prevent evil because even God must obey them. The disadvantage of saying the laws of nature transcend God, however, is that believers may wonder whether we need God to explain the laws of nature. When Laplace was asked how he accounted for the laws of nature, he famously said, "I have no need for a [God] hypothesis." This suggests that the laws of nature somehow exist independent of God.

In light of the stories we read in chapter one, the question of whether God created and upholds the laws of nature should prompt us to wonder if God can interrupt the laws of nature to prevent genuine evils. And we might wonder if God violates such laws to act in the world, especially when enacting miracles. Knowing God's relation to the natural laws is as important as knowing whether God created the standards of morality.

We seem caught on the horns of both a moral and a cosmological dilemma.

---

[45]Hawking and Mlodinow, *Grand Design*, p. 30.

There is a third answer to questions of God's relationship to natural law and morality. I plan to explain this answer in a later chapter, but let me offer a teaser here. My answer says the standards of morality and regularities of existence derive from God's loving nature. God's nature is eternal, without beginning or end. God did not create or choose the attributes of the divine nature. And God cannot change them because the divine nature is immutable.

Because the regularities of existence derive from God's nature, God did not arbitrarily choose the laws of nature and standards of morality. And God cannot supersede them. But the standards of morality or laws of nature neither exist independent of nor transcend God. They emerge from God's loving interaction with creation as God acts from an eternal and unchanging nature of love.

I will explain this third answer later in relation to evil. For now, I conclude this discussion by noting that both chance and regularity pervade life. Random events occur in environments with constraints, regularities and limits. Chance and contingency operating within lawlike regularities make possible, in part, new and creative forms of life and ways of living in our world.[46]

Absolute randomness is a myth. But absolute determinism is too. Forces we cannot see regulate all things, animate and inanimate. Chance and lawlike regularity characterize our world. If chance reigned absolutely, chaos would ensue. If law reigned absolutely, order would eliminate creativity.

Both randomness and regularity persist in the universe.

---

[46]On a biological argument for the directionality of evolution that accounts for randomness and necessity, see Jeffrey P. Schloss, "Divine Providence and the Question of Evolutionary Directionality," in *Back to Darwin: A Richer Account of Evolution*, ed. John B. Cobb Jr. (Grand Rapids: Eerdmans, 2008), p. 334.

3

Agency and Freedom in a World of Good and Evil

*T*he relation between randomness and regularity plays a major role in explaining life. But randomness and regularity are only part of the story—as important as they are. Life also includes free will, good and evil—at least it seems to include them. We need to address these dimensions if we are to answer well life's biggest questions.

The stories in the first chapter directed our attention to tragedies, suffering and evil. Some involved chance: rocks accidentally smashing through windows or random genetic malfunctions. Other stories suggested that humans used free will for evil ends. The Tsarnaev brothers, for instance, freely planned the Boston Marathon bombing. Tutsi rebels freely raped Zamuda and killed her family. Each story prompts those who believe in God to ask questions about divine providence in a world with random events and free will.

In this chapter, we explore free will, good and evil. In particular, we address what philosophers call libertarian free will. We'll also address both the problem of evil and the problem of good. We naturally ask philosophy for help with these issues. But we will draw from science too.

Most theologians think we should align our views of providence with what we believe to be the truth about freedom, goodness and evil. I agree. We cannot make much sense of life without making sense of these features of existence.

STARTING WITH SIMPLE

As a discipline, science has little to say directly about agency and
freedom. When scientists talk about these topics, they leave the realm
of science as commonly understood and move into metaphysics.
After all, we cannot place agency under a microscope or test it in a lab.
We do not see freedom running around the planet or gaze at free will
in our telescopes.

In fact, science cannot observe causation itself in any form. This
point is important because causation is the underlying philosophical
category for agency and freedom. Our senses cannot perceive these
factors of existence directly, but we see movement and creaturely effects of various kinds. We then infer that some movement is self-
caused and expresses agency or freedom.

Although philosophy and theology play central roles in our exploration of freedom, science does profoundly shape our understanding.
Science influences philosophical assumptions and theological proposals. So I begin exploring agency and freedom by thinking scientifically about the simpler and less complex levels of existence. Along
the way, I'll also offer some metaphysical proposals.

The story of life told by many scientists and philosophers says self-
organization exists at various levels of existence. From the simplest
organism to the most complex, we find entities self-organizing.[1]
Self-organization at less complex levels involves the thing or creature
contributing in some way to what it self-becomes. As far as we know,
self-organization is not a conscious activity for simple entities.

Self-organization at life's lower levels derives from the inherent
structures of things in themselves.[2] The form, genes or mere exis-

---

[1]Two of the better-known philosophers who speculate that something like agency or freedom is
present in the smaller entities of existence are Hans Jonas and Alfred North Whitehead. See Hans
Jonas, *The Phenomenon of Life: Towards a Philosophical Biology* (1966; repr., Evanston, IL: North-
western University Press, 2001); and Alfred North Whitehead, *Process and Reality: An Essay in
Cosmology*, ed. David Ray Griffin and Donald W. Sherburne, corrected ed. (1929; New York:
Free, 1978).

[2]One of the better-known advocates for self-organization in biology is Stuart Kauffman. See, for
instance, his book *At Home in the Universe: The Search for the Laws of Self-Organization and
Complexity* (Oxford: Oxford University Press, 1996).

tence of a thing contributes to it becoming what it is, moment by moment. In fact, we cannot understand well even the simplest entities without thinking some features are self-derived. Those who know Aristotle's philosophy see connections between current scientific ideas of self-organization and the basic causes he said influence reality.[3]

At some point in the evolutionary process, the complexity of some creatures reached a threshold. Agency became a possibility and then a reality.[4] It makes little sense to talk about atoms and rocks having agency because they are aggregates of uncoordinated parts. But it does make sense to say that fungi, worms, butterflies, fish, mice and other creatures express agency.[5] Creatures with organizational unity express agency.[6] At least they seem to have agency, given what we observe from their actions. Microorganisms may even possess agency, as far as we know. But if they do, their agency is highly constrained.

Self-organization and agency are not the same as free will, however, as I will explain. However, when exploring the eventual emergence of full-blown freedom, it seems appropriate to begin with the self-organizing capacities and agency found in less-complex creatures. Beginning with less-complex beings fits the logic of evolution because evolutionary history indicates that over long periods life on planet earth diversified, multiplied and became more complex.[7]

---

[3]See Aristotle, "Physics," in *The Basic Works of Aristotle*, ed. Richard McKeon (New York: Random House, 1941), 2:3. See also William Wallace, *The Modeling of Nature: Philosophy of Science and Philosophy of Nature in Synthesis* (Washington, DC: Catholic University of America Press, 1996).

[4]On the issue of emergence, see Philip Clayton, *Mind and Emergence: From Quantum to Consciousness* (Oxford: Oxford University Press, 2004); Philip Clayton and Paul Davies, eds., *The Re-Emergence of Emergence* (Oxford: Oxford University Press, 2006); and Terrence Deacon, "The Hierarchic Logic of Emergence: Untangling the Interdependence of Evolution and Self Organization," in *Evolution and Learning: The Baldwin Effect Reconsidered*, ed. Bruce H. Weber and David J. Depew (Cambridge, MA: MIT Press, 2003), pp. 273-308.

[5]On animal agency as self-direction, see Helen Steward, "Animal Agency," *Inquiry* 52, no. 3 (2009): 217-31.

[6]On the issue of aggregates and organized societies, see David Ray Griffin, *Evil Revisited: Responses and Reconsiderations* (Albany, NY: State University of New York Press, 1991), pp. 102-4, and *Unsnarling the World-Knot: Consciousness, Freedom, and the Mind-Body Problem* (Berkeley: University of California Press, 1998), chap. 9.

[7]For an exploration of agency, freedom and morality among nonhuman animals, see Celia Deane-

Beginning with less-complex creatures also fits our observations of behavior at various levels of existence. We infer self-organization, agency and in some cases free will when we observe entities and creatures of varying complexity. We see the behavior of particles, atoms, cells, basic organisms, insects, vertebrates, fish, reptiles, amphibians, mammals, primates and humans. At each level of complexity, we make judgments about the nature of the activity we observe.

The gradual increase of complex life in evolutionary history eventually led to the emergence of free will. At least that appears to be the case. Identifying the origin of free will is difficult. We doubt atoms have freedom. But it is easy to think dogs, for instance, have at least agency and perhaps free will. The more complex the creature, the more open we are to thinking it expresses some degree of freedom.

Our observations of felines, elephants, cows, dolphins, whales, goats, bonobos, chimpanzees and other animals incline many of us to think they act freely. Many speculate that creatures with mental capacities less complex than ours have free will. However, their freedom appears less developed.[8] Simpler creatures may possess a tiny fraction of the freedom most humans enjoy.

My experiences growing up on a farm led me to believe barnyard animals make free choices among limited options. Hiking the backcountry of Idaho inclines me to think a small measure of freedom—perhaps unconscious—exists in undomesticated animals as well. In my experiences with creatures I meet, I make inferences about the nature and complexity of their self-causation.

We cannot know any of this with certainty, of course. But speculation about free will seems justified, given our experience of our own freedom and our observations of how other humans and creatures behave. These inferences are plausible.

Drummond, *The Wisdom of the Liminal: Evolution and Other Animals in Human Becoming* (Grand Rapids: Eerdmans, 2014).

[8]For instance, see Marc Bekoff, *Minding Animals: Awareness, Emotions, and Heart* (Oxford: Oxford University Press, 2002); and Marc Bekoff and Jessica Pierce, *Wild Justice: The Moral Lives of Animals* (Chicago: University of Chicago Press, 2009).

Beginning with the Complex

Instead of beginning with less-complex creatures when exploring agency and freedom, we could look to humans. In fact, it is easier to account for freedom if we begin with our own experiences. As highly complex creatures, we are aware of our free will, as limited as it is.

If we begin with our experiences, we quickly realize the importance of free will in our lives. We believe we act freely, at least some of the time and to some extent. We cannot easily doubt our deep intuition of free will. And we believe other humans act freely based on our observations of their behavior.

One of the most influential scholars in science and religion research, Ian Barbour, endorses the start-with-our-own-experience method of thinking about how freedom emerged in evolutionary history. We ought to generalize from human experiences of freedom when thinking about freedom among nonhuman creatures. "We are part of nature," Barbour says, and "even though human experience is an extreme case of an event in nature, it offers clues as to the character of other events." Although new phenomena and new properties emerge historically, says Barbour, "we should seek fundamental categories that are as universal as possible."[9]

While humans and other complex creatures have genuine, although constrained, free will, Barbour speculates that rather simple creatures have a degree of what he calls "interiority."[10] This interiority involves some measure of subjectivity. Interiority is present in simple organisms and even cells and is expressed in responsiveness, sentience, anticipation or rudimentary memory. It emerges among complex creatures as consciousness, with the advent of nervous systems. Finally, we find self-consciousness and full-blown freedom among at

---

[9]Ian G. Barbour, "Evolution and Process Thought," in *Back to Darwin: A Richer Account of Evolution*, ed. John B. Cobb Jr. (Grand Rapids: Eerdmans, 2008), pp. 212-13.

[10]Ibid. Arguments for this position—sometimes called panexperientialism—can be found in Christian de Quincey, *Radical Nature: Rediscovering the Soul of Matter* (Montpelier, VT: Invisible Cities, 2002); and Griffin, *Unsnarling the World-Knot*.

least primates and human beings, if not other mammals.[11]

How far freedom descends in the chain of creaturely complexity is hard to know. When exactly some measure of genuine freedom emerged in evolutionary history, simple as such freedom must have first been, we may never know. But it is hard to doubt we humans act freely.

Not everyone affirms the reality of free will, however. Not everyone affirms free will in what they say or write, that is. Skeptics of freedom express various reasons for their skepticism. Some deny free will based upon their observations of behavioral patterns and regularities among large groups of animals. They claim that predictable regularities are irreconcilable with genuine freedom. They believe regularity would only occur if creatures are entirely determined or operate solely by instinct.

The skeptic's denial of freedom to animals can also be used to deny freedom to humans. After all, the behavior of humans, in large numbers, is also highly predictable. A statistical law may tell us something about a particular human population and even produce highly probable predictions.

To illustrate how skeptics discount freedom by observing regularities of large numbers, take as an example the decision some people make to marry. In most cases, numerous factors influence the people making this free choice. Relationships, attraction, biology, chemicals, social pressures and more play a role.

Let us suppose that researchers tallied marriages each year in the total human population. Suppose that year after year for three decades the marriage rate hovered around 50 percent of eligible candidates. Skeptics of free will may observe this regularity and think marriage is inevitable for half the people on the planet. Individuals in this percent, skeptics may say, are not free to remain single. Marriage for them is predestined or fated.

But this way of thinking puts the regularity cart before the free-will horse. Unlike the skeptics, free-will advocates believe statistical av-

---

[11]Barbour, "Evolution and Process Thought," pp. 203-4. See also Deane-Drummond, *Wisdom of the Liminal.*

erages tell us what people freely do in relation to their choices. Averages do not force particular individuals to choose marriage. Instead, statistical averages describe what humans freely choose in their decisions. The predictable percentage of those who marry each year can be reconciled with the idea that each freely chooses to wed.

Those who believe in genuine freedom argue that the chooser makes decisions freely although constraints limit his or her options when freely deciding. For instance, the one choosing to marry may feel marriage is the most compelling option among others. Other factors also influence the person's decision. His or her freedom is limited but real because that person could remain single.

Skeptics also reject free will on other grounds. Some look at random genetic mutations or the regularities supporting our drive to reproduce and then conclude free will does not exist. This seems to be Richard Dawkins's assumption when he says, "we are survival machines—robot vehicles blindly programmed to preserve the selfish molecules known as genes."[12] By accident, says Dawkins, molecules emerged and these replicators "manipulate" us "by remote control."[13] Some sociobiologists agree and consider free will illusory.

Other skeptics think research in neuroscience allows no room for genuinely free choices. They believe that if science can identify brain activity or manipulate brain structures, free will is a misconception.[14] Sam Harris, for instance, says that we "subjectively appear to have complete freedom to behave however [we] please." But in reality, "free will is an illusion."[15] Daniel Wegner says that although "it seems we are agents" and "it seems we cause what we do," it is "ultimately accurate to call all this an illusion." Neuroscientist Patrick Haggard puts it bluntly: "We certainly don't have free will."[16]

---

[12]Richard Dawkins, *The Selfish Gene* (London: Granada, 1978), p. x.

[13]Ibid., p. 20.

[14]For an alternative view, see Carol Rausch Albright and James B. Ashbrook, *Where God Lives in the Human Brain* (Naperville, IL: Sourcebooks, 2001).

[15]Sam Harris, *Free Will* (New York: Free Press, 2012), pp. 5, 9.

[16]Wegner and Haggard are both quoted in Eddy Nahmias, "Is Neuroscience the Death of Free Will?," *The Stone* (blog), *New York Times*, November 13, 2011, http://opinionator.blogs.nytimes.com/2011/11/13/is-neuroscience-the-death-of-free-will.

These skeptics also usually define free will out of existence. The definition of free will they assume ignores the inherent constraints free choosers face. When defining freedom in this way, skeptics think we must decide between believing in unlimited freedom or in no freedom at all.[17]

We all know that we cannot do just anything we might imagine. For instance, we cannot fly to Mars this afternoon. We cannot change from being humans and become toads. We cannot all be president at once. We cannot freely put the entire moon in our basements. There are many things we cannot do, so skeptics say we must not be free at all. They seem to define free will as choosing among unlimited options and having no constraints.

These criticisms of free will are not convincing. Our personal experience of freedom and much research in various academic disciplines— including biology and neuroscience—point toward a third way between unlimited freedom and the absence of free will.[18] The third way says we have limited but genuine freedom. And this third way relies upon information we know best: our own subjective experiences.

The limited-but-genuine-freedom position says we freely choose among a limited number of options. Our environments, bodies, brains, inclinations, genes, history and other factors constrain what is possible in each choosing moment. We are not free to do anything we may imagine. But we are also not entirely determined to do or be just one thing.

The limited-freedom approach says we choose among relevant options, given constraints. Our free will is self-derived and occurs as we face multiple alternatives. Research in science can help to identify constraints to freedom. But science itself cannot fully explain or explain away free will.

Free will is genuine but limited.

---

[17]For a philosophical defense of libertarian free will in light of science, see Richard Swinburne, ed., *Free Will and Modern Science* (Oxford: Oxford University Press, 2011).

[18]For essays with more plausible explanations for the role of neuroscience and morality, see James A. Van Slyke et al., eds., *Theology and the Science of Moral Action: Virtue Ethics, Exemplarity, and Cognitive Neuroscience* (New York: Routledge, 2012).

LIBERTARIAN FREEDOM

I have been using *free will* and *freedom* to talk about choosing among options. The two words, *free* and *will*, capture what most people mean when they talk about the freedom to choose in any particular moment. But philosophers use various terms to talk about free will.

The philosophical label *libertarian free will* describes what I believe is the most plausible view of freedom. Libertarian free will says genuine freedom is irreconcilable with being fully determined to act in a particular way. Libertarian free will supporters are incompatiblists because they believe we cannot be simultaneously free and entirely determined by other forces. In other words, free will and complete determinism are incompatible. We choose among alternatives, and other agents and factors do not completely control us.

Freedom understood in the libertarian free will tradition usually involves two dimensions.[19] One pertains to the power of the chooser, and this dimension sometimes goes by the name *self-determination*. Timothy O'Connor uses the phrase "agent causation" to describe it, and by this he means that the decision of the chooser is necessary for freely selecting an activity.[20] Kevin Timpe calls this dimension "sourcehood," and he says the agent is the source of its actions rather than some other cause.[21] Intention is the exercise of causal influence. Whatever word one prefers, the point is that the agent, individual or actor plays a primary causal role in the choice.

The second dimension of free will is that various possibilities must be available when a free agent chooses. For an agent to act freely, more than one possible and real option must be at hand. Without

---

[19]Gary Watson, "Free Action and Free Will," *Mind* 96 (1987): 145.

[20]Timothy O'Connor, "Agent-Causal Theories of Freedom," in *The Oxford Handbook of Free Will*, ed. Robert Kane, 2nd ed. (Oxford: Oxford University Press, 2011), pp. 309-28. See also Randolph Clarke, "Alternatives for Libertarians," in *The Oxford Handbook of Free Will*, ed. Robert Kane, 2nd ed. (Oxford: Oxford University Press, 2011), pp. 329-48; Robert Kane, *The Significance of Free Will* (Oxford: Oxford University Press, 1998); and Timothy O'Connor, "The Agent as Cause," in *Free Will*, ed. Robert Kane (Oxford: Wiley-Blackwell, 2001), pp. 196-205.

[21]Kevin Timpe, *Free Will: Sourcehood and Its Alternatives*, 2nd ed. (New York: Bloomsbury, 2013), p. 11.

multiple possibilities, a free agent cannot do other than what that agent must do.[22] These various possibilities, says William Hasker, "are crucial to standard definitions of libertarianism," because the ability to choose freely requires more than one option.[23]

A free being is an agent who chooses among options.

As I argued earlier, the most powerful evidence for free will is our own personal experience. In the way we act, we all inevitably presuppose we are, at least to some degree, free. I call this an experiential nonnegotiable. That we presuppose we act freely is evident in the fact that, at least sometimes, we feel remorseful, blameworthy, praiseworthy, self-satisfied, guilty or proud of what we have done.[24] We may say or write that we are not free, but our everyday actions suggest otherwise.

We presuppose free will when we hold others or ourselves accountable to standards of conduct, especially moral standards. We think we can and should freely choose to act according to moral standards. Free will is essential to being accountable to others or ourselves, and we all admit this, at least in how we act and react in life.

Not only do our actions show our fundamental beliefs about free will, but our moral intuitions require the reality of free will. Being morally responsible is impossible if free will is an illusion. "Had people never conceived of themselves as responsible beings," says Richard Taylor, "it is doubtful whether they would ever have thought of themselves as agents either." Taylor adds, "If anyone is responsible for what he has done, then he must have been free."[25]

We cannot be morally responsible unless we are freely response-able.

---

[22]William Hasker, "Divine Knowledge and Human Freedom," in *The Oxford Handbook of Free Will*, ed. Robert Kane, 2nd ed. (Oxford: Oxford University Press, 2011), pp. 40-56. See also Laura W. Ekstrom, "Free Will Is Not a Mystery," in *The Oxford Handbook of Free Will*, ed. Robert Kane, 2nd ed. (Oxford: Oxford University Press, 2011), pp. 366-80.

[23]William Hasker, *The Emergent Self* (Ithaca, NY: Cornell University Press, 1999), p. 86.

[24]David Ray Griffin calls these "commonsense notions" because they inevitably reveal in our actions what we truly believe (*Unsnarling the World-Knot*, pp. 34, 210).

[25]Richard Taylor, "Action and Responsibility," in *Action Theory: Proceedings of the Winnipeg Conference on Human Action*, ed. Myles Brand and Douglas N. Walton (Boston: Reidel, 1976), p. 293.

Free will helps us attribute guilt to those who freely choose evil. Because we think perpetrators of evil at least sometimes freely choose their dastardly deeds, we feel justified in criticizing, reprimanding or even punishing those who freely choose evil when choosing good was possible. Premeditated murder, for instance, is morally reprehensible because we assume the murderer freely planned someone's death. By contrast, an accidental shooting does not carry the same moral responsibility. It was a mistake.

In discussions of moral responsibility, we often overlook free will's importance for making sense of positive moral transformation. When we expect moral or character development of others or ourselves, we believe free choices play a role in the transformative process. Besides, if someone can be blamed for the evil derived from free choices, at least partial credit also goes to the person who freely chooses what is good. For those who think moral progress and character development are possible, affirming free will to do good seems just as crucial as affirming free will to do evil.

Free will also seems necessary for understanding God's providence in light of some tragic stories we read in chapter one. In them, humans used free will wrongly. I believe the evils we encountered are not expressions of God's actions. Most theologians affirm the reality of free will in large part because it helps them make sense of good and evil. We will need to delve deeply into God's relation to creaturely freedom in future chapters.

Let me summarize: self-organization and agency are present among the simpler entities and organisms of existence. Evolutionary science and our observation of behavior suggest that free will emerged at some point in evolutionary history. Our own experience—our deepest intuitions—tells us we are free, at least to some degree. We make free choices among relevant options present at any moment. Although some people deny free will, the way they inevitably act betrays that denial. Free will is an experiential nonnegotiable, and our personal experiences tell us something true about the nature of reality.

Answering life's biggest questions requires believing we can use free will rightly or wrongly.

Of course, answering life's biggest questions—including questions about randomness and evil—involves more than simply saying, it's all about free will! But a fully adequate answer to life's questions cannot ignore freedom. To make sense of life—with its ups and downs, joys and sorrows, good and evil—we must account for free creaturely choices. We cannot understand life well if we ignore free will.

The Values in Life

Just as science cannot put free will under a microscope, it also cannot observe values. Science also cannot explain values, at least not in their ultimate sense.[26] We look to philosophy and theology to ground claims about better and worse, important and unimportant, beautiful and ugly, right and wrong, good and evil.

Value is a conceptual umbrella, under which reside categories such as truth, aesthetics and morality. Making sense of values is essential to making sense of life. We are value-interested creatures. Our belief in the reality of values is fundamental to our lives. At its most elemental level, life involves values.[27] We must account for values because the world teems with them.

To illustrate the power of values, think back to how we responded when reading the stories in chapter one. When we read that gunmen killed Zamuda's family and brutally raped her, we immediately made value judgments. "That is not right!" we said in our minds or felt in our hearts. "This is so sad!" we may have thought, or "this makes me angry!"

When we learned that the Tsarnaev brothers planned the Boston

---

[26]Scientists presuppose values when they say some explanations are better than others. They also presuppose values when they say some discoveries are important. But it is altogether different to presuppose values, which scientists do, than it is to explain values fully, which science alone cannot do.

[27]Tyron L. Inbody expresses the centrality of value well in his search for an adequate answer to the problem of evil: *The Transforming God: An Interpretation of Suffering and Evil* (Louisville, KY: Westminster John Knox, 1997), pp. 14-15, 153-56.

Marathon bombing, our moral intuitions engaged. "This should not have happened," we thought. "Justice must be done," we might have added. Our view of what justice requires may differ from our neighbor's, but our basic sense of fairness points to the fact that we make value judgments. Our moral intuitions prompt us, inevitably, to make value claims about events in our world.

In the way we act, we inevitably reveal our deeply held belief that some ways of living or events in the world are better than others. The act of valuing is another experiential nonnegotiable. Our moral intuitions prompt us to prefer some ways of living to others.

We humans do not always agree, of course, on the specifics of good and evil. Some morally mature people, for instance, think abortion wrong in every instance. Other morally mature people think abortion sometimes justifiable. Some people think polygamy wrong in every situation. Others think having multiple spouses permissible in particular cultures. Some think spitting on the sidewalk inappropriate, other people do not care and some believe such spitting may be good.

We do not need to agree on the details to know that value judgments, in themselves, are inevitable. More specifically, we do not need to agree on moral issues to admit morality matters. Even hardened criminals care about values and retain a moral sense, underdeveloped though these may be.

We are all morally aware.

Issues of value are central to religion because religions and their adherents emphasize value claims. These claims usually involve recommending some ways of living and condemning others. For instance, some religions promote the idea that we ought to live well for our own sakes. Others emphasize living well in relation to other people. Some religions recommend living well in relation to the natural world. Others say we live well in relation to God. Some promote all these ideas and say we act well by loving God, creation, others and ourselves. All religions believe that values matter.

Those of us who believe in God typically think God is the ultimate source of values. God is the source of goodness and promotes it, and God opposes evil. Consequently, say believers, we ought to obey, imitate and praise God. We ought to join God's opposition to evil and promotion of good. Happiness in the present depends, in part, upon how we respond to God's guidance with regard to values. Our status in the afterlife may also depend on our responses.

In sum, we are creatures who value. Making sense of reality involves admitting this. Those of us who believe in God usually think theology plays a role in understanding values—especially good and evil. Making sense of reality, for many of us, involves believing God is the source of goodness and opposed to evil. Most believers say our fundamental moral intuitions, even though they may differ from the intuitions of others, derive from deity.

THE PROBLEM OF EVIL

The struggle comes, as we saw in chapter one, when we try to account for the suffering, tragedy and horrific evil we encounter. Most believers like me think God is good and powerful. Most think God opposes evil and seeks what is good. Most think we ought to imitate God by living lives of love, which means promoting good and opposing evil.

If God is perfectly good, God will *want* to prevent genuine evils. If God can control creatures or circumstances totally, God would be *able* to prevent genuine evils. And yet horrors occur. Genuine evils like those we encountered in chapter one occur often, but even one instance of genuine evil is one too many.

In the face of such evil, some thoughtful people conclude God must not exist. They choose atheism. Others say God must not love perfectly. Still others doubt God has the kind of total control necessary to prevent genuine evil.

Most often, believers who wrestle with the problem of evil say God loves perfectly and can control others entirely. Because these believers cannot reconcile their beliefs with the genuine evil they experience, they appeal to mystery. "We will never understand this side of heaven," they say. "God's ways are not our ways." Making sense of evil, for these people, is impossible.

Those who appeal to mystery still usually say we should oppose genuine evil. "God calls us to work to make the world a better place," they may claim. But it is hard to be motivated to oppose that which an omnipotent God allowed. A God who could control people or situations could have prevented these evils in the first place. Without some clarity about God's ways, opposing what we think is evil may work in opposition to God's plans for good.

Why try to alleviate the suffering a supposedly omnipotent and loving God permits?

Careful readers will notice I have often been adding the adjective *genuine* before evil in paragraphs above. I do so because philosophers sometimes distinguish between necessary evil and gratuitous evil. I call gratuitous evil genuine for various reasons.

Sometimes suffering and pain are required to bring about greater good. For instance, a husband and wife may intentionally become pregnant. They may do so knowing the wife will likely undergo intense pain in the birthing process. But pain in childbirth may be necessary for the greater good of bringing a child into the world and parenting it.

Or consider the discomfort we experience when a nurse injects an antibiotic. The good that comes from fighting infection outweighs the painful prick of the needle. Some pain is necessary for greater good. Without this temporary pain, we are worse off in the long run.

Genuine evils are different in kind from necessary evils. Genuine evils are events that, all things considered, make the world worse than it might have been.[28] The phrase "than it might have been" suggests that better outcomes were possible should choosers have selected or allowed some other viable option. Genuine evils are de-

---

[28]I am grateful to David Ray Griffin for this general understanding of genuine evil. Among his many books, see especially *God, Power, and Evil: A Process Theodicy* (Louisville, KY: Westminster John Knox, 2004). I develop the notion of genuine evil in my book *Defining Love: A Philosophical, Scientific, and Theological Engagement* (Grand Rapids: Brazos, 2010), chap. 6.

structive or injurious occurrences that did not have to take place. They are gratuitous and unnecessary. Something better could have happened instead.

Numerous events qualify as evil. It can be difficult to evaluate which are genuine and which are necessary for greater good. When rain spoils a picnic, some may think the downpour was genuinely evil. But the farmer hoping for moisture may consider the rain good. Earthquakes and tornados, as devastating as they can be, may be instances of necessary evil. After all, they renew soils or replenish ecosystems. We are not always confident in knowing when suffering is genuinely evil.

We do not need to assess all circumstances flawlessly, however, to be justified in believing that genuine evils sometimes occur. I cannot imagine, for example, any instance of rape to be necessary to promote greater good. Genocides are genuine evils too. The Nazi holocaust lands on almost everybody's list of genuine evils, and it is on mine. The vast majority of, if not all, cases of murder, incest, embezzlement, child abuse, cancer and torture are instances of genuine evils.

All stories in the first chapter strike me as examples of genuine evil. They made the world worse than it might have been had some other possible events occurred. Other, better events were possible in each case.

Of course, some good may come from even genuine evils. The rape victim may learn something new, for instance. While learning new things is usually good, such learning does not promote overall well-being. The rape victim is better off, all things considered, had she not been raped. Rape victims would gladly give up learning new information to avoid their pain and humiliation!

Take as another example medical experiments on Jewish prisoners in Nazi camps. Because of those experiments, science made important discoveries. Despite this good, such inhumane experimentation was genuinely evil. The torment caused by tests made the world worse than it might have been had the tests never been done. The costs of suffering and human indignity outweigh the benefits of new discovery. Even if some good can be "squeezed" from them, genuine evils make the world worse than it might have been.

The theological word *sin* offers strong evidence for the reality of genuine evil. Sin presupposes that genuinely evil events occur. Most believers assume God lovingly wants what is best for creatures, creation and the kingdom of heaven. Sin opposes God's loving desires and plans because it makes the world worse than it might have been had sinners freely chosen, instead, to cooperate with God. Sin opposes love.

If the apostle Paul is correct when claiming that all have sinned (Rom 3:23), we have not only witnessed evil, we all have also caused it. Victims of evil know this all too well. Genuine evils occur, and deep down we all know it.

Careful readers may have also noticed I have often talked about God failing to *prevent* evil. Some people think they solve the problem by simply saying God gives freedom and agency to creatures, and, therefore, God does not cause evil. Creatures effect evil, they say, so God should not be blamed.

I also believe God is not the primary cause of evil. But to solve the problem of evil, we must say more than this. After all, a perfectly loving individual would do whatever possible to prevent—not just fail to cause—genuine evil. A person does not have to cause evil directly to be morally culpable for failing to prevent it.

For instance, no one gives an award for Parent of the Year to the mother or father who allows his or her child to drown while saying, "although I could have prevented the drowning, I didn't *cause* it!" The true parent of the year would have done just about everything in his or her ability to prevent the drowning. Allowing this drowning is not loving. And the parent is culpable for failing to prevent the evil.

No one gives an award for Citizen of the Year to the community leader who permits an industrial company to pollute the city's water. The leader may say, "I knew about the polluting and could have stopped it. But don't blame me, because I'm not the cause." We think good leaders work to prevent harm not just avoid causing it. Permitting evil is morally inappropriate.

Similarly, a loving God would not just refrain from causing genuine evil. A loving God would prevent it, if possible. The God who could have prevented a genuinely evil event is culpable for failing to do so. A morally culpable individual—even if divine—has not loved perfectly. A loving God would not allow genuine evil that is preventable.

If we think about it long enough, we all know this. Genuine evils happen, and they have no greater overall purpose. And if we who sometimes do evil know something about goodness, a perfectly loving God would also know and always do what goodness demands (Mt 7:11).

A God worthy of our worship cannot be Someone who causes, supports or allows genuine evil. In fact, I believe it is impossible to worship wholeheartedly a God who loves halfheartedly. We might fear a God who helps sometimes but other times chooses not to, but we cannot admire this God unreservedly.

If God loves perfectly, God must not cause evil nor be culpable for failing to prevent it.

THE PROBLEM OF GOOD

More must be said about the problem of evil. I intend to offer a solution later in this book as we explore my proposed model of providence. Before closing my discussion of values, however, it seems wise to address another, little-discussed "problem": the problem of good.

The problem of evil asks why a good and powerful God does not prevent genuine evil. The problem, left unsolved, seriously challenges those who, like me, believe in God. The problem of evil is a real problem for believers.

By contrast, the problem of good asks whether we can account well for genuine goodness but deny the existence of a good and powerful God. The problem of good, left unsolved, seriously challenges those who do *not* believe in God. The problem of good is a real problem for unbelievers.

I do not raise the problem of good to negate or neutralize the problem of evil. I disagree with believers who think they can leave the problem of evil unsolved because the problem of good presents challenges to atheists. To account well for life, we must offer a plausible solution to why a loving and powerful God does not prevent genuine evil. But we must account for goodness too.

The problem of good reminds us that we encounter a great deal of goodness, love, compassion, generosity and beneficial cooperation in the world. We sometimes focus so intently on evil that we forget the good. To make sense of life, we need to account for both evil and good.

As an example of widespread goodness, take the immense cooperating we do every day. Cooperation often makes better our lives and the lives of others. Although we can cooperate with evil schemes, cooperation is often the means by which immense goodness emerges in day-to-day living. We join together to do good and make the world a better place.

Today, for instance, I cooperated with my wife and three daughters so that we might live good, peaceful and productive lives. We coordinated efforts when doing household chores this morning to begin our day positively. As we traveled to work and school, we cooperated with surrounding drivers to make the commute amazingly well organized. For the most part, our fellow students and colleagues cooperated with us throughout the day.

After school and work, we coordinated transportation so we could participate in evening activities. A few of us fixed the evening meal for the family while others set the table and later cleared dishes. After relaxing, studying or doing more chores, we coordinated schedules for the next day. Setting the house temperature, locking the doors, and shutting off lights and computers—for the good of all—we finally headed to bed.

This "day in the life of the Oord family" does not come close to mentioning all the ways we experienced goodness this day and in others. It does not address the significant self-sacrifices we make, sometimes at significant cost to ourselves, to help others enjoy life or evade suffering. When acting to promote well-being, we sometimes take one for the team. We do so to make our lives, the lives of those we know and even the world better. If we were to list all the ways we act self-sacrificially to benefit others, the list would be long!

Also important for promoting good are the random acts of kindness many do. While less frequent than coordinated cooperation or planned self-sacrifice, spontaneous acts of generosity are powerful examples of goodness. Random acts of kindness may range from an unexpected compliment to a generous gratuity to helping a stranger to picking up trash.

If we look for it, we will notice goodness all around. Virtue is far more common than we may realize. We take for granted good things and good deeds, overlooking them. Sometimes we simply need to open our eyes to the ways we bless others and others bless us. Generosity abounds.

The typical explanation for the ultimate source of goodness—and the explanation I find most plausible—says the inspiration to do good comes from God.[29] God's loving presence pervades reality, and God prompts us to act in good ways and live good lives. God's nature is the measure of what is good. And we do good deeds and become good people when we respond well to God's call to love.[30]

I am not the only one who believes God is the ultimate source of and inspiration for goodness. C. S. Lewis, for instance, says Something exists "which is directing the universe, and which appears to me as a law urging me to do right and making me feel responsible and uncomfortable when I do wrong." Furthermore, Lewis says, "if the universe is not governed by an absolute goodness, then all our efforts are in the long run hopeless."[31]

More recently, theologian Keith Ward argues that we best understand goodness and morality when we believe them grounded in God.

---

[29]Many religious traditions see God as the source and inspiration of what is good, loving or merciful. On this, see selections from Thomas Jay Oord, ed., *The Altruism Reader: Selections from Writings on Love, Religion, and Science* (West Conshohocken, PA: Templeton Press, 2008).

[30]This is a main theme in Thomas Jay Oord and Michael Lodahl, *Relational Holiness: Responding to the Call of Love* (Kansas City, MO: Beacon Hill, 2005).

[31]C. S. Lewis, *Mere Christianity* (1952; repr., New York: HarperCollins, 2000), pp. 25, 31.

Ward postulates the existence of a God who is "of supreme value, and in the mind of which exists all the possibilities of finite being, good and bad." Grounding goodness in God, says Ward, "gives to moral experience an objectivity, authority, and effectiveness that would immensely strengthen the motivating force of morality and its consilience with a more general worldview." In this worldview, God "is supremely good," "creates for the sake of goodness" and offers the "prospect of attaining true human flourishing and well-being."[32]

The problem of good wonders if we can fully explain the goodness in life while denying the existence of God. If God does not exist, why do we encounter beneficial cooperation, positive self-sacrifice, generosity, altruism and love in the world?[33] Why do we judge some actions good or evil, better or worse? And when we make these judgments, why do we think that at least some of them transcend mere personal or social preferences?

Some look to science for an explanation of goodness. To a certain extent, this makes sense. Recent scientific research, especially in sociobiology and evolutionary psychology, seeks an explanation for cooperation and altruistic behavior.[34] Most biologists admit that the behavior of a wide range of species points to altruism, in the sense of acting for the good of others.[35] It is not clear, however, whether this altruistic action is ever primarily other-oriented or always primarily self-oriented.

---

[32]Keith Ward, *Morality, Autonomy, and God* (London: Oneworld, 2013), p. 214.

[33]Although in this book I have generally connected goodness with altruism, cooperation and self-sacrifice, these can also promote ill-being. We can act for the sake of others or cooperate in ways we intend for evil rather than overall well-being. What I reject, however, is that all altruism, cooperation and self-sacrifice have as their primary motive or goal the good of the self. And I reject the notion that altruism, cooperation and self-sacrifice always promote ill-being.

[34]See Edward O. Wilson, *On Human Nature*, 25th anniversary ed. (1978; Cambridge, MA: Harvard University Press, 2004). See also my work on altruism and biology in *Defining Love*, pp. 97-136.

[35]For research on reciprocal altruism, see Robert L. Trivers, "The Evolution of Reciprocal Altruism," *Quarterly Review of Biology* 46, no. 1 (1971): 35-37. For research on kin altruism, see W. D. Hamilton, "The Evolution of Altruistic Behavior," *American Naturalist* 97, no. 896 (1963): 354-56. One of the best books on altruism among groups is by Elliot Sober and David Sloan Wilson, *Unto Others: The Evolution and Psychology of Unselfish Behavior* (Cambridge, MA: Harvard University Press, 1998). A number of more popular books explore various types of altruism. I discuss these and other types of altruism as they relate to love in my book *Defining Love*, pp. 97-136.

Sometimes altruism involves cooperation for mutual benefit, also known as tit-for-tat or reciprocal altruism. Existence is replete with cooperating creatures acting altruistically in this way. If I scratch your back and you scratch mine, both our backs will be less itchy. Many creatures seem to know and act on this general principle.

Other times, self-sacrifice occurs in nature. One creature acts in ways that undermines its own well-being for the good of others. In the behavior of ants, fish, rodents, canines, elephants, primates and other animals, we find examples of creatures acting for the good of others at some cost to themselves.[36] Humans often forgo personal pleasure or endure personal pain for the good of others. Some even die for another's sake.

Of course, observing altruism among humans and animals is different from explaining the ultimate source of goodness. It is difficult, if not impossible, for science to explain this ultimate source because science alone cannot account for values.[37] Science is not built for such comprehensive explanations.

Some sociobiologists argue, however, that the goodness apparent in creaturely altruism and cooperation is not ultimately good at all. Altruism and cooperation are egoism in disguise. Goodness is just another name for reproductive success, say some sociobiologists. Altruists may seem to act for the sake of others, but they do so only if their actions benefit their offspring. "What passes for co-operation turns out to be a mixture of opportunism and exploitation," says

---

[36]For books exploring animal cooperation, see Robert Axelrod, *The Evolution of Cooperation* (New York: Basic, 1984); Samuel Bowles and Herbert Gintis, *A Cooperative Species: Human Reciprocity and Its Evolution* (Princeton, NJ: Princeton University Press, 2011); Lee Alan Dugatkin, *Cheating Monkeys and Citizen Bees: The Nature of Cooperation in Animals and Humans* (Cambridge, MA: Harvard University Press, 1999); Oord, *Altruism Reader*, pp. 213-84; and Matt Ridley, *The Origins of Virtue: Human Instincts and the Evolution of Cooperation* (New York: Penguin, 1996).

[37]Important books exploring this theme include Philip Clayton and Jeffrey Schloss, eds., *Evolution and Ethics: Human Morality in Biological and Religious Perspective* (Grand Rapids: Eerdmans, 2004); Frans DeWaal, *Good Natured: The Origin of Right and Wrong in Humans and Other Animals* (Cambridge: Cambridge University Press, 1996); Andrew Michael Flescher and Daniel L. Worthen, *The Altruistic Species: Scientific, Philosophical, and Religious Perspectives of Human Benevolence* (West Conshohocken, PA: Templeton Press, 2007); and Robert Wright, *The Moral Animal: The New Science of Evolutionary Psychology* (New York: Vintage, 1994).

Michael Ghiselin in support of this view. "Scratch an 'altruist' and watch a 'hypocrite' bleed."[38]

From this perspective, cooperation and self-sacrifice spring from the egoistic desire to further one's genetic lineage.[39] Rather than pursuing mutual aid, the genecentric approach says animals always act with the ultimate goal of passing on their own genes.[40] All self-sacrifice and cooperation—in ants, antelope, elephants, wolves, chimpanzees and humans—is ultimately for the altruist's own benefit. And when one animal cares for its young, the young of the group or even the young of another species, such care is primarily selfish. Morality is merely an evolutionary mechanism for gene replication. Transcendent goodness is a sham.[41]

The idea that creatures are never primarily oriented for the good of others usually springs from a view of reality called *materialism*. For most materialists, nature is all there is, and only science investigates reality rightly.[42] Neither God nor values nor transcendent standards exists by which to assess reality.

To them, matter is all that matters.

The materialist usually intends for the explanation that altruism is really egoism to apply to all creatures, human and nonhuman. In terms of humans, this means that although we may think we act primarily for the good of others, we unconsciously act always and primarily for our own benefit. We have evolved, goes the materialist argument, so that our self-interested motives are hidden even to us. All altruists are self-deceived egoists.[43]

---

[38]Michael T. Ghiselin, *The Economy of Nature and the Evolution of Sex* (Berkeley: University of California Press, 1974), p. 247.

[39]See Wilson, *On Human Nature*, and Dawkins, *Selfish Gene*.

[40]See Petr Kropotkin, *Mutual Aid: A Factor of Evolution*, 3rd ed. (1902; Montreal: Black Rose, 1989). For a great biographical read, see also Oren Harman, *The Price of Altruism: George Price and the Search for the Origins of Kindness* (New York: Norton, 2011).

[41]Perhaps the best-known argument for this position comes from Dawkins in *Selfish Gene*. Alister McGrath offers one of the better responses to Dawkins in *Dawkins's God: Genes, Memes, and the Meaning of Life* (Malden, MA: Blackwell, 2005).

[42]One of the better critiques of scientific materialism comes from John F. Haught, *Is Nature Enough? Meaning and Truth in the Age of Science* (Cambridge: Cambridge University Press, 2006).

[43]Richard D. Alexander advocates this view. See his book *The Biology of Moral Systems* (New York: De Gruyter, 1987), pp. 93-94.

If materialism is true, self-interest rules in the Oord family. Self-sacrifice and random acts of kindness are unwitting self-promotion. All the Oords are utterly selfish, and so are good Samaritans and Mother Teresa.[44] Every soldier who lies on a live hand grenade to save his or her buddies is selfish. Every nurse who willingly accepts exposure to possible infection when attempting to help patients is egotistical. Every foster parent is ultimately motivated by self-gain. The goodness we see in cooperation and self-sacrifice is not really good at all. And we never act primarily for the good of others.

In the end, materialism says *good* is merely a word we use to talk about self-benefit, survival or furthering our genetic lineage. As Richard Dawkins puts it, the world looks exactly as if there is "at bottom . . . no evil and no good, nothing but blind pitiless indifference."[45] Good and evil are ultimately unreal, say some unbelievers, and this is one more reason not to believe in God. Extreme value relativism rules.

I must admit there is a measure of reasonableness to the materialist view. For a short time, I was an atheist, so I understand why some people are attracted to the materialist perspective. Given some of the claims believers make about God, atheistic materialism can seem like an attractive alternative.

I no longer find materialism more plausible than a particular version of theism, however. To me, belief in God makes more sense, overall, than atheistic materialism. My dissatisfaction with how materialism explains (or explains away) good and evil is part of the reason I find atheism less plausible than the particular way of understanding God I offer later in this book.

One major problem with materialism is that we all live as if good and evil are real. I certainly do, and so do you. We all live as if there is, at bottom, more than blind, pitiless indifference. Even Richard

---

[44]For a critique of the view that good Samaritans are ultimately egoists, see Holmes Rolston III, *Genes, Genesis, and God: Values and Their Origins in Natural and Human History* (Cambridge: Cambridge University Press, 1999).

[45]Richard Dawkins, *River out of Eden: A Darwinian View of Life* (London: Weidenfeld & Nicolson, 1995), p. 133.

Dawkins does. We also all live as if we should and sometimes do act primarily for the good of others. A major problem for materialism is the inconsistency between how we all live and the materialist view that good and evil are ultimately unreal.[46] Philosophical materialism doesn't fit with how we all live.

Materialism has other problems too. Some are oriented around materialism's misunderstanding of creaturely motivation. For instance, few of our actions are entirely motivated for our own good. And few are entirely motivated for the good of others. Instead, our motives usually mix. We are motivated partly for our own good and partly for the good of others.

Given this, it is more important to ask what our primary motivation might be among the mix of motivations we have. Almost all of us realize that sometimes our primary motivations are for the good of others. We may be rewarded in some way when acting for the good of others, but our chief intent was not to help ourselves. At other times, we know we should act primarily for the sake of others, even if we fail to do so. Materialism offers no good explanation for motives primarily oriented toward another's good.

Other problems with materialism are ontological. For instance, our experience tells us that we live in an interrelated universe. What I do affects others and me. Isolating my good entirely from the good of others is impossible. I sometimes act primarily for my own sake; other times I may act primarily for the sake of others. Often, my doing good promotes overall well-being in such a way that I help both others and myself.[47] Materialism has difficulty accounting for the interrelatedness and the intermingling of well-being.

The argument that evolution has created us self-deceived is inherently problematic. It backfires on those who make it. After all, if evolution undermines true beliefs about good and evil because we are all

---

[46]One of the better arguments for the reality of ethical law and the natural world is found in Craig A. Boyd, *A Shared Morality: A Narrative Defense of Natural Law Ethics* (Grand Rapids: Brazos, 2007).

[47]I explore this in my essay, "A Relational God and Unlimited Love," in *Visions of Agape*, ed. Craig A. Boyd (Farnham, UK: Ashgate, 2008), pp. 135-48, and in my book *Defining Love*, chap. 4.

self-deceived, the critic of altruism has no grounds to think his beliefs are truer than the believer in altruism. No one can know.

Materialism cannot provide an ultimate explanation for goodness, rightness and morality.[48] Because it denies any transcendent criteria of rightness, we have no fundamental reason to follow materialism's claims about assessing goodness with some degree of objectivity. Some philosophers refer to this problem as the grounding issue. Without a metaphysical foundation or ground, materialists have no objective basis on which to assess good and evil.[49] Without some transcendent ground, the materialist cannot even determine whether his arguments are better than others. The materialist needs a transcendent standard by which to make such value judgments.[50] Because we all inevitably make such judgments—another experiential nonnegotiable—materialism without transcendence cannot offer a satisfying explanation of reality.

Science needs transcendence to explain value.

To account for the ultimate source of goodness, we turn to metaphysics and religion. For many others and for me, a theistic metaphysics—an overall theory of God and the world—provides the best framework for explaining why creatures sometimes do good and why we consider some acts good at all.

Turning to a theistic metaphysics does not mean science plays no role in understanding goodness and morality. We must resist the either/or choice between theology and science.[51] Instead, I believe an adequate theistic metaphysics draws from both religion and science—and other disciplines—when pondering reality, including good and evil. When it comes to theology and science, it's both/and not either/or.

---

[48]For a strong criticism of the materialism of the new atheists, see David Fergusson, *Faith and Its Critics: A Conversation* (Oxford: Oxford University Press, 2009).

[49]For a similar argument, see Haught, *Is Nature Enough?*

[50]Keith Ward argues this point in several books, including *God, Chance, and Necessity* (Oxford: Oneworld, 1996).

[51]For an example of someone who takes an either/or approach to science and religion, see Sam Harris, *The Moral Landscape: How Science Can Determine Human Values* (London: Transworld, 2010), p. 22.

A robust theistic metaphysics proposes that God's loving nature serves as the source and standard of all goodness in the world. When we wonder what is good or evil, right or wrong, or better or worse, we appeal to God. Our appeals are usually unconscious and unreflective. We appeal to God's righteousness when evaluating what is good and evil.

Saying God does good, inspires good and is the source of goodness doesn't go far enough, however. Our experience suggests that creatures do good too. In my view, nonhuman species also sometimes act for the good of themselves, others and the whole. Creatures can live in ways that promote well-being.[52]

Most of the time, creatures must choose to do good. They must respond well to divine inspiration. Unlike God, creatures do not have eternal and unchanging natures necessarily inclined toward love. But they can act in genuinely good ways when they respond well to God's calls.[53]

When creatures respond well to the God whose loving nature is the source and standard of goodness, creatures do what is good in a way appropriate for the context. This may include beneficial cooperation, self-sacrifice, self-enhancement, compassion, generosity, kindness, self-development, self-giving, accepting gifts from others or a host of other activities that promote overall well-being. We can do good in many ways!

When creatures respond poorly, they do evil. Creatures can undermine overall goodness. Some events and ways of living generate ill-being rather than well-being. Christians call these intentional actions *sin*, or a similar word.

Believing that God is the source of goodness provides an overall framework for affirming the work of theology, science and metaphysics. It affirms theology's claim that God exists, does good and is

---

[52]One of the better scholarly examinations of nature and ethics is Celia E. Deane-Drummond, *The Ethics of Nature* (Malden, MA: Blackwell, 2004).

[53]I explore this in more detail in Thomas Jay Oord, "Testing Creaturely Love and God's Causal Role," in *The Science and Theology of Godly Love*, ed. Matthew T. Lee and Amos Yong (DeKalb: Northern Illinois University Press, 2012), pp. 94-120.

the ultimate source of goodness. It affirms scientific research pointing to creaturely altruism, cooperation and self-sacrifice. And it provides an overall metaphysical basis that accounts for the value we find expressed by God and creatures.

In sum, belief in a good God is the best solution to the problem of good. It allows us to answer questions that inevitably arise in our quest to answer well the big questions of life.[54] It also fits well with views of agency and freedom that regard free will as genuine. A theistic metaphysics can help us on a number of issues as we attempt to make sense of existence. The best overall explanation for goodness, love, compassion, generosity and cooperation includes necessary roles for both creatures and the Creator.[55]

Appealing to God doesn't answer all our questions. After all, more than one theology exists. Believers offer multiple ways to think about God's activity in the world.[56] To understand existence in light of what

---

[54]For a powerful defense of this view, see Joseph Bankard, *Universal Morality Reconsidered: The Concept of God* (Cambridge: Cambridge Scholars, 2013), p. 224. See also Alasdair McIntyre, *After Virtue: A Study in Moral Theory* (Notre Dame, IN: University of Notre Dame Press, 1984); and Nancey Murphy and George F. R. Ellis, *On the Moral Nature of the Universe: Theology, Cosmology, and Ethics* (Minneapolis: Fortress, 1996).

[55]For one of the better arguments for the necessity of metaphysics and the greater plausibility of a theistic metaphysics for explaining goodness, see Ward, *Morality, Autonomy, and God*. Some of the better books arguing for altruism or theologies of love include Gary Chartier, *The Analogy of Love: Divine and Human Love at the Center of Christian Theology* (Charlottesville, VA: Imprint Academic, 2007); Colin Grant, *Altruism and Christian Ethics* (Cambridge: Cambridge University Press, 2001); Werner G. Jeanrond, *A Theology of Love* (New York: T & T Clark, 2010); Jacob Neusner and Bruce Chilton, eds., *Altruism in World Religions* (Washington, DC: Georgetown University Press, 2005); George Newlands, *Theology of the Love of God* (Atlanta: John Knox, 1980); Stephen G. Post, Lynn G. Underwood, Jeffrey P. Schloss and William P. Hurlbutt, *Altruism and Altruistic Love* (Oxford: Oxford University Press, 2002); Paul R. Sponheim, *Love's Availing Power: Imagining God, Imagining the World* (Minneapolis: Fortress, 2011); and Amos Yong, *Spirit of Love: A Trinitarian Theology of Grace* (Waco, TX: Baylor University Press, 2012).

[56]Among the better books reconciling divine action and contemporary science in addition to those cited elsewhere in this book, see Ronald Cole-Turner, *The New Genesis: Theology and the Genetic Revolution* (Louisville, KY: Westminster John Knox, 1993); Christopher C. Knight, *Wrestling with the Divine: Religion, Science, and Revelation* (Minneapolis: Fortress, 2001); Samuel M. Powell, *Participating in God: Creation and Trinity* (Minneapolis: Fortress, 2003); Robert John Russell, *Cosmology: From Alpha to Omega* (Minneapolis: Fortress, 2008); Robert John Russell, Nancey Murphy and Arthur R. Peacocke, *Chaos and Complexity: Scientific Perspectives on Divine Action* (Notre Dame, IN: University of Notre Dame Press, 1995); F. LeRon Shults, Nancey Murphy and Robert John Russell, eds., *Philosophy, Science and Divine Action* (Leiden: Brill, 2009); Kirk Wegter-McNelly, *The Entangled God: Divine Relationality and Quantum Physics* (New York: Routledge, 2011); Larry Witham, *The Measure of God: Our Century-Long Struggle*

we've addressed thus far—randomness, regularities, free will, good and evil—we need to explore possible ways to understand God's activity in the world.

We need a plausible model of providence.

to Reconcile Science and Religion (San Francisco: HarperSanFrancisco, 2005); Amos Yong, *The Spirit of Creation: Modern Science and Divine Action in the Pentecostal-Charismatic Imagination* (Grand Rapids: Eerdmans, 2011).

4

Models of God's Providence

I am among the majority of people on planet earth who believe that
a satisfying answer to life's biggest questions includes believing
something true about who God is and how God acts. Theology
matters. As the stories in the opening chapter convey, answering life's
biggest questions involves understanding God's actions, especially in
light of evil and randomness.

Theologians refer to God's activity in the world as providence. But
defining *providence* precisely is difficult. Scriptures seldom use the
term, and when we do find it in holy writ, *providence* can mean
various things. Those who offer definitions of *providence*—theologians in the past and today—usually have a particular theology in
mind when defining it. For now, I simply use *providence* as a way to
talk about God's activity in relation to creatures and the created order
more generally.

My overarching aim for this book is to offer the best way to believe God acts providentially in a world of regularities and randomness, freedom and agency, good and evil. In previous chapters,
I explored what I mean by these aspects of existence and a bit about
God's relation to them. In this chapter, I look at various models of
divine providence.

At the outset, let me say no one speaks for God—myself included.
All models are provisional and likely incomplete. When we propose
theories about any aspect of life—scientific, philosophical, religious,

ethical or otherwise—we should do so with a healthy dose of humility. When we deliberate on the divine, we do so with greater humility and tentativeness.

Pondering providence means seeking the most elusive answers.

Yet I believe we can know *something* about who God is and how God acts. As a Christian, I believe we know something because of the revelation of Jesus Christ. Christians like me think Jesus reveals God's character more clearly than anything or anyone. Because of Jesus, as John's Gospel puts it, God has been made known to us (Jn 1:18), at least to some extent.

I also think we can know something about God because of the revelation we find in Scripture, the natural world, tradition, reason, the arts, sciences and our personal experiences. This connects to the common Christian belief that God is present to and active in all of creation. God's attributes have been seen in what has been created, argues the apostle Paul, and Christians believe in the God in whom "we live and move and have our being" (Acts 17:28; Rom 1:20).

I do not believe, however, that we comprehend God *fully*. I doubt we can ever finally figure out God. We may advance toward deeper knowledge, but I doubt we ever understand in full. We see as if looking through a pair of darkened glasses (1 Cor 13:12). Because our vision is obscured, we should be humble when proposing how we believe God acts providentially.

Theologians throughout the ages have written volume after volume about God's action. Proposals vary, and sometimes subtle nuances separate one theory from another. Other differences are major. The fact that differences exist among theologians should not surprise us of course. If we peer through darkened glasses, no one sees with absolute clarity.

Various forms of God's revelation—including Scripture—are interpreted in diverse ways, further complicating matters. Good-natured, well-intentioned and wise theologians can disagree. No one interprets divine revelation, in whatever form, inerrantly. Our mental processes differ, and no creature knows all things. Not only is humility in order, therefore, but tolerance and generosity of spirit are recommended.

To get a handle on diverse ways theologians think about providence, I offer a figure showing models of God's providence. While not exhaustive, it presents seven major models of how believers think God acts providentially.[1] The figure should help us make sense of various ways of thinking about divine providence. And it should help as I move toward proposing the new model I find most plausible.

1	2	3	4	5	6	7
God is the omnicause.	God empowers and overpowers.	God is voluntarily self-limited.	God is essentially kenotic.	God sustains as impersonal force.	God is initial creator and current observer.	God's ways are not our ways.

Figure 4.1. Models of God's providence

Whole books could be written about each model in this figure.[2] But I explain each in this chapter with basic sketches. I note implications of the models, including how they portray randomness, free will, goodness, evil, and God's love and power. I hope that, despite my brevity, the key ideas of each providence model will become evident.

1. God Is the Omnicause

The basic idea of this model is that God causes all things. What appear to be random events or the activities of free will are in accordance with God's will, such that God ultimately makes them happen, as they happen. God is in complete control.

The Heidelberg Catechism promotes this model of providence. It

---

[1]Theologians and scientists use models to explore the validity and fruitfulness of competing theories. Frederick Ferré defines a model, in this sense, as "that which provides epistemological vividness or immediacy to a theory by offering as an interpretation of the abstract or unfamiliar theory-structure something that fits the logical form of the theory and is well known." Frederick Ferré, "Mapping the Logic of Models in Science and Theology," in *New Essays on Religious Language*, ed. Dallas M. High (New York: Oxford University Press, 1969), p. 75.

[2]For a book proposing eleven models, see Terrance Tiessen, *Providence and Prayer: How Does God Work in the World?* (Downers Grove, IL: InterVarsity Press, 2000). See also Charles M. Wood, *The Question of Providence* (Louisville, KY: Westminster John Knox, 2008).

says God "rules in such a way that . . . everything comes to us not by chance but by his fatherly hand."[3] And everything means everything!

Those in the Reformed tradition of Christianity often promote this model. An advocate, B. B. Warfield, puts it succinctly, "There is nothing that is, and nothing that comes to pass, that [God] has not first decreed and then brought to pass by His creation or providence."[4] This means, says Warfield, that God's "will is the ultimate account of all that occurs."[5]

Exactly *how* God controls all things, says this model, is a mystery. God's actions are inscrutable. Although humans may seem to act freely and other creaturely causes exist in the universe, in some unfathomable way, God totally causes every event.[6] The catechism statement we saw above uses the phrase "in such a way" when pointing to this mystery, and many advocates of this model use it too. Although it is impossible to understand how God can control all things and yet creatures act freely or exert creaturely causation of some sort, advocates of the omnicause model claim it to be so.

According to this model, all occurrences are part of the "secret providence of God," to quote John Calvin.[7] "The great works of the Lord are carefully crafted in respect of all that he wills," says Calvin, "so that in a wonderful and ineffable way nothing happens contrary to his will, even that which is contrary to his will!"[8]

Paul Kjoss Helseth, a contemporary advocate of the model, calls it "divine omnicausality." God alone preserves and governs all things. In

---

[3]*The Heidelberg Catechism*, trans. Allen O. Miller and M. Eugene Osterhaven (Philadelphia: United Church Press, 1962) as reprinted in *Confessions and Catechisms of the Reformation*, ed. Mark Noll (Grand Rapids: Baker, 1991), pp. 141-42.

[4]B. B. Warfield, "Predestination," in *Biblical Doctrines*, vol. 2 of *The Works of Benjamin B. Warfield* (1929; repr., Grand Rapids: Baker Books, 1991), p. 21.

[5]Ibid., p. 9.

[6]See Herman Bavinck, *God and Creation*, vol. 2 of *Reformed Dogmatics*, ed. John Bolt, trans. John Vriend (Grand Rapids: Baker Academic, 2004), pp. 614-15; and Francis Turretin, *Institutes of Elenctic Theology*, ed. James T. Dennison Jr., trans. George Musgrave Giger (Phillipsburg, NJ: P & R, 1992), 1:500-517.

[7]John Calvin, *The Secret Providence of God*, ed. Paul Helm, trans. Keith Goad (Wheaton, IL: Crossway, 2010).

[8]Ibid., p. 81.

light of this, says Helseth, "we are called to place our confidence in the character and promises of our Father, even when we have no idea precisely what he is doing as he works out the particulars of his sovereign will."[9]

Advocates of the omnicause model have a particular view of divine power in mind. They often use the word *sovereignty* when describing it, and they typically mean that God exerts control. Advocates find comfort in this model because it reassures them that whatever occurs—no matter how bad—is part of God's meticulous plan.

Several passages of Scripture seem to portray God as the omnicause. Isaiah, for instance, reports God saying,

> I form light and create darkness,
>> I make weal and create woe;
>> I the LORD do all these things. (Is 45:7)

The prophet Amos asks an apparently rhetorically question: "Does disaster befall a city, unless the LORD has done it?" (Amos 3:6). And the writer of Proverbs declares what some think supports the compatibility of God causing all things and creatures intending some:

> The human mind plans the way,
>> but the LORD directs the steps. (Prov 16:9)

The model that sees God as the omnicause has plenty of critics, and I am one. Critics argue, for instance, that a better interpretation of most biblical passages and the overall drift of Scripture do not present God as determining all that occurs, especially evil events. Critics say the omnicausal view goes against our commonsense understanding of the world, including our intuitions about randomness and free will. Besides, it makes no sense to say that God totally causes something and that creatures also cause it.

To critics, this model appears to imply that God promotes sin and evil. It is hard—in fact, impossible for me—to believe God perfectly

---

[9]Paul Kjoss Helseth, "God Causes All Things," in *Four Views on Divine Providence*, ed. Dennis W. Jowers (Grand Rapids: Zondervan, 2011), p. 52.

loves while also being the ultimate cause of every rape, torture, disease and terrorist act. This model says God caused all of the tragic evils we encountered in chapter one. To me, this model makes little, if any, sense.[10]

2. GOD EMPOWERS AND OVERPOWERS

Although I have no survey data to support this claim, I would guess this providence model is most common among "average" believers. It says God creates and sustains all creation. God empowers humans by giving them free will, at least sometimes. But God also sometimes overpowers human free will or interrupts the causal regularities of existence. God's will is sometimes permissive and sometimes controlling.

The model that portrays God as empowering and overpowering embraces both the idea that humans act freely and that God sometimes overrides human freedom. Sometimes humans act freely because God allows it. Other times, God entirely controls humans by withdrawing, overriding or failing to provide freedom. This model embraces both randomness and supernatural control. Events sometimes happen by accident. Other times God or the devil, acting alone, brings about a result. Sometimes God invites creatures to cooperate.

Those who embrace this model of divine providence usually distinguish between general and special providence. "General providence" usually refers to God's superintending the processes of history without interrupting or controlling them entirely. "Special providence" describes God controlling actions or events so that God guarantees an outcome. God uses special providence to control people or situations to ensure important ends.

Marc Speed embraces this model of divine providence. "God sometimes overrides His intelligent creatures' free will," says Speed. God does so, because "God needs certain people to do good things at certain times, and certain people to do 'bad' things at certain times,

---

[10]For books arguing that Calvinism is problematic, see Don Thorsen, *Calvin vs. Wesley: Bringing Belief in Line with Practice* (Nashville: Abingdon, 2013); and Jerry L. Walls and Joseph R. Dongell, *Why I Am Not a Calvinist* (Downers Grove, IL: InterVarsity Press, 2004).

in order to meet His long-term educational goal for humanity." God must "make sure important/convincing events occur, so He can make them part of His 'videotape' (so to speak) of human history to show humanity at the white throne judgment." For this reason, says Speed, "God can and does, at times, superimpose upon and override the will of individual human beings in certain circumstances, in order to cause particular aspects of His grand plan to come to pass."[11]

Some versions of Arminian theology embrace this model.[12] Arminian theologian Jack Cottrell says that "even though [God] bestowed relative independence on his creatures, as Creator he reserved the right to intervene if necessary. Thus he is able not only to *permit* human actions to occur, but also to *prevent* them from occurring if he so chooses." This means God, says Cottrell, can "remain in complete control."[13]

Roger Olson, another Arminian theologian, appeals to the notion that God permits evil without willing it. "Nothing can happen that God does not *permit*," says Olson, "but that is not the same as saying he *causes* or renders certain everything and certainly not evil, sin, or innocent suffering."[14]

Those who embrace this model of providence often use the word *intervene* to describe how God acts in special ways. Type the phrase "God intervenes" into an Internet search engine, and you'll find personal stories in which the authors say God interrupted the natural order or overrode human freedom to do something special. God permits most occurrences in life, says this model, but God sometimes intervenes to prevent others.

---

[11]Marc Speed, "God Is Sovereign—Why God Sometimes Overrides People's Free Will," accessed January 15, 2014, www.bible-questions-and-answers.com/God-Is-Sovereign.html. I thank Brendan Engen for alerting me to this website.

[12]One of the better summaries of Arminian theology is Roger E. Olson's book, *Arminian Theology: Myths and Realities* (Downers Grove, IL: InterVarsity Press, 2006).

[13]Jack Cottrell, "The Nature of Divine Sovereignty," in *The Grace of God, the Will of Man*, ed. Clark H. Pinnock (Grand Rapids: Zondervan, 1989), p. 112.

[14]Roger E. Olson, "What's Wrong with Calvinism?," *My Evangelical Arminian Theological Musings* (blog), Evangelical Channel, *Patheos*, March 22, 2013, www.patheos.com/blogs/rogereolson/2013/03/whats-wrong-with-calvinism.

It's not clear what advocates of this model mean when they say "God intervenes." It is one thing to say God acts influentially in our lives; several models of providence affirm this. It is another to say God controls people or situations entirely by withdrawing, overriding or failing to grant freedom or agency. Philosophers call this acting as a sufficient cause.

Many theologians say God influences the natural order and sustains the law or regularities of nature. But saying God intervenes to interrupt the regularities of existence and perform special deeds goes beyond saying God acts influentially. This divine intervention disrupts in a controlling way the natural causes or lawlike regularities of life.

Philosopher Alvin Plantinga appeals to an interventionist God. According to him, God sometimes intervenes by overpowering or usurping the regularities of existence. "God will intervene (if that's the right word) when he has a good reason for doing so," says Plantinga. "But why suppose we human beings would be in a position to know when he does and when he doesn't have a good reason?" After all, says Plantinga, God's "options and possibilities are far beyond our ken; his ways are 'past finding out.'"[15] Intervention likely occurs, Plantinga says, but it is fundamentally mysterious. Although God can and does sometimes intervene, we cannot know why.

Plantinga's statements help us see a major reason to criticize the God-empowers-and-overpowers model of providence: explanatory inconsistency. In response to a "happy accident" or fortuitous event, advocates may say God caused it. Or they may say it was the result of chance. To explain evil, they may blame sinful humans. They may say God allows evil as part of some secret plan. Some may blame the devil, whom God permitted to wreak havoc. In this model, one never knows whom to blame or praise. The result: explanatory inconsistency.

Those who embrace this approach to providence typically say, of course, that God does not cause evil. They usually blame human

---

[15]Alvin Plantinga, *Where the Conflict Really Lies: Science, Religion, and Naturalism* (Oxford: Oxford University Press, 2011), pp. 101-2.

freedom gone awry, chance or demonic forces. But as we saw from the quotations above, advocates also typically believe God permits or allows evil because God has the kind of controlling power to prevent such evil.[16]

Although this model may allow its advocates to say God is not the source of evil, its view of divine power makes God responsible for failing to *prevent* genuine evil. It is hard to believe God loves perfectly if God is capable of total control but fails to prevent genuine evil. God remains culpable.

Advocates of this model may respond to this criticism by saying, "Who cares about explanatory consistency? We're talking about God!" But this response simply appeals to mystery. God's ways are inscrutable, this approach ultimately argues. Such appeals do not help us make sense of life, which is what we are all trying to do. Besides, we should be wary of worshiping the entirely inscrutable God because we never know who the devil he may be!

If this model of God's providence is the most common, it's no wonder believers get confused. We can't make sense of life when this level of explanatory inconsistency prevails. This model offers little hope for understanding why genuinely evil events occur, whether those evils were generated randomly or by free will. We need a better model of divine providence.

3. God Is Voluntarily Self-Limited

This model starts with the premise that God essentially has the kind of power to create something from nothing (*creatio ex nihilo*) and control others entirely. Despite having the capacity to be all-controlling, however, God made a voluntary decision to give at least some creatures freedom. When doing so, God voluntarily gave up total control. God made this decision when initially creating, and

---

[16]Michael D. Robinson's version of what he calls "augmented Arminianism" argues that God permits evil, and I believe his proposal is subject to several of my criticisms here. Robinson, *The Storms of Providence: Navigating the Waters of Calvinism, Arminianism, and Open Theism* (Lanham, MD: University Press of America, 2003).

God (usually) stands by it. Most advocates of this model say love is God's motive for not creating humans as robots, allowing randomness and not controlling the created order entirely.

Some advocates of the model of God as voluntarily self-limited slip in and out of the model that supposes a God who empowers and overpowers. They generally think God gives freedom and agency to creatures and respects the fundamental regularities/laws of the universe. But they also think that, on a truly special occasion, God overpowers a creature or situation. Such overpowering may have been necessary for Jesus' resurrection, for instance. It may be necessary for God's final victory at the end of time. It may have occurred in particular awe-inspiring, law-breaking, freedom-trumping miracles recorded in Scripture or witnessed today. When this model says God, on the rare occasion, controls others, it differs only in degree, not in kind, from the God-empowers-and-overpowers model.

Several passages of Scripture support the idea that God gives freedom to creation. But advocates of this model of providence often cite Philippians 2:5-11. In it, the apostle Paul talks about Jesus self-giving or self-emptying in a sacrificial way. The word in the passage related to this self-giving comes from *kenoō*, and the concept is commonly known as kenosis. Advocates of this model say Jesus' self-giving reveals that God voluntarily self-limits, in the name of love, to allow a measure of independence to creatures and to grant freedom or agency.[17] This involves what Thomas Tracy calls God's "intentional self-restraint."[18] It implies that God could be all-controlling, but God usually chooses not to control entirely.

Scientist and theologian John Polkinghorne is among many well-known advocates of the model of God as voluntarily self-limited. God's "act of creation involves a voluntary limitation," says Polking-

---

[17]A number of theologians and philosophers propose some version of kenosis theology. For instance, see Nancey Murphy and George F. R. Ellis, *On the Moral Nature of the Universe: Theology, Cosmology, and Ethics* (Minneapolis: Fortress, 1996); and Jürgen Moltmann, "God's Kenosis in the Creation and Consummation of the World," in *The Work of Love: Creation as Kenosis*, ed. John C. Polkinghorne (Grand Rapids: Eerdmans, 2001).

[18]Thomas F. Tracy, *God, Action, and Embodiment* (Grand Rapids: Eerdmans, 1984), p. 44.

horne, "in allowing the other to be."[19] This kenotic vision of voluntary self-limitation, says Polkinghorne, means "God does not will the act of a murderer or the destructive force of an earthquake but allows both to happen in a world in which divine power is deliberately self-limited to allow causal space for creatures."[20]

Philip Clayton's version of this model is especially noteworthy because he rejects any divine control in the ongoing history of the universe. Clayton's proposal might be named the not-even-once version of voluntary self-limitation. After God created the universe from nothing, Clayton says, God voluntarily decided not to control creatures or situations—ever![21]

The divine decision not to intervene and overpower creatures raises questions about suffering in the world. Clayton believes God has good reasons for not preventing innocent suffering, although God could do so. Such suffering "is a necessary consequence of God's creating a universe in which autonomous beings can evolve."[22] If God were to break the natural laws or override creaturely freedom even once, says Clayton, "God would incur a responsibility to intervene in most or all cases of suffering."[23] To maintain the integrity of the world God created and avoid the responsibility that comes with occasionally interventions, God never intervenes to control a situation or person, even though God could.

In my opinion, the model of God as voluntarily self-limited is in many ways commendable, especially models like Clayton's. It sup-

---

[19]John C. Polkinghorne, "Chaos Theory and Divine Action," in *Religion and Science*, ed. W. Mark Richardson and Wesley J. Wildman (New York: Routledge, 1996), p. 249. See also Craig A. Boyd and Aaron D. Cobb, "The Causality Distinction, Kenosis, and a Middle Way: Aquinas and Polkinghorne on Divine Action," *Theology and Science* 4 (2009): 391-406.

[20]John C. Polkinghorne, "Kenotic Creation and Divine Action," in *The Work of Love: Creation as Kenosis*, ed. John C. Polkinghorne (Grand Rapids: Eerdmans, 2001), p. 102.

[21]See Philip Clayton's essay in which he affirms *creatio ex nihilo*: "Creation *ex Nihilo* and Intensifying the Vulnerability of God," in *Theologies of Creation: Creatio ex Nihilo and Its New Rivals*, ed. Thomas Jay Oord (New York: Routledge, 2014).

[22]Philip Clayton and Steven Knapp, *The Predicament of Belief: Science, Philosophy, Faith* (Oxford: Oxford University Press, 2011), p. 66. See also Clayton's book *Adventures in the Spirit: God, World, and Divine Action* (Philadelphia: Fortress, 2008).

[23]Clayton and Knapp, *Predicament of Belief*, p. 52.

ports the commonsense view that random events occur. It supports our basic intuition that we act freely, at least to some degree. It blames genuine evil upon free creatures or random events in the world. It says love motivates God's self-limitation. And in versions like Clayton's, it offers a high degree of explanatory consistency. This model goes a long way toward helping us make sense of our world.

But I also have problems with this model. My main problem derives from the voluntary aspect of God's self-limitation. This model maintains a view of God's power that says God *could* withdraw, override or fail to offer freedom/agency to creatures. God *could* momentarily violate the regularities/natural laws of the universe. God could intervene in these ways if God chose to do so because God can control others.

This model implies that God could stop random events or prevent free choices that cause genuine evil. God could have prevented the events in the stories we read at the outset of this book. But God permitted them. God essentially possesses the kind of all-controlling power to prevent evil although God rarely or never uses it. God could stop evil but doesn't.

The God who could control others entirely but voluntarily self-restrains could prevent genuine evil. The God who voluntarily self-limits could, in principle, and sometimes should become un-self-limited. Nothing but divine choice prevents God from stopping genuine evil.

I can think of numerous evil events a voluntarily self-limited God should have prevented by momentarily becoming un-self-limited. Victims of horrific evils likely have their list of events too. Saying God allowed or permitted but did not will evil offers little comfort. A perfectly loving God should and would prevent genuine evil if it were possible. Consequently, I cannot believe that the God described in this model loves perfectly.

Although I disagree with John Calvin on many things, he rightly criticizes those who say God permits evil but does not will it. We should make "no distinction between God's will and God's permission," says Calvin. "Why shall we say 'permission' unless it is because God so wills?"[24] In his commentary on Genesis, he puts it bluntly: "What else is the permission of Him who has the power of preventing and in whose hand the whole matter is placed but his will?"[25] If the God who could control others permits something to occur, God must want that occurrence—at least more than the alternatives.

Advocates for this model typically respond to this criticism with one of two answers. The first says God has made a voluntary promise at the creation of the universe to control others rarely or never. God aims to keep this promise because God is faithful. The second answer says that if God occasionally controlled others, this would interrupt the world's natural or moral regularities of life in some unsatisfactory way. God chooses not to intervene to control some situation entirely, they say, because natural or moral laws would become untrustworthy.

I am not satisfied with either answer. The first appeals to a voluntary divine promise made in the beginning and kept (mostly) throughout history. But, I wonder, which is more important: keeping promises or loving steadfastly? When the two conflict, I choose love. Besides, a wise God would not make a promise that love may eventually require breaking.[26] I find it difficult if not impossible to obey in good faith—let alone worship—a God who, to keep a promise, allows genuine evil.

Loving steadfastly is more important than keeping promises that contradict love.

The other answer says God cannot voluntarily interrupt the regularities of existence without causing greater negative consequences. This is one version of what some call the free-process view of God's

---

[24]John Calvin, *Institutes of the Christian Religion*, ed. John T. McNeill, trans. Ford Lewis Battles (Philadelphia: Westminster, 1960), 2:3.23.8.

[25]John Calvin, *Commentaries on the First Book of Moses Called Genesis*, vol. 1, trans. John King, Christian Classics Ethereal Library, Grand Rapids, www.ccel.org.

[26]I agree with William Alston when he argues that God cannot be bound by promises in the same way humans are. Human promises and obligations are grounded in that which is external to themselves. But God is not bound by anything external to himself, except insofar as God's nature requires this. When the Bible talks about God making promises, this must be understood as an expression of God's essential nature in relation to others. William Alston, "Some Suggestions for the Divine Command Theorists," in *Divine Nature and Human Language* (Ithaca, NY: Cornell University Press, 1989), p. 265.

relation to the created order. The voluntary-self-limitation version of the free-process view, however, does not take seriously enough the perspective of evil's victims. And there are so many victims! This view says God chooses not to interrupt the free processes of existence to prevent evil. But I cannot see why occasional interruptions would throw the whole universe off kilter.

In sum, I find the model of providence as voluntarily self-limited attractive in many ways. I like that it says love motivates God to give freedom/agency to others and to uphold the regularities/laws of the universe. But I can't embrace the model fully because its view of voluntary divine self-limitation leads to a major problem: if God has the ability *not* to give freedom/agency or *not* to uphold the regularities/laws of the universe, God should sometimes use those abilities, in the name of love, to prevent genuine evil. A loving God would become un-self-limited, if God were able, in order to stop evil. Claiming that a God capable of control nevertheless permits evil leaves crucial questions unanswered.

4. GOD IS ESSENTIALLY KENOTIC

Spoiler alert: I find this providence model most convincing. Actually, I created it, so I will explain and defend it later in detail. But let me give the basic ideas here.

The model of God as essentially kenotic says God's eternal nature is uncontrolling love. Because of love, God necessarily provides freedom/agency to creatures, and God works by empowering and inspiring creation toward well-being. God also necessarily upholds the regularities of the universe because those regularities derive from God's eternal nature of love. Randomness in the world and creaturely free will are genuine, and God is not a dictator mysteriously pulling the strings. God never controls others. But God sometimes acts miraculously, in noncoercive ways. God providentially guides and calls all creation toward love and beauty.

I should also briefly note that this model uses the word *kenosis*, which, as we saw, some advocates of model three also use. In light of this similarity, let me quickly distinguish kenosis in the two models. The model of God as voluntarily self-limited thinks self-limitation is a free divine choice. It begins with the idea that God essentially has the capacity to control others entirely, and God could choose not to self-limit. But God freely chose at creation or, usually, chooses in history thereafter not to exercise the capacity to control others entirely.

The model of providence as essentially kenotic, by contrast, portrays God's self-limitation as involuntary. God's nature of love logically precedes God's sovereign will. This means that God's self-limiting kenosis derives primarily from God's eternal and unchanging nature of love and not from voluntary divine decisions. Because God's nature is love, God always gives freedom, agency and self-organization to creatures, and God sustains the regularities of nature.

How's that for a teaser? More on this model later . . .

5. God Sustains as an Impersonal Force

This model's basic idea is that God exists as an impersonal force creating and sustaining all creation. Randomness, creaturely freedom and the regularities/laws of the natural world are real. God's steady-state influence never violates the integrity of the universe and its creatures that God now sustains.

This model differs from others because it says God's steady and impersonal presence never varies. God never engages in give-and-receive relationships. For this reason, miracles never occur, at least not miracles that involve any change in God's interaction with creatures. This means, for instance, that while the practice of prayer may help psychologically, it makes no difference to the God described by this model. Although God is a necessary cause in whatever happens, advocates of this model typically assume a view of causal closure in which natural causes—which God sustains moment by moment—explain reality.

Advocates of the impersonal-force model use static names for God. They may call God the Ground of Being, Pure Act, Depth or Holy Reality. They think of God as an infinite, impersonal ultimate and not a determinate or objective being.[27] These names emphasize God's existence as the underlying support of all creation without attributing to God agency or interactive personhood.

Paul Tillich, an influential mid-twentieth-century theologian, advocates this model of providence. The person "who believes in providence does not believe that a special divine activity will alter the conditions of finitude and estrangement," says Tillich.[28] Providence is not God's action but our reassurance that when evil and misfortune come, all of this cannot separate us from the love of God.[29] After all, says Tillich, "it is an insult to the divine holiness to treat God as a partner with whom one collaborates or as a superior power whom one influences by rites and prayers."[30]

One way to say God sustains but never interacts is to argue that God only acts once: a timeless master act.[31] Gordon Kaufman proposes this view of providence. It involves "the whole course of history, from its initiation in God's creative activity to its consummation when God ultimately achieves his purposes."[32] In this one providential act, God "gives the world the structure [that] it has and gives natural and historical processes their direction."[33] Consequently, says Kaufman, "there is no God who 'walks with me and talks with me' in close interpersonal communion, giving his full attention to my complaints, miraculously extracting me from difficulties into which I have gotten myself by invading nature and history with *ad hoc* rescue operations from on high."[34]

In the model of God as a sustaining impersonal force, God does

---

[27]See Wesley J. Wildman, "Ground-of-Being Theologies," in *The Handbook of Religion and Science*, ed. Philip Clayton (New York: Oxford University Press, 2006), pp. 612-32.
[28]Paul Tillich, *The Shaking of the Foundations* (New York: Charles Scribner's Sons, 1948), pp. 106-7.
[29]Ibid., pp. 271-72.
[30]Ibid.
[31]Friedrich Schleiermacher leans toward this view. See *The Christian Faith*, ed. H. R. MacKintosh and J. S. Stewart (1830; repr., Edinburgh: T & T Clark, 1989), pp. 149-56.
[32]Gordon D. Kaufman, "On the Meaning of 'Act of God,'" *Harvard Theological Review* 61 (April 1968): 191.
[33]Ibid., p. 192.
[34]Ibid., p. 200.

not enter into a give-and-receive relationship. In fact, God does not have intentions or an interacting will. God's permeating influence—the divine force field, we might say—never changes in content and consistency. God is like a diffuse gas, something similar to what early scientists called "ether."

This model has some advantages. In it, the freedom we experience and the randomness we encounter are genuine. God isn't controlling. Like glue holding all things together, God plays a necessary role in the existence of all things. One should not blame God for evils, unless one thinks God's mere presence makes deity blameworthy.

But the impersonal-force model has disadvantages, at least for those who think providence involves more than God sustaining creation in a non-interactive way. This model ignores vast amounts of Scripture, which often describes God as interacting with creatures in various ways. Writers of holy writ say God gives and receives; God influences others and others influence God.

Based on Scripture and their own religious experiences, many think God acts purposefully in their day-to-day, moment-by-moment lives. Giving up belief in miracles and the difference-making possibility of petitionary prayer is too high a price. Most believers want to believe God can be both consistent and innovative, in the sense of being faithful yet also responsive. I want this too, and the model I offer supports these beliefs.

Scripture and Christian experience describe God in relational terms, but this model does not account well for these witnesses. Biblical writers often call God a parent, lover or friend. By contrast, the impersonal-force model sees God as a kind of "metaphysical iceberg," as one critic put it.[35] Like an unresponsive chunk of ice, the God of this model does not engage in mutually influencing relationships. God is impassible, which means God remains unaffected by what occurs in the world.

Overall, this view helps in terms of what it says about God's con-

---

[35]Clark Pinnock makes this argument in "An Interview with Clark Pinnock," *Modern Reformation*, November-December 1998, p. 37.

stancy. God sustains the natural laws, creates conditions for creaturely freedom and makes chance possible. But this model fails to support the idea that God is personal, interactive and involved in give-and-receive relations with creation. It fails to give hope that God will act any differently to help when we encounter challenges or that God will rejoice when creatures do well. And it fails to support the idea that we make any difference to God.

6. GOD IS INITIAL CREATOR AND CURRENT OBSERVER

This model is similar to the previous one because it says God's influence on creation never varies. After creating the universe, says this model, God did not stick around. God created all things, set natural laws in motion and has since withdrawn. God is now, to quote Bette Midler, "watching us from a distance."[36]

Historians often identify several thinkers active during the Enlightenment with this model. It typically goes under the name *deism*, although deism comes in many forms. Advocates share the view that God is not currently involved with the world.

Scholars typically describe the rise of deism by telling the story of the scientific revolution. As science churned out explanations for events previously thought caused by God, some intellectuals saw no need to believe in God's ongoing creating, sustaining and interacting with creatures. Scientific explanations were welcomed by deists skeptical of claims about special revelation, or any revelation beyond what we learn through reason and the natural world. Besides, if God is omnipotent and wise, argue this model's advocates, God would have created a universe capable of running well without needing additional tinkering.

The model that portrays God as merely an observer of his creation usually says God initially created the universe out of nothing and set up its fundamental laws in that creative act. But after this initial burst, God left the world alone to follow these laws. While the regularity of

---

[36]Bette Midler, vocal performance of "From a Distance," by Julie Gold, released in 1990 on *Some People's Lives*, Atlantic Records, CD.

the laws and the initial fine-tuning of the universe suggest God initially created, the absence of empirically verified miracles suggests that God now has a hands-off policy toward creation.

One early deist, Matthew Tindal, called this model "natural religion." He argues that "it is evident by the light of nature that there is a God . . . who is the source of all other beings." However, events that some people call miracles, says Tindal, rely upon superstition rather than reason.[37] God does not "act arbitrarily," he says, nor "interpose" in the world.[38] This also seems to be Charles Darwin's view of God's activity.[39]

More recently, Michael Corey embraces the basics of this providence model. Corey endorses "deistic evolution," which says, "God has indirectly guided the evolutionary process along by designing the miraculous property of self-organization into the first atoms and molecules."[40] God's creative activity "is confined to the initial moments of creation," says Corey, and afterward God "allowed [the first atoms and molecules] to develop on their own entirely according to natural cause-and-effect processes."[41]

The deistic evolution model is superior, believes Corey. After all, "a God who continually has to intervene to accomplish His creative purposes is clearly inferior . . . in the same way that a car-maker who is clever enough to design self-building cars is far more impressive than one who has to be directly involved during each step of the creative process."[42]

The current-observer model is similar to the impersonal-force model. The main difference is the causal role God plays in each. In the impersonal-force model, God is a necessary ongoing cause of all

---

[37]Matthew Tindal, *Christianity as Old as the Creation* (Whitefish, MT: Kessinger, 2004), p. 232.
[38]Ibid., p. 115.
[39]See, for instance, Ronald W. Clark, *The Survival of Charles Darwin* (New York: Random House, 1984), p. 121; and Neil C. Gillespie, *Charles Darwin and the Problem of Creation* (Chicago: University of Chicago Press, 1979), pp. 130-31.
[40]Michael A. Corey, *Back to Darwin: The Scientific Case for Deistic Evolution* (Lanham, MD: University Press of America, 1994), p. 15.
[41]Ibid.
[42]Ibid., p. 18.

things. By contrast, advocates of the current-observer model emphasize the lack of divine causation in the present. Life required God's initial creating, but the universe currently runs on its own.

The current-observer model has advantages. It does not clash with much of what scientists say about the world. It believes the natural world can tell us true things about God. It takes reason seriously and rejects nonsensical religious views based on logical contradictions and superstition. This model fits with our intuitions about randomness, agency and freedom.

This model seems to get around the problem of evil. After all, an uninvolved and uncontrolling God cannot be the direct cause of evils we experience, nor should we expect deity to prevent evil. An uninvolved God is neither praiseworthy for the good we experience today nor blameworthy for the bad.

By putting God's action only at initial creation, however, this model has difficulty explaining how an omnipotent God would have created a world with so much evil. One wonders, is this the best an omnipotent God can create? To use Corey's car illustration, couldn't a *really* clever carmaker design self-building cars that function reliably?

This model also feels hollow to those who believe God acts in daily life. John Wesley, for instance, criticized the God of this model for fostering what he called "practical atheism."[43] While advocates of this model believe God exists, their belief allows for no divine action in the present. Critics call this model's God an "Absentee Landlord" because God is never available when creation's tenants need help.[44]

This model will not appeal to people who, like me, believe they have felt God's presence in their lives. It will not appeal to those who, like me, believe God acts miraculously. This model will not appeal to those who, like me, pray expecting that at least sometimes our prayers influence how God acts. And it will not appeal to people who, like

[43]John Wesley, "On Living Without God," sermon 130, in *The Works of John Wesley*, ed. Albert C. Outler (Nashville: Abingdon, 1987), 4:171, § 1.7.
[44]John C. Polkinghorne, *Science and Providence: God's Interaction with the World* (West Conshohocken, PA: Templeton Press, 2005), p. 8.

me, think some forms of revelation are special, e.g., Scripture, because these forms give a clearer understanding of God than does nature or reason alone.

The more I list reasons why this model of providence will not appeal to many people, the more I realize why it is unpopular. But more than lacking popularity, this model fails to offer hope that God makes a difference in our attempts to make sense of evil and randomness. It offers no hope that God acts to overcome evil or console those in pain.

7. GOD'S WAYS ARE NOT OUR WAYS

Versions of this final model vary widely. Each shares the fundamental belief that while God acts providentially, we ultimately have no idea what God's actions are finally like. No language, no analogy and no concepts can tell us the nature of divine providence. All is mystery.

The technical term sometimes used for this model is *apophatic theology*. The basic idea is that we cannot describe God or divine activity positively. This negative theology claims we can only talk about what God is not.

This model typically expresses itself more subtly than bluntly saying, "we don't know." One version says God is wholly other. Those who appeal to "wholly other" language often do so to undermine any comparison between God and creation. God is not a being, they say, and God has no unique traits. God's traits—if any—differ entirely from creation.

At least in his early writings, Karl Barth represents the view that God differs entirely from creation. Barth says an "infinite qualitative difference" exists between the Creator and creatures.[45] "There is no way from us to God," says Barth, and we cannot even find God through paradox.[46] All presumed knowledge of God is ignorance or

[45]Karl Barth, *The Epistle to the Romans* (Oxford: Oxford University Press, 1933), p. 10. For one of the best overall explanations of Barth's theology, see John R. Franke, *Barth for Armchair Theologians* (Louisville, KY: Westminster John Knox, 2006).
[46]Karl Barth, *The Word of God and the Word of Man*, trans. Douglas Horton (Boston: Pilgrim, 1928), p. 177.

comes only through the paradox of faith because God is wholly other.

Barth eventually says, however, that some knowledge of God is possible due to the revelation in Jesus Christ. But it remains a mystery how, through Jesus, we know something about the utterly unknowable God. If we take seriously Barth's fundamental claim that God differs from us in all respects—God is wholly other—this approach renders divine providence incomprehensible. Emphasizing Jesus Christ as God's way to self-reveal means the difference between God and creation cannot be infinite. After all, most Christians say Jesus is human as well as divine, and most believers think that at least humans are made in God's image.

Some embrace this model of providence through the deconstructive philosophy of Jacques Derrida. In Derrida, we find one who adopts the idea that God is "wholly other" (*tout autre*) but without also claiming that the revelation of Jesus Christ gives knowledge of God. Derrida's best-known theological interpreter, John Caputo, argues that Derrida's work should not be entirely understood as negative theology. But in "this failure of knowledge [of God]," says Caputo, "the knowing which un-knows the un-known God is a sweeping success that keeps God safe."[47]

Advocates of deconstructive theology say it helps us avoid idolatry. After all, we will not idolize a God we cannot know. But I believe this approach fails to provide constructive proposals to make sense of life. It fails to answers our deepest questions about how God acts in the world. Although it overcomes idolatry, it also offers no content for affirmative worship.

A sophisticated version of this model appeals to what Thomas Aquinas calls "primary" and "secondary" causation. Theologians have proposed various understandings of the primary/secondary scheme.[48]

One influential version says God, as primary cause, acts providen-

---

[47]John D. Caputo, *The Prayers and Tears of Jacques Derrida: Religion Without Religion* (Bloomington: Indiana University Press, 1997), p. 44. See also Jacques Derrida, *Acts of Religion* (New York: Routledge, 2002).

[48]Etienne Gilson, *The Christian Philosophy of St. Thomas Aquinas* (Notre Dame, IN: University of Notre Dame Press, 1994).

tially through creaturely secondary causes. When asked what this primary/secondary scheme tells about *how* God acts as a cause, advocates answer by appealing in some way to mystery. They say God's activity cannot be thought of as one cause among others, so we cannot compare it to other causes.[49] As Aquinas puts it, "we cannot know what God is, but rather what He is not." And, he continues, "we have no means for considering how God is, but rather how He is not."[50] This means, says Aquinas, "it must nowise be admitted that God is like creatures."[51]

Theologian Michael J. Dodds endorses the primary/secondary scheme we find in Aquinas. "The notion of primary and secondary causality of the creature," Dodds says, "will make sense only if we remember that these causes do not belong to the same order."[52] God's ways are totally unlike creaturely ways because "God's actions are fundamentally different from that of creatures."[53]

The primary/secondary scheme allows us to say God acts through chance. But in chance events, says Dodds, "all that God wills happens unfailingly."[54] God's causal action in random events is altogether different from anything we understand. "The effect intended by God does unfailingly occur since no creaturely cause can impede divine causality and that effect unfailingly occurs precisely in the way that God intends it to occur, whether by necessity, contingency, freedom, or chance."[55] In short, we cannot comprehend God's action in any way.

---

[49]For a modified Thomistic account of primary and secondary causation not subject to the criticisms I offer here, see Boyd and Cobb, "Causality Distinction, Kenosis, and a Middle Way," pp. 391-406.

[50]Thomas Aquinas, *Summa Theologica*, 1.3, prologue.

[51]Ibid., 1.4.3, ad 4.

[52]Michael J. Dodds, *Unlocking Divine Action: Contemporary Science and Thomas Aquinas* (Washington, DC: Catholic University of America Press, 2012), pp. 191-92. For a similar interpretation of Aquinas, see Gilson, *Christian Philosophy*, p. 182.

[53]Dodds, *Unlocking Divine Action*, p. 171. Dodds follows Aquinas in appealing to the language of analogy—and rejecting univocity—when talking about how God's actions compared with creaturely actions. But analogy understood in the Thomistic tradition goes only one way: our actions are analogous to God's, but God's are not analogous to ours. This use of *analogy* is at odds with the more usual way of using the word *analogy*, which involves two-way not one-way comparisons.

[54]Ibid., p. 224.

[55]Ibid., p. 225.

The primary and secondary causation scheme, in most forms, is an elaborate appeal to mystery. The appeal to inscrutability is especially evident when difficult issues arise. For instance, Dodds appeals to mystery when addressing the problem of evil because the primary/secondary scheme cannot solve it.[56] "To bring something forth from nothing, the Creator must be infinitely powerful. To do so freely, bespeaks of unbounded goodness and love," says Dodds. But "the only answer to evil and suffering . . . is not a logical solution, but a mystery."[57] In other words, this model of providence cannot provide a satisfying answer to why a loving and powerful God fails to prevent evil.

The God's-ways-are-not-our-ways model of providence sometimes takes center stage after other models fail. Those who appeal to the omnicause and God-empowers-and-overpowers models are especially prone to appeal to mystery. When explanatory inconsistency or outright contradiction arise, advocates of these models often say, "Remember: God's ways are not our ways." The mystery card becomes an out when preferred models of providence fail to shed light on dark and difficult questions.

This model that says "God's ways are not our ways" is the least helpful of all models of divine providence. It is least helpful because it purports to give answers that end up not being answers. Proponents at first may say God exerts real influence and acts in the world, but eventually they claim we cannot understand God's influence. Divine action is utterly incomprehensible.

I believe we cannot comprehend God fully. And mystery must play some role in discussions of how God acts in the world. But this model offers no constructive proposal. Although its advocates may sound humble when saying finite creatures only know in part, they end up implicitly or explicitly declaring we cannot understand divine providence. We may appreciate their humility, but we should not feel obliged to adopt their mystery model.

In fact, the God's-ways-are-not-our-ways model is probably not a

---

[56]Ibid., pp. 230-43.
[57]Ibid., p. 230.

model of providence at all. It doesn't offer a constructive proposal for understanding God's work in the world. Instead, it subtly denies that theology can help us make progress in addressing the fundamental project of this book: making sense of life. I have included it in my discussion because many who affirm divine providence explicitly or implicitly appeal to it.

CONCLUSION

As I said at the outset of this chapter, I have not offered an exhaustive list of models of God's providence. But these are what I consider the main ones. The brief sketches of each help us get a handle on the issues at stake. And these sketches should make us aware of the relative adequacy or inadequacy of each model of divine providence.

In the final chapters, I explore elements of the providence models positioned near the center of the figure above. I will proffer the essentially kenotic God as the model that I think best accounts for randomness, regularity, freedom, good, evil and God's providence of uncontrolling love.

5

The Open and Relational Alternative

*I*n recent decades, a compelling way to answer life's biggest questions has emerged. This way includes a variety of ideas under the overarching label "open and relational theology." The label covers a diverse set of views, and its adherents range from conservative to progressive. Open and relational theology also draws from various resources to offer an attractive proposal for how God acts providentially.

Open and relational theology embraces the reality of randomness and regularity, freedom and necessity, good and evil. It asserts that God exists and that God acts objectively and responsively in the world. This theology usually embraces at least these three ideas:

1. God and creatures relate to one another. God makes a real difference to creation, and creation makes a real difference to God. God is relational.

2. The future is not set because it has not yet been determined. Neither God nor creatures know with certainty all that will actually occur. The future is open.

3. Love is God's chief attribute. Love is the primary lens through which we best understand God's relation with creatures and the relations creatures should have with God and others. Love matters most.

Advocates of open and relational theology may describe their views a little differently from the way I have here.[1] Some add other beliefs.

---

[1]Among the open and relational theology books of importance and in addition to those cited

But most advocates embrace at least these three statements.

Open and relational theology offers a unique and, I think, helpful approach to understanding God's providence. This general theological movement fits models near the center of the options that we explored in the previous chapter. The model of providence I will propose, essential kenosis, represents one version of open and relational theology.

Believers have trod diverse paths on their journey to embrace open and relational theology. These paths indicate why this way of thinking about God and life's biggest questions is attractive. Each path tells us something interesting about those who walked it. And each points to reasons an open and relational theological perspective helps us understand divine providence.

SCRIPTURE

In 1994, a quintet of scholars—David Basinger, William Hasker, Clark Pinnock, Richard Rice and John Sanders—wrote a groundbreaking and provocative book, *The Openness of God*.[2] Although they offered many reasons to embrace the openness view, the book's subtitle points to the chief role of Scripture: *A Biblical Challenge to the Traditional Understanding of God.*

The authors of *The Openness of God* believe Scripture's overall message fits best with the three basic ideas of open and relational

---

elsewhere in this chapter, see Vaughn W. Baker, *Evangelism and the Openness of God: The Implications of Relational Theism for Evangelism and Missions* (Eugene, OR: Pickwick, 2013); David Basinger, *The Case for Freewill Theism: A Philosophical Assessment* (Downers Grove, IL: InterVarsity Press, 1996); Karen Baker-Fletcher, *Dancing with God: The Trinity from a Womanist Perspective* (St. Louis: Chalice, 2006); Gregory A. Boyd, *God of the Possible: A Biblical Introduction to the Open View of God* (Grand Rapids: Baker Books, 2000); John B. Cobb Jr. and Clark H. Pinnock, eds., *Searching for an Adequate God: A Dialogue Between Process and Free Will Theists* (Grand Rapids: Eerdmans, 2000); William Hasker, *The Triumph of God over Evil: Theodicy for a World of Suffering* (Downers Grove, IL: InterVarsity Press, 2008); Michael Lodahl, *God of Nature and of Grace: Reading the World in a Wesleyan Way* (Nashville: Kingswood, 2003); Brint Montgomery, Thomas Jay Oord and Karen Winslow, *Relational Theology: A Contemporary Introduction* (San Diego: Point Loma, 2012); and Richard Rice, *God's Foreknowledge and Man's Free Will* (Minneapolis: Bethany, 1980).

[2]Clark Pinnock et al., *The Openness of God: A Biblical Challenge to the Traditional Understanding of God* (Downers Grove, IL: InterVarsity Press, 1994).

theology I mentioned. They believe God gives freedom and relates to creatures as the living God of history. Although God knows all that is knowable, God cannot know with certainty now all that will actually happen in the future. Future events do not yet exist and therefore are, in principle, not yet knowable. Love is God's primary attribute, and God calls us to live lives of love.

Clark Pinnock is one of the better-known authors of *The Openness of God*, and many identify his name with this evangelically oriented version of open and relational theology. Pinnock's journey to the open view began in a Baptist context shaped by Calvinist writings.[3] Pinnock originally considered himself, as he put it, "a Calvinist who regarded alternate evangelical interpretations as suspect and at least mildly heretical."[4]

While studying the Bible carefully, however, Pinnock came to believe he needed course corrections in his spiritual journey. He needed to "listen more carefully to what the Scriptures actually say and teach."[5] This led him to believe "reform in the doctrine of God is needed precisely because of the Bible." He came to believe Scripture "authorizes the open view in significant ways."[6]

Old Testament writings witness to a relational deity as God enters into covenant through give-and-receive relations with others. In this covenant, God makes promises whose fulfillment depends on creaturely responses. The Lord says, for instance, "if my people who are called by my name humble themselves, pray, seek my face, and turn from their wicked ways, then I . . . will forgive their sin and heal their land." But if they "turn aside and forsake my statutes and my commandments," says the Lord, "I will pluck you

[3]Barry L. Callen tells the story of Pinnock's journey in *Clark H. Pinnock: Journey Toward Renewal, an Intellectual Biography* (Nappanee, IN: Evangel, 2000).

[4]Clark H. Pinnock, "From Augustine to Arminius: A Pilgrimage in Theology," in *The Grace of God and the Will of Man: A Case for Aminianism*, ed. Clark H. Pinnock, rev. ed. (Minneapolis: Bethany, 1995), p. 17.

[5]Clark H. Pinnock, "A Response to Rex A. Koivisto," *Journal of Evangelical Theological Society* 24 (1981): 153-54.

[6]Clark H. Pinnock, *Most Moved Mover: A Theology of God's Openness* (Grand Rapids: Baker Books, 2001), p. 60.

up from the land that I have given you" (2 Chron 7:14, 19-20).

In this covenant and others, God waits for Israel's response. God is not sure which action will be taken until creatures respond. We find covenants such as this among numerous Old Testament passages, and they indicate that God does not always know what will happen in the future.

In the Old Testament, biblical authors also say God has regrets, learns and changes plans. In fact, God sometimes has a change of mind. In the Genesis flood story, for instance, God "saw . . . the wickedness" and "was sorry that he had made humankind" (Gen 6:5-6). If God knows the future exhaustively, God will not have regrets.

In the story of Abraham taking Isaac to be sacrificed, the angel of the Lord says, "Do not lay your hand on the boy . . . ; for now I know that you fear God" (Gen 22:12). The Lord learns something from Abraham's actions, something not known previously. To say God learns is to say God comes to know something not previously knowable.

The Lord says to Hezekiah, "Set your house in order, for you shall die; you shall not recover." But Hezekiah prays and weeps. The Lord sees this repentance and says, "I will add fifteen years to your life" (Is 38:1-5). God's plans change because of Hezekiah's actions.

The word of the Lord prompts Jonah to proclaim: "Forty days more, and Nineveh shall be overthrown!" (Jon 3:4). But the king of Nineveh and his people repent. They say, "Who knows? God may relent and change his mind." God does just that. "When God saw what they did," says Scripture, "God changed his mind" (Jon 3:9-10). In fact, forty or more Old Testament passages say God has a change of mind, which suggests God does not foreknow the future in its entirety.

Pinnock also listened carefully to the New Testament. While this segment of the Bible says less about God's knowledge of the future, we find in it a record of Jesus' life and teachings. Christians believe Jesus offers the fullest revelation of God's character.

New Testament writers report that God expresses sacrificial love, including love for enemies and strangers. This love tells us something about God's relational power. "God's true power is revealed in the cross of Jesus Christ," says Pinnock. "In this act of self-sacrificing, God deploys power in the mode of servanthood, overcoming enemies not by annihilating them but by loving them." This means that "the power of love is the power that wills genuine relationships," and this view "is certainly not a diminished or inferior view of power."[7]

In light of Scripture, these passages of Scripture and those describing God's relationship with the early church, Pinnock found himself "giving up the view according to which God is thought to relate primarily to us as all-determining monarch and law-giver." This meant "shifting to the paradigm in which God relates to us primarily as parent, lover, and covenant partner."[8] According to Pinnock, "what we find in Scripture is a range of images designed to disclose something of God's nature. They seem to tell us that creation is a dynamic project and that God is personal and relational."[9] This open and relational perspective, he came to believe, is "the dynamic theism of the scriptural witness."[10]

The open and relational perspective rejects the idea that God controls all things. "In the biblical narrative," says Pinnock, "one does not find a predestinarian decree operating behind the scenes, to ensure that God's will is always done." This means "history is not a printout of pre-programmed events, all videotaped and decided."[11] History is open, and creatures join God in writing it.

Pinnock's view of God changed partly because he discovered that "the Bible assumes libertarian freedom when it posits personal give-and-take relationships and when it holds people responsible for their actions."[12] "God, in grace, grants humans significant freedom to co-operate with or work against God's will for their lives," says Pinnock,

---

[7]Clark H. Pinnock, "God's Sovereignty in Today's World," *Theology Today* 53 (April 1996): 20.
[8]Clark H. Pinnock, foreword to *Clark Pinnock on Biblical Authority*, by Ray Roennfeldt (Berrien Springs, MI: Andrews University Press, 1993), pp. xx-xxi.
[9]Pinnock, *Most Moved Mover*, p. 60.
[10]Pinnock, in Clark H. Pinnock and Delwin Brown, *Theological Crossfire: An Evangelical/Liberal Dialogue* (Grand Rapids: Zondervan, 1990), p. 96.
[11]Pinnock, *Most Moved Mover*, p. 41.
[12]Ibid., p. 115.

"and he enters into dynamic, give-and-take relationships with us."[13] All of this implies that God's relation to time is similar to ours. God "remembers the past, savors the present, and anticipates the future."[14]

One of the more influential biblical scholars today, Terence Fretheim, also embraces open and relational themes because he sees them in the biblical text.[15] Fretheim argues, for instance, that creation is "not a finished product or static state of affairs but a dynamic process in which the future is open to a number of possibilities and in which God's engagement with creaturely activity is crucial for creational developments."[16] "Any talk about divine omniscience in the Old Testament must be limited when it comes to talk about the future," he says. "It is limited in such a way as to include a genuine divine openness to the future."[17]

Pinnock and Fretheim are among Christians who, through biblical studies, embrace open and relational theology.[18] According to the overall drift of Scripture, they say, open and relational themes dominate.[19] Christians who regard the Bible as their primary theological resource must take the open and relational perspective seriously.

---

[13]Clark Pinnock et al., *Openness of God*, p. 7.

[14]Pinnock, *Most Moved Mover*, p. 41.

[15]Terence E. Fretheim has many publications that document the biblical support for open and relational theology. See, for instance, *Creation Untamed: The Bible, God, and Natural Disasters* (Grand Rapids: Baker Books, 2010); *God and World in the Old Testament: A Relational Theology of Creation* (Nashville: Abingdon, 2005); *The Suffering of God: An Old Testament Perspective* (Philadelphia: Fortress, 1984); "Genesis," in *The New Interpreter's Bible*, vol. 1 (Nashville: Abingdon, 1994); *Exodus* (Philadelphia: John Knox, 1991); "The Bible in a Postmodern Age," in *The Bible Tells Me So*, ed. Richard P. Thompson and Thomas Jay Oord (Nampa, ID: SacraSage, 2011); "Divine Foreknowledge, Divine Constancy, and the Rejection of Saul's Kingship," *Catholic Biblical Quarterly* 47 (October 1985): 595-602; and "The Repentance of God: A Key to Evaluating Old Testament God-Talk," *Horizons in Biblical Theology* 10 (June 1988): 47-70.

[16]Fretheim, *Creation Untamed*, p. 150.

[17]Fretheim, *Suffering of God*, p. 57.

[18]In addition to Pinnock and Fretheim, biblical scholars whose work is especially congenial to open and relational theologies include William A. Beardslee, Michael Brown, William P. Brown, Walter Brueggemann, C. S. Cowles, Ronald Farmer, John Goldingay, Gerald Janzen, George Lyons, David J. Lull, Richard Middleton, Russell Pregeant and Karen Winslow.

[19]For discussions of the suffering and changing God of the Old Testament, see also Brevard Childs, *Biblical Theology in Crisis* (Philadelphia: Westminster, 1970), pp. 44-47; Fretheim, *Suffering of God*; and Claus Westermann, *Elements of Old Testament Theology*, trans. Douglas W. Stott (Atlanta: John Knox, 1982), pp. 138-49.

CHRISTIAN THEOLOGIES

Some adherents to open and relational theology followed themes already present in the Christian tradition as their path to embracing the open and relational perspective. These traditions include Adventist, Arminian, Lutheran, Mennonite, Pentecostal, Restorationist and Wesleyan.[20] This does not mean everyone who identifies with or works from these traditions embraces open and relational theology. Rather, some members in these traditions follow the logic of particular themes on their way to embracing open and relational thought.[21]

For example, Lutheran theologian Marit Trelstad says, "Lutheran theology provides an emphasis on justification rooted in God's unswerving love and promise." God's covenant "describes the fundamental promise and reality of relationship God offers to creation," and "covenantal love is essential to God's nature." This covenant "provides creative possibilities for new forms of becoming" and "indelibly knits humanity to God."[22]

Contemporary Anabaptists draw from Menno Simons's emphasis upon pacifism, freedom and peace. Some Anabaptists find these themes congruent with the emphasis upon noncoercion and divine persuasion typical of open and relational theology. Rod Thomas, for instance, argues that "the theological openness that Jesus embodied and the idea

---

[20]One could add Latter-Day Saint (Mormon) theology to this list, although scholars debate whether the Latter-Day Saint movement is rightly considered part of the Christian tradition. For Mormon views compatible with open and relational themes, see Blake Ostler, *Exploring Mormon Thought: The Attributes of God*, vol. 1 (Draper, UT: Kofford, 2001). See also the discussion between evangelical Clark Pinnock and Mormon David Paulsen, "A Dialogue on Openness Theology," in *Mormonism in Dialogue with Contemporary Christianity*, ed. Donald W. Musser and David L. Paulsen (Macon, GA: Mercer University Press, 2007), pp. 489-553.

[21]I am grateful to friends and scholars on Facebook discussion groups for helping me think through how members in Christian traditions follow themes when embracing open and relational theologies. In particular, I thank David Cole, Chris Fisher, James Goetz, Simon Hall, Randy Hardman, John D. Holloway, Curtis Holtzen, William Lance Huget, Jacob Matthew Hunt, Dave Huth, Richard Kidd, Richard Livingston, Jay McDaniel, T. C. Moore, Quinn Olinger, Bryan Overbaugh, Matt Perkins, David Saleeba, Neil Short and Rod Thomas.

[22]Marit A. Trelstad, "Putting the Cross in Context: Atonement Through Covenant," in *Transformative Lutheran Theologies: Feminist, Womanist and Mujerista Perspectives*, ed. Mary J. Streufert (Minneapolis: Fortress, 2010), p. 109.

that God is relational rely on persuasion as the primary form of engagement." This involves what Thomas calls "nonviolent politics."[23]

Some contemporary Baptists extrapolate from their belief that believers must freely choose baptism. This extrapolation leads them to embrace open and relational theology, with its emphasis upon creaturely freedom. Frank Tupper, for instance, believes we should think of God as persuasive and empowering. Worship of Abba, says Tupper, "includes the renunciation of dominating power and overwhelming force as the way to accomplish the will of God."[24]

Pentecostals believe we must cooperate with God when exercising the gifts of the Spirit, and this Creator-creature-cooperation theme prevails in open and relational theology.[25] Pentecostal theologian Joshua D. Reichard says, "God's activity in the world is not primarily unilateral but relational." God shares power with believers through *concursus*, which means God cooperates with creatures to accomplish the divine will.[26] Pentecostal-charismatic affirmations, such as contemporary spiritual gifts and the possibility of miracles, says Reichard, "have inherent compatibility with open and relational theology."[27]

The Stone-Campbell Restorationist movement emphasizes freedom in the Spirit. This fits the emphasis upon free will found in open and

[23]Rod Thomas, "Rebooting Political Jesus Part 3, Nonviolent Politics," *Resist Daily*, http://resistdaily.com/rebooting-political-jesus-part-3-nonviolent-politics.

[24]E. Frank Tupper, *A Scandalous Providence: The Jesus Story of the Compassion of God* (Macon, GA: Mercer University Press, 1995), p. 133.

[25]In addition to Joshua D. Reichard's writing (see below), see Kenneth J. Archer, "Open Theism View: 'Prayer Changes Things,'" *Pneuma Review* 5, no. 2 (2002): 32-53; and idem, *The Gospel Revisited: Towards a Pentecostal Theology of Worship and Witness* (Eugene, OR: Pickwick, 2011).

[26]See Joshua D. Reichard, "Relational Empowerment: A Process-Relational Theology of the Spirit-filled Life," *Pneuma: The Journal of the Society for Pentecostal Studies* 36, no. 2 (2014): 1-20. See also idem, "Toward a Pentecostal Theology of Concursus," *Journal of Pentecostal Theology* 22 (2013): 95-114.

[27]Joshua D. Reichard, "Of Miracles and Metaphysics: A Pentecostal-Charismatic and Process-Relational Dialog," *Zygon: Journal of Religion and Science* 48 (2013): 274-93. See Reichard's other essays, including "Beyond Causation: A Contemporary Theology of Concursus," *American Journal of Theology and Philosophy* 34 (2013): 117-34; "An 'Improbable Bond of the Spirit': Historical Perspectives on the Christian Life in Pentecostal-Charismatic and Process-Relational Theologies," in *The Holy Spirit and the Christian Life*, ed. Wolfgang Vondey (New York: Palgrave Macmillan, 2014), pp. 179-98; and "From Causality to Relationality: Toward a Wesleyan Theology of Concursus," in *Wesleyan Theological Journal* 49, no. 1 (2014): 122-38.

relational theology.[28] William Curtis Holtzen, a theologian in this tradition, says "God's real power in relational theism is not about compulsion or coercion but rather a love that lures, prompts, and leads humans to become what God desires them to become and transform into the *Imago Dei*." Holtzen believes God "has to become vulnerable, take risks, and share power with humanity thus allowing us the ability to alter or conform to God's plans."[29]

Many attracted to Jacob Arminius's affirmation of creaturely cooperation with God for salvation and denial of individual predestination find themselves drawn to open and relational theology.[30] Although Arminius believed God foreknows all things, other Arminian themes are identical to themes in open and relational theology. Arminian theologian Roger Olson, for instance, says that "free will is a key idea of Arminian theology, and prevenient grace is the source of free will with regard to a person's acceptance of the gospel. . . . Free will is *for the sake* of God's character." Open and relational theology agrees. Open and relational theology, says Olson, is "closer to the 'heart' of Arminianism."[31]

Christians who believe love is central for faith and practice are likely to embrace open and relational theology. In their own ways, many Christian traditions say God's primary attribute is love, and God lovingly gives to and receives from creatures. Many say God calls

---

[28]See C. Leonard Allen and Richard T. Hughes, *Discovering Our Roots: The Ancestry of the Churches of Christ* (Abilene, TX: Abilene Christian University Press, 1988). For an early Restorationist tract compatible with open theology, see T. W. Brents's late nineteenth-century arguments against the predestining and foreknowing God of Calvinism, *The Gospel Plan of Salvation*, 8th ed. (Nashville: Gospel Advocate, 1890), www.oldpaths.com/Archive/Brents/Thomas/Wesley/1823/gosplan.html.

[29]William Curtis Holtzen, "Bruce (Not So) Almighty: Divine Limitation and Human Transformation," in *Essays of Hope*, ed. Joseph Grana (Fullerton, CA: Hope International University Press, 2012), p. 56.

[30]For expositions of Arminian theology, see Carl Bangs, *Arminius: A Study in the Dutch Reformation* (Grand Rapids: Zondervan, 1985); W. Stephen Gunter, *Arminius and His "Declaration of Sentiments": An Annotated Translation with Introduction and Theological Commentary* (Waco, TX: Baylor University Press, 2012); and Keith D. Stanglin and Thomas H. McCall, *Jacob Arminius: Theologian of Grace* (Oxford: Oxford University Press, 2012).

[31]Roger Olson, "Is Open Theism a Type of Arminianism?," *My Evangelical Arminian Theological Musings* (blog), Evangelical Channel, *Patheos*, November 10, 2012, emphasis original, www.patheos.com/blogs/rogereolson/2012/11/is-open-theism-a-type-of-arminianism/.

us to cooperate with divine providence by living lives of love.

The central themes of the Wesleyan tradition fit well with open and relational theology. Wesleyans typically follow John Wesley's efforts to understand divine sovereignty in light of God's love.[32] Wesley preached that God "strongly and sweetly influenc[es] all, and yet without destroying the liberty of his rational creatures."[33] He understood God's power, says Randy Maddox, "fundamentally in terms of *empowerment*, rather than control or *overpowerment*." Wesleyans should believe "God's grace works powerfully, but not irresistibly," says Maddox, at least "in matters of human life and salvation."[34]

Many in the Wesleyan tradition follow Wesley's lead and emphasize love as the center of Christian theology.[35] Mildred Bangs Wynkoop, for instance, wrote her magnum opus, *A Theology of Love*, to envision holiness through the lens of God's relational love.[36] "When each doctrine of the Christian faith is identified and defined by [Wesley]," argued Wynkoop, "the basic meaning invariably comes out 'love.'"[37]

John Wesley's "thought is like a great rotunda with archway entrances all around it," says Wynkoop. "No matter which [archway] is

---

[32]Among helpful Wesleyan resources, see J. Gregory Crofford, *Streams of Mercy: Prevenient Grace in the Theology of John and Charles Wesley* (Lexington, KY: Emeth, 2010); and Rem B. Edwards, *John Wesley's Values—And Ours* (Lexington, KY: Emeth, 2012). See also sources listed in footnotes below.

[33]John Wesley, "On the Omnipresence of God," sermon 118, in *The Works of John Wesley*, ed. Albert C. Outler (Nashville: Abingdon, 1987), 4:42, § 2.1.

[34]Randy L. Maddox, *Responsible Grace: John Wesley's Practical Theology* (Nashville: Kingswood, 1994), p. 55.

[35]See, for instance, the work of Barry L. Callen, *God as Loving Grace: The Biblically Revealed Nature and Work of God* (Nappanee, IN: Evangel, 1996); John B. Cobb Jr., *Grace and Responsibility: A Wesleyan Theology for Today* (Nashville: Abingdon, 1995); Kenneth J. Collins, *The Theology of John Wesley: Holy Love and the Shape of Grace* (Nashville: Abingdon, 2007); Timothy J. Crutcher, *The Crucible of Life: The Role of Experience in John Wesley's Theological Method* (Lexington, KY: Emeth, 2010); Diane Leclerc, *Discovering Christian Holiness: The Heart of the Wesleyan-Holiness Theology* (Kansas City, MO: Beacon Hill, 2010); Lodahl, *God of Nature and of Grace*; Randy L. Maddox, *Responsible Grace*; K. Steve McCormick, "The Heresies of Love: Toward a Spirit-Christ Ecclesiology of Triune Love," in *Wesleyan Theological Journal* 37 (Spring 2002): 35-47; Thomas Jay Oord and Michael Lodahl, *Relational Holiness: Responding to the Call of Love* (Kansas City, MO: Beacon Hill, 2005); and Theodore Runyon, *The New Creation: John Wesley's Theology Today* (Nashville: Abingdon, 1998).

[36]Michael Lodahl and I make the same argument in *Relational Holiness*.

[37]Mildred Bangs Wynkoop, *A Theology of Love: The Dynamic of Wesleyanism* (Kansas City, MO: Beacon Hill, 1972), p. 10.

entered, it always leads to the central Hall of Love."[38] This love "creates freedom," she says, and it links "every doctrine together into one dynamic architectonic and [shows] the theological stature and integrity of John Wesley."[39]

Theologians in all these traditions wrestle with how to understand God's foreknowledge in light of divine love and creaturely freedom. Most deny that God foreordains or predestines all things. But many believe God foreknows all future occurrences. For them, God knows with absolute certainty what we will do tomorrow and in the entire future, and yet we are free to do otherwise. These theologians embrace traditional positions on God's omniscience typically labeled "simple foreknowledge" or "middle knowledge," which I will explain later.[40]

Others in these traditions, however, believe emphasis upon God's love and creaturely freedom does not fit traditional views of God's foreknowledge. God does not foreknow the future exhaustively. They believe God experiences time in a way similar to the way creatures experience it. The future is full of possibilities, and, being omniscient, God knows them all. But God cannot foreknow with absolute certainty which possibilities will become actual.

Although Pinnock's book *The Openness of God* and other works brought this view of God's knowledge to the center of contemporary conversation, theologians in the nineteenth and early twentieth centuries also affirmed it.[41] For instance, Methodist theologian Lorenzo

---

[38]Ibid.

[39]Ibid., pp. 10, 11.

[40]For more on middle knowledge, see Thomas Flint, *Divine Providence: The Molinist Account* (Ithaca, NY: Cornell University Press, 1998). For more on simple foreknowledge, see David Hunt, "The Simple-Foreknowledge View," in *Divine Foreknowledge: Four Views*, ed. James K. Beilby and Paul R. Eddy (Downers Grove, IL: InterVarsity Press, 2001), pp. 65-103; and for a criticism of simple foreknowledge see Dean Zimmerman, "The Providential Usefulness of 'Simple Foreknowledge,'" in *Reason, Metaphysics, and Mind: New Essays on the Philosophy of Alvin Plantinga*, ed. Kelly James Clark and Michael Rea (Oxford: Oxford University Press, 2012), pp. 174-202.

[41]For a list of leading voices preceding and including contemporary open theologians, see John Sanders, "Who Has Affirmed Dynamic Omniscience and the Open Future in History?," *Open Theism Information Site*, updated January 27, 2014, http://opentheism.info/information/affirmed-dynamic-omniscience-open-future-history/#_edn11. Tom Lukashow has done signifi-

D. McCabe (1817–1897) extensively defended the view that God's omniscience does not entail exhaustive foreknowledge.[42] "As to pure contingencies prior to their creation," argued McCabe, "[God] may have theories, ideals, fancies, possibilities or probabilities, but cannot have certain knowledge."[43] "In the divine omniscience," he says, "there must be an element of growth," which means new knowledge will become available to God in the future.[44]

Lutheran theologian Isaak Dorner (1809–1884) said a consistent view of God working with us in history requires that God knows future, free acts of creatures as possibilities, not actualities. "We cannot be satisfied with the assertion that for God there can be nothing past and nothing future as such," argued Dorner. God's knowledge "presupposes a movement, a change even in the knowing activity of God himself."[45]

Stone-Campbell Restorationist thinker T. W. Brents (1823–1905) believed God voluntarily chooses not to know some things. Brents argued that "if God knew before He gave Adam the law in the garden that [Adam] would violate it, then [Adam] was not free; for he could not have falsified God's foreknowledge." For this reason, God "saw fit to avoid knowledge of everything incompatible with the freedom of the human will."[46]

The Roman Catholic theologian Jules Lequyer (1814–1862) followed what he believed the logic of free will implied by God's foreknowledge.[47] "I believe that God has only a conjectural knowledge of the

---

cant historical work on advocates of the open view of the future, and his work can be found on the web: "Open Theism Time Line by Tom Lukashow," published by Terri Churchill, March 28, 2013, www.scribd.com/doc/132763616/Open-Theism-Timeline-by-Tom-Lukashow.

[42]See Lorenzo Dow McCabe, *Divine Nescience of Future Contingencies a Necessity* (New York: Phillips & Hunt, 1882); and idem, *The Foreknowledge of God* (Cincinnati: Cranston & Stowe, 1887).

[43]McCabe, *Divine Nescience*, p. 24.

[44]Ibid., p. 27.

[45]Isaak August Dorner, "On the Proper Version of the Dogmatic Concept of the Immutability of God," in *God and Incarnation in Mid-Nineteenth Century German Theology*, ed. and trans. Claude Welch (New York: Oxford University Press, 1965), pp. 135-36.

[46]T. W. Brents, *The Gospel Plan of Salvation*, 1st ed. (Cincinnati: Chase & Hall, 1874), p. 96, www .oldpaths.com/Archive/Brents/Thomas/Wesley/1823/gosplan.html.

[47]See Donald Wayne Viney, "Jules Lequyer and the Openness of God," *Faith and Philosophy* 14

acts determined by human activity," said Lequyer.[48] God's knowledge depends, in part, upon creaturely decisions.

Adventist scholar Uriah Smith (1832–1903) wrote commentaries on the prophecies of Daniel and Revelation and yet denied exhaustive foreknowledge. "God made [humans], as he must make all intelligences who are to serve him, as free moral agents," argued Smith, "that such service may not be mechanical and constrained, but voluntary and free." "God knew of course that [humans] *might* sin," he says, "but this would be a very different thing from saying he knew that [humans] *would* sin."[49]

Several Methodist theologians in the early twentieth century rejected exhaustive foreknowledge.[50] One of the best known, Edgar S. Brightman (1884–1953), put his rejection of exhaustive definite foreknowledge this way: "God cannot be said to have complete foreknowledge. Although a divine mind would know all that was knowable and worth knowing, including the consequences of all possible choices, it would not know what choices a free mind would make."[51] God cannot know because God's "consciousness is an eternal time movement, the soul of the ongoing of all reality."[52]

In the latter part of the twentieth century, some followed the newly emerging process theology tradition as their path to open and relational theology.[53] Process theology is notoriously difficult to define,

---

(April 1997): 212-35.

[48]Jules Lequyer quoted in Charles Hartshorne and William L. Reese, *Philosophers Speak of God* (Chicago: University of Chicago Press, 1953), p. 230.

[49]Uriah Smith, *Looking unto Jesus or Christ as Type or Antitype* (Battle Creek, MI: Review & Herald, 1898), p. 49, ¶2.

[50]See Randy L. Maddox's work on Methodists who rejected exhaustive foreknowledge in "Seeking a Response-Able God: The Wesleyan Tradition and Process Theology," in *Thy Nature and Thy Name Is Love: Wesleyan and Process Theologies in Dialogue*, ed. Bryan P. Stone and Thomas Jay Oord (Nashville: Kingswood, 2001), pp. 111-42.

[51]Edgar Sheffield Brightman, *The Finding of God* (New York: Abingdon, 1931), p. 136. See also idem, *The Problem of God* (New York: Abingdon, 1930).

[52]Brightman, *Finding of God*, p. 132.

[53]Process theology comes in a variety of forms. In addition to those by Cobb, Griffin and Hartshorne, whose works are mentioned above, these books represent some of the variety: Bradley Shavit Artson, *God of Becoming and Relationship: The Dynamic Relationship of Process Theology* (Woodstock, VT: Jewish Lights, 2013); Joseph A. Bracken, *Does God Roll Dice: Divine Providence for a World in the Making* (Collegeville, MN: Liturgical, 2012); Philip Clayton, *Adventures*

and scholars debate how best to describe its essence.[54] But Christian process theologians typically affirm the centrality of love for theology, genuine creaturely freedom, randomness and regularities in the world, and that God's current knowledge does not include future occurrences.[55] They are open and relational theologians.

Most process thinkers agree with Charles Hartshorne, who argues for "growth in God's knowledge." "The creative process produces new realities to know."[56] This means "God does not already or eternally know what we do tomorrow," says Hartshorne, "for, until we decide, there are no such entities as our tomorrow's decisions."[57]

Process theologian John B. Cobb Jr. agrees. "If one reads the Bible in any straightforward way," he argues, "there is no question but that creaturely events have an impact on God that is not already predetermined. The Bible often speaks of God's interacting with human beings, of this interaction as even changing God's mind." The Bible does not make much sense, says Cobb, if God eternally knows all events as already completed.[58]

Other theological traditions and theologians propose beliefs congenial with or identical to open and relational theology. My aim for

in the Spirit: God, World, and Divine Action (Philadelphia: Fortress, 2008); Monica A. Coleman, Making a Way out of No Way: A Womanist Theology (Minneapolis: Fortress, 2008); Bruce Epperly, Process Theology: A Guide for the Perplexed (London: T & T Clark, 2011); Roland Faber, God as Poet of the World: Exploring Process Theologies (Louisville, KY: John Knox Westminster, 2004); Catherine Keller, Face of the Deep: A Theology of Becoming (New York: Routledge, 2003); idem, On the Mystery: Discerning God in Process (Minneapolis: Fortress, 2008); Jay McDaniel and Donna Bowman, eds. Handbook of Process Theology (St. Louis: Chalice, 2006); Schubert Ogden, The Reality of God and Other Essays (Norwich, UK: SCM Press, 1967); Marjorie Hewitt Suchocki, God, Christ, Church: A Practical Guide to Process Theology (New York: Crossroad, 1993); and Daniel Day Williams, The Spirit and the Forms of Love (New York: Harper & Row, 1968).

[54]John B. Cobb Jr., a leading representative for process theology, does not identify an essence to process theology. His colleague and also a leading spokesman for process thought, David Ray Griffin, lists ten core doctrines. David Ray Griffin, Reenchantment Without Supernaturalism: A Process Philosophy of Religion (Ithaca, NY: Cornell University Press, 2001).

[55]For introductions to process theology, see John B. Cobb Jr., The Process Perspective: Frequently Asked Questions About Process Theology, ed. Jeanyne B. Slettom (St. Louis: Chalice, 2003); and Epperly, Process Theology. See also McDaniel and Bowman, Handbook of Process Theology.

[56]Charles Hartshorne, Omnipotence and Other Theological Mistakes (Albany: State University of New York Press, 1984), p. 27.

[57]Ibid., p. 39.

[58]Cobb, Process Perspective, p. 31.

this section, however, has been to make two main points. First, ideas at the heart of some Christian traditions prompt some members to follow the logic of those ideas as their path to open and relational theology. Second, although open and relational theology as a comprehensive way of thinking is a recent phenomenon, some theologians from the distant past championed its ideas. Significant theologians of yesteryear even championed the idea that God's omniscience does not include knowing now with certainty all that will occur sometime in the future.

PHILOSOPHY

A third path some have taken to open and relational theology is philosophical. Philosophers divide their discipline into various traditions, divisions and emphases. In the current scene, analytic and continental philosophical approaches dominate. Among those two, analytic philosophers have engaged themes of open and relational theology most directly, especially the issue of divine foreknowledge.

A number of important philosophers accept an open and relational view of God's knowledge. William Hasker is one of the best known. Hasker was convinced early in life that humans have free will, in the sense of libertarian freedom. And this conviction played a key role in his journey to open and relational thought.

As a Wheaton College student, Hasker began to discover problems with affirming libertarian free will and believing some traditional theological ideas. "I was torn between my love and admiration for Augustine (which still persist today)," he says, "and the deeply troubling aspects of his doctrines of election and reprobation. Eventually I concluded that the God of holiness, love, and justice in whom both Augustine and I believed simply could not be the author of an eternal, unconditional decree of reprobation."[59]

During these early years, Hasker held the simple foreknowledge view of God's omniscience. This view says humans are genuinely free,

---

[59]William Hasker, *Providence, Evil and the Openness of God* (New York: Routledge, 2004), p. 98.

and yet God foreknows all free choices in the future and the results of those choices. Most who accept simple foreknowledge think God timelessly foreknows future free actions.

Later in life, Hasker was introduced to the middle-knowledge view of God's omniscience, also known as Molinism. This view says God knows all the actual decisions free creatures will make before creatures make them. God also knows what free creatures would have done in any possible situation, even if the choices were never actually made. Philosophers call the alleged actions creatures might have done "counterfactuals of freedom."

Hasker's reaction to Molinism was and remains negative. "Right from the beginning, this theory struck me as being entirely implausible," he says. As Hasker sees it, "there is nothing whatever either in the circumstances involved or in the nature and character of the chooser that determines in advance the decision that will be made."[60] Until a free agent makes an actual choice, God cannot foreknow that choice except the possibilities involved.

In 1973, Hasker began to move away from the simple-foreknowledge perspective. In that year, he read Nelson Pike's argument for the incompatibility of divine foreknowledge and human freedom.[61] "The argument at once struck me as extremely compelling, and I have never wavered from that first impression," he reports. "None of the ingenious ways of evading the argument has seemed to me at all satisfactory."[62] We now call the alternative Hasker began to consider "the open view" of God's knowledge.

Hasker also began to question the traditional view of God's relation to time, especially timeless eternity. During this period, he "began to write a paper exploring the difficulties of this doctrine."[63] The paper eventually led to a book, *God, Time, and Knowledge*,

---

[60]Ibid., p. 99.

[61]See Nelson Pike, *God and Timelessness* (New York: Shocken, 1970).

[62]William Hasker, *Providence, Evil and the Openness of God*, p. 100.

[63]William Hasker's paper was eventually published as "Concerning the Intelligibility of 'God Is Timeless,'" *New Scholasticism* 57 (1983): 170-95.

and to Hasker rejecting divine timelessness.[64]

The idea that God is essentially timeless makes little philosophical sense to Hasker, and "it clearly is not the biblical way of thinking about God." "For me personally, the decisive consideration was that a timeless God would be able to know us human beings only as timeless representations," he explains. "This detracts seriously from the personalism and intimacy which are so important to our relationship with God."[65]

In his journey to an open and relational perspective, Hasker also came to believe that neoplatonic-inspired metaphysics, not the Bible, motivated the traditional Christian view of God's relation to time. In contrast to neoplatonism, a more adequate view says God experiences the passage of time in a manner similar to the way creatures experience it: moment by moment.

"God's knowledge of the future, incomparably greater though it is than any knowledge we could possess, is not the complete, certain, and infinitely detailed knowledge posited by most of the theological tradition," says Hasker. "Though this conclusion is not one that I am now reluctant about, it was arrived at with considerable reluctance and after extended reflection."[66]

Hasker and other open and relational thinkers believe God is omniscient. They believe God knows everything that can be known. God knows now what might occur in the future, but God cannot know now all events that will actually occur. To put it philosophically, God knows all possibilities and all actualities, but God cannot know which possibilities will become actual until they are actualized.

Open and relational thinkers believe God's alleged foreknowledge of actual events is incompatible with creaturely free will. But they do not say God's foreknowledge exerts causal force to determine what will happen. Open and relational thinkers believe, however, that the exhaustive-foreknowledge view implies the future is complete, settled

[64]William Hasker, *God, Time, and Knowledge* (Ithaca: Cornell University Press, 1989).
[65]Hasker, *Providence, Evil and the Openness of God*, p. 100.
[66]Ibid., p. 101.

and fixed. Free will only makes sense if the future is not complete, not settled and not fixed because free will requires multiple options and the ability to do otherwise than what one might have done. For free will to be genuine, the future must be open, not settled.

In addition to denying that God knows the actual future, most for whom philosophy was their path to open and relational theology reject additional views of God common in Christian history. Most reject traditional ways of thinking about God's timelessness, simplicity, impassibility and immutability. These attributes interrelate, at least loosely, and rejecting one often means rejecting the others.

For instance, the open and relational view of foreknowledge is tied, as Hasker realized, to God's relation to time. Process philosopher Alfred North Whitehead is perhaps best known for postulating that God exists everlastingly in the process of time. Whitehead's early twentieth-century contributions continue to influence scholars today.

Some outside the process tradition now also make this argument, however. Nicholas Wolterstorff, for instance, says that "at least some of [God's] aspects stand in temporal order-relations to each other. Thus God, too, has a time-strand. His life and existence is itself temporal." Furthermore, says Wolterstorff, "the events to be found on God's time-strand belong within the same temporal array as that which contains our time-strands."[67] God exists everlastingly in time.

For a significant period, process philosophers and theologians were the most prominent among those reevaluating the classic doctrine of divine impassibility.[68] The impassibility doctrine says creatures do not essentially affect God. According to the traditional view, God has only logical relations with creation, not real and mutually

---

[67]Nicholas Wolterstorff, "God Everlasting," in *God and the Good: Essays in Honor of Henry Stob*, ed. Clifton Orlebeke and Lewis Smedes (Grand Rapids: Eerdmans, 1975), pp. 181-203; reprinted in *Philosophy and Faith: A Philosophy of Religion Reader*, ed. David Shatz (New York: McGraw, 2002), pp. 62-69. See also selections from Gregory E. Ganssle, ed., *God and Time: Four Views* (Downers Grove, IL: InterVarsity Press, 2001); Gregory E. Ganssle and David M. Woodruff, eds., *God and Time: Essays on the Divine Nature* (New York: Oxford University Press, 2002); and Amos Yong, "Divine Knowledge and Relation to Time," in *Philosophy of Religion: Introductory Essays*, ed. Thomas Jay Oord (Kansas City, MO: Beacon Hill, 2003), pp. 136-52.

[68]See especially Charles Hartshorne, *Man's Vision of God* (New York: Harper & Row, 1941).

influencing relations. Rather than relational, the impassible God is not susceptible to creaturely causation.[69]

By the end of the twentieth century, it seemed the majority of Christian scholars rejected the classical view of impassibility. Most believed God to be relational because God affects others and others affect God. Ronald Goetz even argues that the doctrine of the suffering God—the view that God is relational and passible rather than unaffected and impassible—has become the new orthodoxy among Christians.[70]

Richard E. Creel is among contemporary philosophers who now believe God is relational rather than impassible. If God loves, Creel says, God must sympathize with those whom God loves. "Any being which is insensitive or indifferent to the joys and sufferings of others," he argues, "is unloving and therefore unworthy of the title 'God.'" A personal God enters into dialogue with others, which means God must "take such input into account in decisions about and response to [creatures]."[71] If God truly takes "such input into account," creatures affect deity.

Closely related to passibility is God's mutability. To be mutable is to change, and the classic doctrine of divine immutability says God never changes in any respect. Charles Hartshorne's views on this subject may be the most influential, historically speaking, among open and relational thinkers.[72] Hartshorne rejected the idea found

---

[69]Richard E. Creel, "Immutability and Impassibility," in *A Companion to Philosophy of Religion*, ed. Philip L. Quinn and Charles Taliaferro (Oxford: Blackwell, 1997), p. 314.

[70]Ronald Goetz, "The Suffering God: The Rise of a New Orthodoxy," *Christian Century* 103 (1986): 385-89. Jürgen Moltmann has become well known for his emphasis upon God experiencing suffering, which is the same as saying God is passible or relational. See especially Moltmann, *The Crucified God* (London: SCM Press, 1974). More recently, Wesley Hill has argued that impassibility has returned to general favor. Hill's characterization of a suffering-God motif is not robust enough, however, to account for the view held by most relational theologians that God has both passible and impassible aspects. Wesley Hill, "The New 'New Orthodoxy': Only the Impassible God Can Help," *First Things*, January 15, 2015, www.firstthings.com/web-exclusives/2015/01/the-new-new-orthodoxy.

[71]Creel, "Immutability and Impassibility," p. 315. For a slightly different and earlier argument from Richard Creel, see his book *Divine Impassibility: An Essay in Philosophical Theology* (1986; repr., Eugene, OR: Wipf & Stock, 2005).

[72]For a summary of Hartshorne's philosophical views on God, see Donald Wayne Viney, *Charles Hartshorne and the Existence of God* (Albany: State University of New York Press, 1985).

in Thomas Aquinas, for instance, which says God is pure act without any potential for change. For Aquinas, God is immutable in all respects. For Hartshorne, God is immutable in some respects and mutable in others.

Hartshorne says God's eternal nature never changes. It is immutable. But God's living experience changes in moment-by-moment relations with others. It is mutable. As the greatest conceivable being, God's essence is perfectly unchanging. But in experience, God as the greatest conceivable being perfectly changes when taking in new information and experiences.[73]

If God is a living person with moment-by-moment experiences, God's experience in one moment could be surpassed by God's experience in the next. In this sense, God changes, but this change is perfect. "The numerically distinct God-tomorrow will also be perfect," says Hartshorne, "though He will exhibit perfection in an enriched state of actuality."[74]

In sum, Christian open and relational philosophers are rethinking traditional views of God.[75] They remain committed, however, to

---

[73]See Charles Hartshorne, *The Divine Relativity: A Social Conception of God* (New Haven, CT: Yale University Press, 1948).

[74]Charles Hartshorne, *The Logic of Perfection* (LaSalle, IL: Open Court, 1962), p. 66. See also my essay "Attaining Perfection: Love for God and Neighbor," in *Spiritual Formation: A Wesleyan Paradigm*, ed. Diane Leclerc and Mark A. Maddix (Kansas City, MO: Beacon Hill, 2011), pp. 65-73.

[75]For other philosophically oriented works on open and relational thought, see Basinger, *Case for Freewill Theism*; Daniel A. Dombrowski, *Analytic Theism, Hartshorne, and the Concept of God* (Albany: State University of New York Press, 1996); Peter Geach, *Providence and Evil* (Cambridge: Cambridge University Press, 1977); Charles Hartshorne, *Man's Vision of God* (New York: Harper & Row, 1941); William Hasker, *Providence, Evil and the Openness of God*; idem, *God, Time, and Knowledge*; J. R. Lucas, *The Future: An Essay on God, Temporality, and Truth* (London: Blackwell, 1989); Derek Malone-France, *Deep Empiricism: Kant, Whitehead, and the Necessity of Philosophical Theism* (Lanham, MD: Lexington, 2006); Timothy O'Connor, *Theism and Ultimate Explanation: The Necessary Shape of Contingency* (London: Wiley-Blackwell, 2012); Alan Rhoda, "Beyond the Chessmaster Analogy: Game Theory and Divine Providence," in *Creation Made Free: Open Theology Engaging Science*, ed. Thomas Jay Oord (Eugene, OR: Pickwick, 2009); idem, "The Philosophical Case for Open Theism," *Philosophia* 35 (2007): 301-11; Alan Rhoda, Gregory A. Boyd and Thomas G. Belt, "Open Theism, Omniscience, and the Nature of the Future," *Faith and Philosophy* 23 (2006): 432-59; George W. Shields and Donald W. Viney, "The Logic of Future Contingents," in *Process and Analysis: Whitehead, Hartshorne, and the Analytic Tradition*, ed. George W. Shields (Albany: State University of New York Press, 2004), pp. 209-46; Richard Swinburne, *The Coherence of Theism* (Oxford: Oxford University Press, 1977); Dale

overarching Christian beliefs that say God loves, creates, sustains, knows all, is powerful, is holy, etc. In these commitments, they remain traditional. But the ways open and relational philosophers understand God's attributes differ from the understanding of many philosophers and theologians of yesteryear.

SCIENCE

Science is the fourth major path that some have taken to open and relational theology. Many who engage the science-and-religion dialogue are attracted to open and relational themes, in large part because aspects of science harmonize with aspects of open and relational theology. For these science and religion scholars, it makes sense to say an open and relational God creates an open and relational universe.[76]

John Polkinghorne came to open and relational theology primarily through his studies in science. After earning a PhD in physics at Cambridge University, Polkinghorne began a career in the sciences, writing his first book on particle physics. He worked with some of the foremost scientists of his day and contributed to scientific research, specifically theoretical elementary particle physics. He also served as university lecturer in prominent universities in the United Kingdom.

Around the age of fifty, Polkinghorne decided to leave the laboratory and pursue ordination in the Church of England. "I simply felt that I had done my little bit for particle theory," he said, "and the time had come to do something else."[77] In the decades that followed, he served as the dean and chaplain at Trinity Hall, Queens College,

---

Tuggy, "Three Roads to Open Theism," *Faith and Philosophy* 24 (2007): 28-51; Donald Wayne Viney, "God Only Knows? Hartshorne and the Mechanics of Omniscience," in *Hartshorne, Process Philosophy and Theology*, ed. Robert Kane and Stephen Phillips (Albany: State University of New York Press, 1989), pp. 71-90; Keith Ward, *Divine Action* (San Francisco: Torch, 1991); idem, *God, Chance, and Necessity* (Oxford: Oneworld, 1996); and a compilation of Ward's work, *By Faith and Reason: The Essential Keith Ward*, ed. William Curtis Holtzen and Roberto Sirvent (London: Darton, Longman & Todd, 2012).

[76]For philosophical essays on science from open-view philosophers, see Thomas Jay Oord, William Hasker and Dean Zimmerman, eds., *God in an Open Universe* (Eugene, OR: Wipf & Stock, 2011). For theological essays from open and relational thinkers, see Thomas Jay Oord, ed., *Creation Made Free: Open Theology Engaging Science* (Eugene, OR: Pickwick, 2009).

[77]John C. Polkinghorne, *From Physicist to Priest, an Autobiography* (London: SPCK, 2007), p. 71.

Cambridge, in addition to becoming a prolific author. As a leading voice among those who work to reconcile science and theology, he tried to "be two-eyed, looking with both the eye of science and with the eye of religion, and such binocular vision enables [him] to see more than would be possible with either eye on its own."[78]

Training in physics led Polkinghorne to approach the world in a particular way. As I noted earlier, physics suggests that events in our world are at least partly random and unpredictable. Twentieth-century science saw the death of mechanism as scientists discovered in nature widespread and intrinsic unpredictability. The subatomic level first revealed this, but intrinsic unpredictability also became evident at the everyday level of chaos theory.

Polkinghorne came to believe the randomness in the world tells us something true about the openness of reality itself. This belief stems from his commitment to philosophical realism, which says our observations tell us something true about the world.[79] "Affirming that what we know or cannot know should be treated as a reliable guide to what is the case," he explains. Or to put it more philosophically, "intelligibility is the reliable guide to ontology."[80]

The realist position is persuasive because it considers reality when trying to make sense of life. As a critical realist, Polkinghorne believes reality is at least somewhat like it appears to be.[81] When the realist sees intrinsic unpredictabilities, he takes them "as being signs of a genuine ontological openness," says Polkinghorne.[82]

Extrapolating from the scientific idea that observation tells us something true and from the theological idea that God works creatively in the

---

[78]Ibid., p. 134.

[79]For analysis of Polkinghorne's understanding of realism in relation to other understandings, see Niels Henrik Gregersen, "Critical Realism and Other Realisms," in *Fifty Years in Science and Religion: Ian G. Barbour and His Legacy*, ed. Robert John Russell (Burlington, VT: Ashgate, 2004), chap. 4.

[80]John C. Polkinghorne, *Belief in God in an Age of Science* (New Haven, CT: Yale University Press, 1998), p. 10.

[81]Polkinghorne explains what he means by critical realism in *The Polkinghorne Reader: Science, Faith, and the Search for Meaning*, ed. Thomas Jay Oord (West Conshohocken, PA: Templeton Press, 2010), pp. 21-24.

[82]Polkinghorne, *From Physicist to Priest*, pp. 139-40.

world, Polkinghorne came to believe God faces an open future. "If I can act in this way in a world of becoming that is open to its future," he says, "I see no reason to suppose that God, that world's creator, cannot also act providentially in some analogous way within the course of its history."[83]

Consistent with open and relational theology, Polkinghorne says God is not a Cosmic Tyrant who does everything and allows no independent power to creatures. But neither is God a Deistic Spectator who just stands aside and lets it all happen. Instead, "the Christian God is the God of love who neither abandons creatures nor prevents them from being themselves and making themselves."[84]

The idea that creatures play a role in "making themselves" is partly Polkinghorne's way of interpreting evolution theologically. "God interacts with creatures," he says, but God "does not overrule the gift of due independence which they have been given."[85] Evolution requires contributions from both creatures and the Creator. The created order comes from God's creating and creatures co-creating.

Polkinghorne is one of many contemporary thinkers who find kenotic theology satisfying, and kenotic theology influences how he thinks about God's foreknowledge. He believes "the creation of a world of real becoming" must have involved "not only a kenosis of divine power but also a kenosis of divine knowledge." This means "even God does not yet know the unformed future, for it is not yet there to be known."[86]

God's lack of foreknowledge signifies no imperfection in God's nature. It only means God's relation to time is similar to creation's relation. "The eternal God, in bringing a temporal world into being," says Polkinghorne, "has condescended also to engage with the reality of time." Postulating both eternity and temporality in God's nature, although in different respects, "has been an important ingredient in much contemporary theology."[87]

---

[83]Ibid., p. 140.
[84]Ibid., pp. 140-41.
[85]Ibid.
[86]Polkinghorne, *Belief in God in an Age of Science*, p. 73.
[87]Polkinghorne, *From Physicist to Priest*, p. 141.

Open and relational theologies are well situated to accept the randomness many report in the world, in general, and in evolution, in particular. They assume that God is not all-controlling and that creation exhibits genuine causality. They also affirm with most of science that all causation is forward oriented. In open and relational theologies, the forward flow of time is a necessary feature of those things that actually exist. In other words, effects cannot precede their causes.

Polkinghorne has his own version of open and relational thought, but other scholars leading the science-and-theology conversation offer their versions of open and relational thinking. Among prominent voices are Ian Barbour,[88] Philip Clayton,[89] John Haught[90] and Arthur Peacocke.[91] In each, we see not only theological arguments about God's knowledge, presence, power and love. Each also accepts dominant perspectives in the sciences, especially physics and biology.

Open and relational scholars do not agree on all the specifics, of course. The details of their visions of providence, for instance, differ depending on their interests, expertise, inclinations and primary concerns. The open and relational umbrella is broad enough to include a diversity of ideas.

Having looked at the various paths scholars have taken to open and relational theology, I turn now to a specific view of providence offered

---

[88]Among Ian Barbour's many books, see especially *Nature, Human Nature, and God* (Minneapolis: Fortress, 2002); *When Science Meets Religion: Enemies, Strangers, or Partners?* (New York: HarperCollins, 2000); *Religion in an Age of Science* (Norwich, UK: SCM Press, 1990); and *Issues in Science and Religion* (Upper Saddle River, NJ: Prentice Hall, 1966).

[89]Among Philip Clayton's many books, see especially *Adventures in the Spirit*; *Mind and Emergence: From Quantum to Consciousness* (Oxford: Oxford University Press, 2004); *Explanation from Physics to Theology: An Essay in Rationality and Religion* (New Haven, CT: Yale University Press, 1989); *God and Contemporary Science* (Grand Rapids: Eerdmans, 1997); and Philip Clayton and Jeffrey Schloss, eds., *Evolution and Ethics: Human Morality in Biological and Religious Perspective* (Grand Rapids: Eerdmans, 2004).

[90]Among John Haught's many books, see especially *Christianity and Science* (Maryknoll, NY: Orbis, 2007); *Is Nature Enough? Meaning and Truth in the Age of Science* (Cambridge: Cambridge University Press, 2006); *Deeper Than Darwin: The Prospects for Religion in the Age of Evolution* (Cambridge, MA: Westview, 2003); and *God After Darwin: A Theology of Evolution*, 2nd ed. (Cambridge, MA: Westview, 2007).

[91]Among Arthur Peacocke's many books, see especially *Paths from Science Toward God: The End of All Our Exploring* (London: Oneworld, 2001); *God and Science: A Quest for Christian Credibility* (Norwich, UK: SCM Press, 1996); and *Theology for a Scientific Age: Being and Becoming; Natural, Human and Divine* (Minneapolis: Fortress, 1993).

by John Sanders, an open and relational theologian. I want to explore Sanders's model not only to note its helpfulness and not only because it has been highly influential. I also explore Sanders's model of providence to show how it is both similar to and different from the essential kenosis model I will propose as an alternative.

6

Does Love Come First?

*I*n the previous chapter, we looked at paths some have taken to open and relational theology. Whether through study of Scripture, theology, philosophy or science, all who journey to open and relational theology ponder divine providence to some degree. The far-reaching issues of providence drive open and relational reflections.

Open theologian John Sanders offers one of the most thorough and best-known theologies of providence written from an open and relational perspective. His book, *The God Who Risks*, has as its subtitle *A Theology of Divine Providence*. The book has rightly been hailed as a benchmark contribution to the theology of providence.[1]

In this chapter, I explore key features of Sanders's thought. While I agree with him on most issues, I highlight areas of disagreement to contrast Sanders's views with my alternative open and relational theology proposal. My version of open and relational theology and the model of providence it offers—what I call "essential kenosis"—is similar to Sanders's version. But my version also has some key differences.

In all this, I aim to provide another step toward making better sense of our lives.

---

[1]A number of endorsers of Sanders's book offer high praise. William Abraham says, for instance, that "Sanders's book is a benchmark treatment of the theology of providence." John Sanders, *The God Who Risks: A Theology of Providence*, rev. ed. (Downers Grove, IL: InterVarsity Press, 2007), back cover.

The God Who Risks

Sanders affirms most if not all the features of open and relational theology mentioned in the previous chapter. In *The God Who Risks: A Theology of Divine Providence*, Sanders says he understands providence as "the way God has chosen to relate to us and provide for our well-being."[2] He offers what he calls a "risk model of providence," which says God voluntarily decided to create a world with free creatures.[3] When creating in this way, God made a covenant to be open to creatures. This covenant "is not a detailed script but a broad intention that allows for a variety of options regarding precisely how it may be reached."[4]

As an open and relational theologian, Sanders rejects the idea that God constantly controls others. "God grants humans genuine freedom to participate in this project, and he does not force them to comply."[5] Creating genuinely free creatures means that God gives up the ability to control all creatures all the time.

God acts providentially, but the divine plan has "a broad intention with flexible strategies that allow for a variety of options."[6] God works with his creatures, seeking to obtain various goals. In this providential activity, says Sanders, "God genuinely enters into dynamic give-and-take relationships with humans, loving them, providing for them, and soliciting their collaboration in the fulfillment of God's purposes for creation."[7]

God's providence involves risk. This means, says Sanders, God "does not get everything he desires."[8] But this is the nature of love: "love takes risks and is willing to wait and try again if need be."[9] Love may result in deep interpersonal relationship. But it may also be scorned, as creatures reject God's invitation. This does not make God

---

[2]Ibid., p. 12.
[3]Ibid., p. 16.
[4]Ibid., p. 244.
[5]Ibid., p. 174.
[6]Ibid., p. 15.
[7]Ibid., p. 38.
[8]Ibid., p. 207.
[9]Ibid., p. 179.

helpless because "there is much the lover can do," says Sanders. "But success is not guaranteed."[10]

The risk model of providence will not appeal to everyone, Sanders admits. Some believers prefer guarantees.[11] But the alternative to a risk-taking God model is some form of theological determinism. Outcomes are guaranteed only if God controls others. Robots can be trusted to comply, but free creatures may hinder divine plans.

Sanders affirms open and relational beliefs about God's knowledge and relation to time. "God is everlasting through time," he says, "rather than timelessly eternal." God knows all that can be known, given the sort of world God chose to create. The future is not entirely knowable because it is contingent upon creaturely choices. Sanders calls this "dynamic omniscience." In this view, "God knows the past and present with exhaustive definite knowledge and knows the future as partly definite (closed) and partly indefinite (open)."[12]

Love motivates divine providence. "Love is the preeminent characteristic of God," says Sanders.[13] And "the commitment to love his creatures and bring them into a reciprocal relationship of love is fundamental." God does not give up on covenantal commitments but responds with a strategy for redeeming each situation.[14] Sanders believes that "God loves his creatures and desires to bless them with all that is in their best interest." The relationship God offers "is not one of control and domination but rather one of powerful love and vulnerability."[15]

Some criticize open and relational theologians for using creaturely analogies when conceiving of the Creator. The technical word for this practice is *anthropomorphism*, which means "humanlike." Open theists use creaturely images, analogies and language to describe God, who is not a creature.

---

[10]Ibid.
[11]Ibid., p. 175.
[12]Ibid., p. 15.
[13]Ibid., p. 181.
[14]Ibid., p. 244.
[15]Ibid., p. 71.

Sanders answers this criticism by saying that biblical writers use anthropomorphic language often. Consequently, biblically oriented open and relational theologians feel warranted when following this biblically derived practice. Furthermore, Scripture reveals that God is like us in some respects but not in others. Our language describes something about who God truly is. After all, the Bible says we are created in God's image.

The clearest revelation of God comes in Jesus Christ, himself human and divine. Sanders makes a strong christological case for open and relational theology. "If Jesus is *the* ultimate revelation of who God is and what humans are supposed to be in relationship to God," he says, "then we should pay particular attention to the way divine providence works in the life of Jesus."[16] If we look to Jesus, says Sanders, "we see the genuine character of God, who is neither an omnipotent tyrant nor an impotent wimp."[17]

Jesus reveals that God intimately relates to us by giving and receiving love. "God is intimate and near, not remote or disengaged," says Sanders.[18] Because creatures affect God, the evangelical emphasis on "a personal relationship with God" is correct.[19] God's way is to respond to creatures and be receptive to what they say and do.[20]

What creatures do makes a difference to God.

According to the witness of Jesus, God opposes evil. "If Jesus is the paradigm of providence," says Sanders, "then God is fundamentally opposed to sin, evil, and suffering." Jesus' life, death and resurrection reveal that "God is not the all-determining power responsible for sending everything, including suffering, on us." Rather, "the almighty God wins our hearts through the weakness of the cross and the power of the resurrection," says Sanders. "Love does not force its own way

---

[16]Ibid., p. 93, emphasis original.

[17]Ibid., p. 94.

[18]Ibid., p. 115.

[19]John Sanders, "Divine Providence and the Openness of God," in *Perspectives on the Doctrine of God: Four Views*, ed. Bruce A. Ware (Nashville: B & H, 2008), pp. 196-97.

[20]Sanders, *God Who Risks*, p. 116.

on the beloved."[21] In sum, "the way of God is love."[22] In the work of John Sanders, we find a powerful model of divine providence.

PROBLEMS WITH SANDERS'S VIEW

Up to this point in my summary of Sanders's version of open and relational theology, I completely agree with him. I might articulate some points slightly differently, but we both endorse main themes of open and relational theology. We agree on so much!

I disagree, however, with Sanders's view of how God's love and power relate. I also disagree when Sanders says God allows or permits genuine evil. These disagreements matter when it comes to thinking about how God acts providentially in a world of randomness and evil.

In *The God Who Risks*, Sanders often says God permits evil when evil could have been prevented.[23] "Evil is allowed but not desired by God," he says.[24] "God permits things to happen, both good and bad, that he does not specifically intend." General sovereignty "allows for pointless evil."[25] And "God has the power to prevent sin and evil from coming about."[26]

When Sanders talks about evil, he apparently means genuine evil. Genuine evils have no specific purpose; they are gratuitous or pointless. "Some evil is simply pointless because it does not serve to achieve any greater good," says Sanders.[27] "Horrible events happen that God did not want to occur."[28]

---

[21]Ibid., p. 193.

[22]Ibid.

[23]An accessible book comparing an open-theology theodicy to other theodicies is Richard Rice's book *Suffering and the Search for Meaning: Contemporary Response to the Problem of Pain* (Downers Grove, IL: IVP Academic, 2014). Other important writings on theodicy from an open-theism perspective include Gregory A. Boyd, *Satan and the Problem of Evil: Constructing a Trinitarian Warfare Theodicy* (Downers Grove, IL: InterVarsity Press, 2001); William Hasker, *Providence, Evil and the Openness of God* (New York: Routledge, 2004); idem, *The Triumph of God over Evil: Theodicy for a World of Suffering* (Downers Grove, IL: InterVarsity Press, 2008); and Alan Rhoda, "Gratuitous Evil and Divine Providence," *Religious Studies* 46 (2010): 281-302.

[24]Sanders, *God Who Risks*, p. 198.

[25]Ibid., p. 226.

[26]Ibid., p. 230.

[27]Ibid., p. 272.

[28]Ibid., p. 276.

But God has a reason for not preventing evil, says Sanders. The reason has to do with "the nature of the divine project."[29] The divine project involves what Sanders calls "general sovereignty." God's general sovereignty "does not allow for each and every such evil to be explained" because "God is only responsible for the structures within which we operate and for those specific acts in history God elects to do."[30] God's creational project makes possible the structures of existence in which evil and suffering could occur. But according to Sanders, God does not directly intend or cause evil.

God is ultimately responsible for evil, according to Sanders. "It may be said that God, in permitting significant others who have in fact done evil, takes responsibility for creating a world in which such evil could obtain. But God cannot be blamed for the actual evil of the creatures, since God did not intend it."[31] Here, Sanders seems to distinguish between God's ultimate decision to create a specific type of universe with freedom, structures and processes and the belief that God does not want particular evils.

But is this distinction ultimately meaningful?

A critic might respond that the God Sanders describes fails to act like a loving human, let alone a perfectly loving God. A loving mother would prevent pointless harm to her child if she were able. She would not stand by to allow others to assault her youngster. Loving parents prevent evil when they can.

While in some respects God acts like a loving parent, says Sanders, God does not act so in others. "Unlike a human parent, God is uniquely responsible for upholding the ontological, moral, and relational structures of the universe."[32] In other words, God does not prevent genuine evil in specific cases because God is concerned about the whole.

Sanders also believes God does not act like a teacher whom we

---

[29]Ibid., p. 272.
[30]Ibid., p. 273.
[31]Ibid., p. 233.
[32]Ibid.

might think should halt trouble in a chaotic classroom. We might think a loving teacher, if he or she were able, would prevent one student from bullying another, for instance. Bullying is evil activity a loving person wants to thwart, if possible.

With regard to the classroom analogy, Sanders says the almighty God "could veto any specific act" by a student. But if God "made a habit of it, then he would turn the beloved into an automaton and thus find himself alone," says Sanders. "God cannot prevent all the evil in the world and still maintain the condition of fellowship intended by his overarching purpose in creation."[33] God fails to prevent specific evils because God has to manage the entire universe, with its structures and processes.

Notice that Sanders talks about God "making a habit" of vetoing specific acts. This suggests he believes God can and perhaps does occasionally veto acts by controlling others or situations.[34] For instance, he says that "in the God-human relationship, God sometimes decides alone what will happen."[35] There are "specific acts in history God elects to do."[36] "Sometimes God unilaterally decides what shall be."[37] And "there are some things that the almighty God retains the right to enact unilaterally."[38] Assuming God acts in relation to creatures, which these quotes imply, the divine actions Sanders mentions seem to require God to control creatures completely.

We might summarize Sanders's overall explanation in this way: God decided to create a world in which free creatures might exist and enjoy unforced relationship. Sometimes, however, free creatures do evil. God can control specific acts, thereby preventing genuine evil.

---

[33]Ibid., p. 269.

[34]In private and public settings since the publication of *The God Who Risks*, Sanders has said that he no longer thinks it necessary to affirm that God occasionally intervenes or interrupts nature. But because his statements in this book lead in that direction and because, as I will argue soon, Sanders believes sovereignty logically precedes love in God's nature, I feel I should criticize his views here.

[35]Ibid., p. 174.

[36]Ibid., p. 273.

[37]Ibid., p. 198.

[38]Ibid., p. 247.

But God does not usually do so, which means God voluntarily chooses not to prevent evil. God allows it. Controlling others too often would result in a world of robotlike creatures instead of free ones. God manages the whole and rarely, if ever, intervenes to prevent specific evils.

If I have summarized Sanders's view correctly, I wonder how the victims of evil we encountered in the first chapter would respond to it. How would the victims of the Boston bombing, the woman killed by an errant rock, the parents of a child born with severe disabilities or Zamuda, who was raped and whose family was killed, respond to this explanation? I doubt they would find it satisfying.

Sanders's view says God could prevent these instances of real-life evil. But God chooses not to. God's choosing to allow genuine evils is somehow for the good of overall creation. "God elects not to renege on the conditions he established," to use Sanders's words.[39] Instead of preventing these specific evils, God chooses to "maintain the conditions of fellowship intended by his overarching purpose in creation."[40] Sanders seems to believe God cannot maintain the overall conditions of creation while preventing specific horrors and atrocities.

God's failure to prevent evil, Sanders believes, derives from God's voluntary commitments. "God does not give up power," says Sanders, "but he does promise to adhere to the creational structures he made." And this "divine self-restraint should be understood as the restraint of love in concern for his creatures."[41]

I doubt, however, that the voluntary self-restraint Sanders alleges that God chooses sounds loving to Zamuda and other victims of genuine evil. I cannot imagine God saying to Zamuda, "I could have prevented your rape and family's death, but I voluntarily restrained myself from doing so. Despite this, please believe that I love you."

I'm sure Zamuda and other victims think authentic concern involves preventing the genuine evil they endured, if such prevention were pos-

---

[39]Ibid., p. 233.
[40]Ibid., p. 269.
[41]Ibid., p. 241.

sible. Sanders believes preventing these evils is possible for God, and God could stop horrific suffering instantly. The God who throughout history has had the capacity to control others, however, apparently has not thought the suffering we have witnessed in the world and our personal lives was bad enough to prevent. Evidently, God's preventing these evils would have been worse than allowing them.

By contrast, I believe the almighty and loving God who could enact some things unilaterally should avert pointless misery, rape and death. The God who can veto any specific act should veto acts of genuine evil. Not to do so means God is morally culpable. In my view, failure to prevent genuine evil doesn't sound like God is, as Sanders claims, "fundamentally opposed to sin, evil, and suffering."[42] It sounds more like God's primary commitment is never or rarely to tamper with the structures, conditions and processes of creation. This God sounds more like a project manager and less like the personal Lover who cares for each creature.

At stake is whether Zamuda's rape and the other atrocities we encountered in chapter one are genuine evils. Genuine evils are events that, *all* things considered, make the world worse than it might have otherwise been. Sanders believes that God allows pointless evils, so he apparently thinks genuine evils occur. And he would likely say the atrocities we encountered were genuine evils.

The version of open and relational theology Sanders offers, however, does not actually consider these atrocities *genuinely* evil, at least in light of overall creation. His view implies that although God could intervene and prevent them, God would be unloving if God did so. Intervening in specific cases would mean tampering with the general structures and processes of the world.

Had God prevented the actual rapes, murders, genocides and incest we have witnessed in history, this would not have been the best for God. Preventing the Boston Marathon, for instance, would have been the wrong thing for God to do, even though it was possible.

---

[42]Ibid., p. 116.

Preventing such evil, in Sanders's view, is apparently not loving because it would have meant tampering with the processes of existence.
Evidently, God's preventing the grossest evils of history would have
been worse, all things considered, than allowing them.

I find it difficult to imagine how God's preventing rape and murder
in any particular instance would make the world worse. I am not
convinced the creation project requires God to allow genuine evils—
including the Boston Marathon bombing, the woman killed by an
errant rock, the debilitating condition of infant Eliana Tova, the rape
of Zamuda and murder of her family, and countless other atrocities.
This doesn't sound to me like God, as Sanders alleges, desires to "bless
them with all that is in their best interest."[43]

Sanders's position seems to imply that voluntarily giving freedom
to others is always the most loving thing God can do. But is this true?
Is giving freedom when it could be restrained always an act of love?

If we can restrain freedom to prevent horrific evil, most of us think
we should do so. While it may be our general policy to "live free and
let be," we can also imagine times that, if we were able, constraining
others would be the way of love. We lock up hardened criminals, for
instance, because we think restricting their freedom is for the good
of all. We restrict the freedom of severely mentally ill people, at least
temporarily, for their own good and the good of others.

If we could have restrained those who freely raped Zamuda and
killed her family, we would have done so. If we could have temporarily restrained the freedom of the Tsarnaev brothers and prevented the Boston Marathon bombing, we would have done so. We
can think of other scenarios in which constraining freedom, to
some degree, would be an act of love. While we cannot entirely
control others, we think love sometimes requires restraining them,
if restraining is possible.

The God who could prevent any genuine evil unilaterally is responsible for *allowing* genuine evil. The one who could stop genuine evil

---

[43]Ibid., p. 71.

by restraining the perpetrator of evil is morally responsible—or better, culpable—for permitting the painful consequences. We don't consider morally exemplary those who fail to intervene to prevent horrific events and atrocities, if such prevention were possible.

Sanders's view resembles what many call the free-process defense to the problem of evil.[44] This defense says God created a dynamic world with various processes, conditions and structures. The existence God created included the possibility of freedom and a measure of spontaneity. The free processes of the world include freedom and novelty.[45] But they also allow for pain, suffering and destruction.

For instance, we read in chapter one the story of the woman killed when a tire flung a rock through her car windshield. And we read the true story of infant Eliana Tova, whose tiny body was the victim of genetic abnormalities. The free-process defense says these evils are possible because God created an open, dynamic universe that makes novel, free and random events possible.

The free-process defense comes in two forms. The two forms differ on whether God could entirely control the open systems, processes and conditions of life to prevent genuine evil. Sanders and most free-process-defense theologians accept that form that says God can momentarily suspend the processes, conditions and laws of the universe to prevent evil. But if God could have prevented instances of death and severe physical defect such as we have noted, either God is not perfectly loving or these tragedies are not genuinely evil. I can't believe either is true.[46]

Finally, Sanders believes open and relational theology supports well the idea that we can have a personal relationship with God. I agree. Love includes both personal and communal interaction, and it makes sense that God can do both perfectly. But in the personal

---

[44]For a nice overview of the free-process defense, see Garry DeWeese, "Natural Evil: A 'Free Process' Defense," in *God and Evil: The Case for God in a World Filled with Pain*, ed. Chad Meister and James K. Dew Jr. (Downers Grove, IL: InterVarsity Press, 2013), pp. 53-64.

[45]John Polkinghorne defends a version of the free-process defense. See *Science and Providence: God's Interaction with the World* (West Conshohocken, PA: Templeton Press, 2005).

[46]I will offer the other form of the free-process defense in the following chapter.

stories of suffering, tragedy and horror we have encountered, Sanders apparently believes God allowed those atrocities for the good of the whole. God's preventing them would have been worse. Sanders's position makes us wonder if God really cares about particular people, particular instances and particular pain.

The theodicy that Sanders proposes suggests a lack of divine concern for helping individuals avoid becoming the victims of evil. It rejects the idea that God acts selectively to stop suffering. To its advantage, this rejection overcomes questions about God helping some and not others. But it fails to present a God who lovingly intercedes for individuals by preventing their individual tragedies. It says to the Zamudas of the world, "I could have prevented your suffering, but doing so would have meant withdrawing the freedom of those who violate you. Overriding their freedom meant tampering with creation. I chose not to do that."

In sum, Sanders fails to solve the problem of evil.

Without a solution to this problem, we cannot make sense of numerous events in our world. Sanders's overall version of open and relational theology is largely helpful, and I agree with the majority of what he proposes. But it fails to answer well this crucial question: Why doesn't a powerful and loving God prevent *all* evil that is genuinely evil, especially specific instances of horror in our personal lives?

WHAT COMES FIRST IN GOD'S NATURE?

In the next chapter, I offer a solution to the problem of evil when I present the essential kenosis model of providence. But looking a bit more at Sanders's view to conclude this chapter can help us see why it fails to solve the problem of evil. This further look may also help move us toward a more adequate model of providence.

The heart of the problem is this: Sanders's version of open and relational theology does not make love God's foremost and governing attribute. Love does not come first.

This charge may seem odd. Like most open and relational theologians, Sanders says love is God's chief attribute. "Love is the preeminent characteristic of God," as he puts it.[47] And "the way of God is love."[48] Like all open and relational theologies, love plays a central role in Sanders's providence proposal.

Sanders's other statements, however, suggest that when God initially decided to create, divine sovereignty existed prior to love and was preeminent. God's power logically precedes divine love in divine decision making. These statements from Sanders reveal this:

> If God wants a world in which he tightly controls every event that happens, then God is free to do so.[49]

> God sovereignly chooses not to govern the world without our input.[50]

> It was solely God's decision to do things this way instead of exercising meticulous providence.[51]

> God is free to sovereignly decide not to determine everything that happens in history.[52]

> God, in sovereign freedom, decided not to tightly control human affairs.[53]

> In *sovereign freedom*, God has decided to make some of his actions contingent upon our requests and actions.[54]

The point Sanders makes is that nothing essentially constrains God's decisions, at least when initially creating. God's sovereign freedom is unconstrained. This fits his view, which we saw earlier, that God has the power to prevent genuine evil but instead allows it.

Sanders apparently believes we must choose among three options when thinking about God creating and acting providentially. The first option is a form of process theology. Sanders is wary of process theologies that say, as he puts it, that God is "pervasively conditioned by

---

[47]Sanders, *God Who Risks*, p. 181.
[48]Ibid., p. 116.
[49]Ibid., p. 185.
[50]Ibid., p. 52.
[51]Ibid., p. 198.
[52]Ibid., p. 174.
[53]Ibid., p. 198.
[54]Ibid., p. 14, emphasis original.

creatures." He wants to avoid saying that God, by necessity or by nature, depends on the world. Sanders believes God can unilaterally act on the world, and he doubts process theologians can affirm this.[55] Let's call the first option "The world conditions God."

The second option Sanders wants to avoid is a form of Calvinism. He is wary of Calvinist theologies that say, as he puts it, that "the divine nature necessarily must create a world in which God is omnidetermining." This view says God's ongoing providential control is "a manifestation of the divine nature."[56] Creatures are not really free, and randomness and chance are illusions. Let's call this second option "God constantly controls the world."

The option Sanders prefers says God sovereignly gives freedom but allows evil. Sovereign activity lays the framework of the creation project. "The divine nature is free to create a project that involves loving relations with creatures," says Sanders.[57] But God could have created a world without free creatures. And God could (and perhaps occasionally does) control creatures or situations to bring about some outcome. Let's call Sanders's third option "God sovereignly, not of necessity, decided to create a world with free creatures."

I prefer a fourth option to these. We might call my view "God's loving nature requires God to create a world with creatures God cannot control." This option is part of the essential kenosis model I describe in the next chapter. But let me compare my preferred option with Sanders's view, which says God sovereignly, not of necessity, decided to create a world with free creatures.[58]

Open and relational theology says a relational God of love collabo-

---

[55]Ibid., p. 162.

[56]Ibid., p. 231.

[57]Ibid.

[58]The position that God's loving nature requires God to create a world with creatures God cannot control can apply either to the traditional view that God initially created something from absolutely nothing (*creatio ex nihilo*) or the view that God always creates from that which God previously created (*creatio ex creatione*). I explain the latter view in my essay "God Always Creates out of Creation in Love: *Creatio ex Creatione a Natura Amoris*," in *Theologies of Creation: Creatio ex Nihilo and Its New Rivals*, ed. Thomas Jay Oord (New York: Routledge, 2014), pp. 109-22.

rates with creatures. God's love takes risks in relationship, as Sanders puts it. Because love does not control others, the risk model of providence does not offer the guarantees divine determinism does. God's relationship with creatures, says Sanders, "is not one of control and domination but rather one of love and vulnerability."[59] God "does not force [creatures] to comply."[60] In sum, Sanders believes "love does not force its own way on the beloved."[61] I agree.

If God's preeminent attribute is love and love invites cooperation without forcing its own way, however, it makes little sense to say "sovereign freedom" allows God to create in an unloving way. It makes little sense, for instance, to say that God voluntarily decided against "exercising meticulous providence." If love comes first and love does not force others to comply, it makes little sense to say "God is free to sovereignly decide not to determine everything." If love comes first, God *cannot* exercise meticulous providence or determine everything.

To put it in question form using Sander's own language, why should we think a loving God who "does not force the beloved" is truly free "to tightly control every event that happens"? Why should we think a loving God is free to control others entirely, even if God never exercised that freedom? If love doesn't force the beloved and God is love, God *can't* force the beloved.

Let me illustrate my point: mermaids cannot run marathons.

Mermaids cannot run marathons because they have no legs. It is the nature of a mermaid to be legless. We might imagine how a mermaid would flap her tail when trying to cross land. But running marathons requires legs, and mermaids have none. Consequently, marathon-running mermaids cannot exist.

Likewise, it makes no sense to say God could control events if God's preeminent attribute is uncontrolling love. If God's love cooperates rather than controls and if God risks rather than forces guarantees, love as the logically prior attribute prevents God from

---

[59]Sanders, *God Who Risks*, p. 71.
[60]Ibid., p. 174.
[61]Ibid., p. 193.

determining totally. God cannot force the beloved because, as Sanders rightly says, love does not force its own way.

To put the analogy succinctly: mermaids cannot run marathons because a mermaid's nature includes leglessness. God cannot create controllable creatures because God's nature is uncontrolling love.

Sanders's main problem is that he does not take love as the logically preeminent attribute in God's nature. Unfortunately, Sanders believes God's "nature does not dictate the sort of world God must make."[62] At least when creating and perhaps also when relating, love does not come first in God in Sander's model.

By contrast, I *do* think God's nature dictates the sort of world God must make.[63] God must act according to the divine nature, and the preeminent attribute of God's nature is love. For this reason, I think love is God's ultimate guide when creating any world. In my view, love logically precedes power in God's nature. And the logical preeminence of love over sovereignty affects how we should think about God's ongoing creating and relating with creatures.

If love seeks collaboration instead of control, takes risks instead of forcing guarantees and does not force others to comply, a perfectly loving God cannot sovereignly control every event, exercise meticulous providence or absolutely determine everything. God cannot control others because, as Sanders rightly says, love does not force its own way on the beloved. Rather than saying God sovereignly decided to create a free world, we should say God's loving nature requires making undetermined creatures in any world God creates.[64]

---

[62]Ibid., p. 185.

[63]Sanders is aware of the possibility that the divine nature may prevent God from doing some things. He notes biblical passages supporting this view. But in response to such passages, Sanders says, "Although there is no attempt by biblical writers to reconcile the notion that God can do anything with the idea that God does not get everything he wants, it must be remembered that both sets of statements occur within the framework of God's relationship with the people to whom these particular statements are made" (ibid., p. 193). This suggests that he believes such statements are relative to certain times and places. At the least, he seems to think statements in Scripture pertaining to God's inabilities do not describe conditions in God's eternal nature.

[64]In a footnote, Sanders admits he engages in speculation when he talks about whether the divine nature requires God to create a world. He says he bases his speculation on his prior doctrine of creation (ibid., p. 328). Because Sanders affirms *creation ex nihilo*, I assume he is referring to

Although I agree with the vast majority of Sanders's version of open and relational theology, his misstep, as I see it, is failing to follow through on his claim that God's preeminent attribute is love. He believes God's sovereign will logically precedes God's loving nature, at least when it comes to initial creation. And given Sanders's statements that God sometimes acts alone to bring about outcomes and allows genuine evil, his view also implies the sovereign will logically precedes love in history.[65]

For Sanders, love does not come first in God's nature.

My criticism of Sanders leads to my alternative version of open and relational theology, what I call "essential kenosis." At the heart of essential kenosis is the belief that uncontrolling love is logically preeminent in God. To this theology we now turn.

---

this theory of initial creation when he speaks of his prior creation doctrine. My alternative position says love precedes sovereignty in God's nature. But my theory is essentially neutral on this issue of *creation ex nihilo*. One can affirm creation out of nothing or deny it while agreeing with me that God's love is the preeminent attribute of God's nature and therefore God could not create a world devoid of freedom or agency.

[65]I appreciate John Sanders's response to some of the material in this chapter. It helped clarify my thinking although it did not fundamentally change my criticism. Find his helpful response at the conclusion of my blog essay, "Problems with Sanders's View of Providence," *Thomas Jay Oord* (blog), July 21, 2014, http://thomasjayoord.com/index.php/blog/archives/problems_with_sand erss_view_of_providence/#.U-KJI-NdV8E.

7

The Essential Kenosis Model
of Providence

We began our efforts to make sense of life by looking at true stories of genuine evil. In each account, aspects of randomness and free will were present. We also encountered unsatisfying explanations for why a loving and powerful God did not prevent these horrific events. We need persuasive answers to life's puzzling questions.

Genuinely random, chance and accidental events occur often in the world. From quantum events to genetic mutations to human interactions and beyond, existence bubbles with randomness. We also find structure, order and consistency in creation. Lawlike regularities persist in everyday life and the world explored by science. Existence as we know it depends upon regularities. Neither absolute randomness nor absolute regularity, however, reigns absolutely. The lawlike regularity of the world combined with spontaneous randomness provides a context for both creative novelty and faithful reliability.

Humans (and perhaps other complex creatures) act freely although all creaturely freedom is limited. Most if not all humans have libertarian free will, even if some deny it. We may not find full-blown freedom among simpler entities and less complex organisms, but we do find self-organization and in some a measure of agency. Freedom and agency used wrongly cause genuine evil. But evils can also have random causes.

Life is not all about evil. We encounter much good in life too. It makes sense to me and to many others that a good God is the source of goodness.

Explanations of existence that include a prominent role for God are more satisfying overall. In fact, it makes sense that God uses creaturely free choices and random events in ongoing creating and providential activity. However, believers are right to wonder why this good God fails to prevent genuine evils that free choices and random events cause.

Those who believe in God offer various theories—models of providence—to account for divine action. Providence models that deny randomness and freedom do not correspond with life as we know it. Models that say God is impersonal, uninvolved or unaffected by creation cannot account well for religious experiences, goodness and love, or sacred Scripture. Models that say God sometimes entirely controls others or, in principle, could do so fail to provide plausible answers to the problem of evil. Models of providence appealing to utter mystery or an inscrutable divine will are especially unhelpful. Although we will never understand God completely, we need a plausible model of providence if we are to make sense of reality.

Open and relational theology offers helpful answers to life's questions. It affirms genuine randomness and lawlike regularity. This theology embraces self-organization, agency and libertarian free will. Open and relational theology believes that values are real, including genuine evil; that God is good; and that it is possible for creatures to do what is good. The active and relational God of this perspective knows all that can be known, but the future remains authentically open to both Creator and creatures.

Even though open and relational theologies are attractive, unresolved questions remain. One of the most thorough expositions of open and relational theology to date, for instance, fails to solve the problem of evil. This version of open and relational theology fails largely because it says God permits pointless evil. It considers sovereignty, rather than love, to come first logically in God's nature.

In previous chapters, I promised a version of open and relational theology I call essential kenosis. I said this theology would answer remaining questions and provide a model of providence that includes randomness and regularity, free will and necessity, goodness and evil, and more. This model would emphasize that God loves all creation steadfastly because God's nature is uncontrolling love. And it would offer a plausible solution to the problem of evil.

It is time to make good on my promise.

KENOSIS

Let's begin with Jesus Christ and kenosis. The verb form of *kenōsis* appears about a half dozen times in the New Testament. One of the most discussed appearances comes in the apostle Paul's letter to believers in the city of Philippi. The text is powerful for what it says about God, Jesus and the way we ought to live.

Here is the Philippians text, including the verses surrounding *kenōsis*, to provide context for help in finding its meaning:

> Let each of you look not to your own interests, but to the interests of others. Let the same mind be in you that was in Christ Jesus,
>
> who, though he was in the form of God,
> > did not regard equality with God
> > as something to be exploited,
> but emptied himself [*ekenōsen* = kenosis],
> > taking the form of a slave,
> > being born in human likeness.
> And being found in human form,
> > he humbled himself
> > and became obedient to the point of death—
> > even death on a cross.
> Therefore God also highly exalted him
> > and gave him the name
> > that is above every name,
> so that at the name of Jesus
> > every knee should bend,
> > in heaven and on earth and under the earth,
> and every tongue should confess
> > that Jesus Christ is Lord,
> > to the glory of God the Father.

Therefore, my beloved, just as you have always obeyed me, not only in my presence, but much more now in my absence, work out your own salvation with fear and trembling; for it is God who is at work in you, enabling you both to will and to work for his good pleasure. (Phil 2:4-13)

This passage begins with Paul's ethical instructions: look to the interests of others, not your own. He points to Jesus Christ, who divinely acts as the primary example of someone who expresses other-oriented love. Jesus' love is evident, says Paul, in his diminished power and his service to others. The weakness of the cross is an especially powerful example of Jesus acting for the good of others.[1] God endorses Jesus' other-oriented love, and God enables those who follow Jesus' example to pursue salvation. Paul tells readers to pursue salvation earnestly.

All Scripture requires interpretation. Theologians interpret this passage in various ways and apply it to various issues. When considering the meaning of *kenōsis*, theologians in previous centuries typically focused on the phrase just prior to *kenōsis* in this passage: "[Jesus] did not regard equality with God as something to be exploited" (Phil 2:6). They believed it provides clues for explaining Jesus' humanity and divinity.

At a fifth-century meeting in Chalcedon, Christian theologians issued a statement saying Jesus Christ has two natures "communicated to" one person. Jesus is the God-human, said many who attended the meeting. He is fully divine and fully human. These early church leaders arrived at this view after rejecting other options for understanding Jesus as the Christ.

Theologians thereafter pondered which divine attributes Jesus retained in human life and which, apparently as a result of self-emptying, he did not. The Chalcedonian creed offers little to no help in answering the specifics of this issue. Theologians today still ponder how Jesus is both human and divine.[2]

---

[1]Jürgen Moltmann has become well known for this idea, and he explains it in *The Crucified God* (London: SCM Press, 1974).

[2]On the historical debate of kenosis and Jesus' two natures, see David Brown, *Divine Humanity:*

In recent decades, however, discussions of kenosis have shifted.[3] Instead of appealing to kenosis in the debate over which divine attributes Jesus possesses, theologians today use *kenosis* primarily to describe how Jesus *reveals* God's nature. Instead of imagining how God may have relinquished attributes when becoming incarnate, many now think Jesus' kenosis tells us who God is and how God acts.

The contemporary shift to thinking of kenosis as Jesus revealing God's nature moves theologians away from phrases in the passage preceding *kenōsis*. Following the lead of some biblical scholars, many theologians now read *kenōsis* primarily in light of phrases such as "taking the form of a slave," "humbled himself" and "death on a cross." These phrases immediately follow *kenōsis*, and they focus on Jesus' diminished power and service to others.[4] They suggest that God's power is essentially persuasive and vulnerable, not overpowering and aloof. We especially see God's noncoercive power revealed in the cross of Christ, which suggests that God's power is cruciform (see also 1 Cor 1:18-25).[5] Phrases in the Philippians passage describe forms of other-oriented love.

Kenosis and the Construction of a Christian Theology (Waco, TX: Baylor University Press, 2011); and Thomas R. Thompson, "Nineteenth-Century Kenotic Christology: Waxing, Waning and Weighing of a Quest for a Coherent Orthodoxy," in *Exploring the Kenotic Christology: The Self-Emptying of God*, ed. C. Stephen Evans (Vancouver: Regent College, 2006).

[3]Among recent helpful texts on kenosis, see Brown, *Divine Humanity*; Peter J. Colyer, *The Self-Emptying God: An Undercurrent in Christian Theology Helping the Relationship with Science* (Cambridge: Cambridge Scholars, 2013); C. Stephen Evans, ed., *Exploring Kenotic Christology: The Self-Emptying of God* (Vancouver: Regent College, 2006); and John C. Polkinghorne, ed., *The Work of Love: Creation as Kenosis* (Grand Rapids: Eerdmans, 2001).

[4]See the work of biblical scholars such as John Dominic Crossan and Jonathan Reed, *In Search of Paul: How Jesus's Apostle Opposed Rome's Empire with God's Kingdom* (San Francisco: HarperSanFrancisco, 2004), p. 290; James D. G. Dunn, *Christology in the Making: An Inquiry into the Origins of the Doctrine of the Incarnation*, 2nd ed. (London: SCM Press, 1989), p. 116; Michael J. Gorman, *Inhabiting the Cruciform God: Kenosis, Justification, and Theosis in Paul's Narrative Soteriology* (Grand Rapids: Eerdmans, 2009), chap. 1; Donald Macleod, *The Person of Christ*, Contours of Christian Theology (Leicester: Inter-Varsity Press, 1998), p. 215; Ralph P. Martin, *Carmen Christi: Philippians 2:5-11 in Recent Interpretation and in the Setting of Early Christian Worship*, rev. ed. (Grand Rapids: Eerdmans, 1983), p. 170; and N. T. Wright, *The Climax of the Covenant* (Minneapolis: Fortress, 1993), p. 84.

[5]For the relation between God's holiness and cruciformity, see Michael Gorman, "'You Shall Be Cruciform for I Am Cruciform': Paul's Trinitarian Reconstruction of Holiness," in *Holiness and Ecclesiology in the New Testament*, ed. Kent E. Brower and Andy Johnson (Grand Rapids: Eerdmans, 2007), pp. 148-66.

I follow the contemporary trend of interpreting kenosis primarily as Jesus' qualified power, other-orientation and servant love. This interpretation seems more fruitful overall than discussions about what might be communicated between Christ's two natures, although I think such discussions have their place. My interpretation also helps us consider God's essential power, in light of God's loving nature and orientation toward creation. Consequently, I refer to kenosis to talk not so much about how God became incarnate as to understand God's nature in light of incarnate love. For as the writer of Hebrews puts it, Jesus is the "exact representation of [God's] nature" (Heb 1:3 NASB).

We can know something about God's nature in the light of Jesus' kenotic love.

Scholars also debate how best to translate the word *kenōsis*. While most believe it tells us something true about God, no one knows precisely what the word means. *Kenōsis* sits in the midst of what biblical scholars believe to be a poem or hymn, and this genre allows for an especially wide range of interpretations. Scholars interpret *kenōsis* variously as "self-emptying," "self-withdrawing," "self-limiting" or "self-giving."

Some of these translations are less helpful than others. "Self-emptying," for instance, does not make much sense if taken literally. To say God is emptied sounds like deity is a container whose contents pour out. This is not the personal language of love, and love seems the central point of the passage. Biblical scholar Gordon Fee, for instance, says the idea that God self-empties is at best metaphorical because "the suggestion that Christ 'emptied himself' *of* something is quite foreign to Paul's own concern."[6] Kenosis is not "a divestiture of something," says biblical scholar Michael Gorman.[7] Relational language, rather than container language, is more helpful if kenosis pertains primarily to love.

---

[6]Gordon D. Fee, "The New Testament and Kenosis Christology," in *Exploring Kenotic Christology: The Self-Emptying of God*, ed. C. Stephen Evans (Vancouver: Regent College, 2006), p. 29. See also Gordon D. Fee, *Paul's Letter to the Philippians* (Grand Rapids: Eerdmans, 1995), p. 210.
[7]Gorman, *Inhabiting the Cruciform God*, p. 22.

Jürgen Moltmann sometimes uses "self-withdrawing" to describe kenosis. God "withdrew himself into himself in order to make room for the world," says Moltmann. In kenosis, God "distances himself" from the world "to concede space for the presence of creation."[8] In this, says Moltmann, "the omnipotent and omnipresent God withdraws his presence and restricts his power."[9] This involves "a restriction of God's omnipotence, omnipresence, and omniscience for the sake of conceding room to live to those he has created."[10]

Moltmann's intent is laudable because he seeks to account for divine love and creaturely freedom.[11] But self-withdrawing language is problematic for several reasons. Saying God withdraws from space, if taken literally, implies God is no longer omnipresent. Saying God self-restricts knowledge suggests God does not know all that is knowable, which negates omniscience. Saying divine power is self-restricted suggests God is not doing all God could do, which opens self-withdrawing theology up to the criticism that it promotes a deity not fully engaged with creation. Understanding kenosis as withdrawing introduces serious complications.

Perhaps the most common understanding of kenosis is that God, out of love, voluntarily self-limits for the sake of others. Jeff Pool describes this view of kenosis as "volitional divine self-limitation" because "God restricts the divine self."[12] Vincent Brümmer affirms voluntary self-limitation and says God's power does not derive from a "limitation or a dependence which is imposed on God from outside."[13] Polkinghorne says "divine power is deliberately self-

---

[8]Jürgen Moltmann, "God's Kenosis in the Creation and Consummation of the World," in *The Work of Love: Creation as Kenosis*, ed. John C. Polkinghorne (Grand Rapids: Eerdmans, 2001), p. 146.

[9]Jürgen Moltmann, *God in Creation* (London: SCM Press, 1985), p. 87.

[10]Moltmann, "God's Kenosis," p. 147.

[11]Moltmann often unites his understanding of kenosis with the notion of zimzum, a concept he explores in several books. Zimzum is God withdrawing into Godself. It's is God's self-limitation for the other (*God in Creation* [San Francisco: Harper & Row, 1985], p. 86). See Anna Case-Winters's critique in *Reconstructing a Christian Theology of Nature* (Burlington, VT: Ashgate, 2007), chap. 7.

[12]Jeff B. Pool, *Divine Vulnerability and Creation*, vol. 1 of *God's Wounds: Hermeneutic of the Christian Symbol of Divine Suffering* (Cambridge: James Clarke, 2009), p. 139.

[13]Vincent Brümmer, *What Are We Doing When We Pray? A Philosophical Enquiry* (London: SCM Press, 1984), p. 67.

limited."[14] Notice that self-limitation in each of these cases is thought to be voluntary. God essentially retains the capacity to control others, but God willingly self-restricts.

Several problems emerge when we think of kenosis as God's voluntary self-limitation, and we have mentioned these in previous chapters.[15] The primary one is that voluntary self-limitation says God does not always use for good the power God essentially possesses.[16] We see this plainly when, for instance, Polkinghorne spells out what voluntary self-limitation means for questions of evil. "God does not will the act of a murderer or the destructive force of an earthquake," he says, "but allows both to happen in a world in which divine power is deliberately self-limited to allow causal space for creatures."[17]

Theologians who understand kenosis as voluntary self-limitation believe God voluntarily chooses not to prevent genuine evil.[18] Instead, God permits it. We are right to think, however, that the God who voluntarily self-limits ought to become un-self-limited, for the sake of love, to prevent genuine evil. In other words, kenosis understood as voluntary self-limitation leaves God culpable for failing to prevent genuine evil. Kenosis as voluntary self-limitation fails to make good sense in light of genuine evil.

These three interpretations of kenosis—self-emptying, self-withdrawing or voluntary self-limitation—present significant problems. Some don't match relational notions of other-oriented love, which seem the overall point of the passage. Others imply that God is not present in all places or not as influential as God could be. And each

---

[14]John C. Polkinghorne, "Kenotic Creation and Divine Action," in *The Work of Love: Creation as Kenosis*, ed. John C. Polkinghorne (Grand Rapids: Eerdmans, 2001), p. 102.

[15]The voluntary divine self-limitation approach aligns with the voluntarist rather than the intellectualist/nature tradition of philosophical theology. I explored these traditions briefly in chapter two.

[16]Anna Case-Winters argues similarly in *God's Power: Traditional Understandings and Contemporary Challenges* (Louisville, KY: Westminster John Knox, 1990), p. 204.

[17]Polkinghorne, "Kenotic Creation and Divine Action," p. 102.

[18]One of the better scholarly examinations of divine power in relation to evil is Atle Ottesen Søvik, *The Problem of Evil and the Power of God: On the Coherence and Authenticity of Some Christian Theodicies with Different Understandings of God's Power* (Oslo: Unipub AS, 2009).

leaves the problem of evil unresolved. These portrayals of kenosis offer little help for understanding the relation between God's power and love in the face of evil.

Although no translation is perfect, the most helpful rendering of *kenōsis* may be "self-giving." Interpreting kenosis as self-giving and therefore others-empowering love has the advantage of fitting well the opening context of the Philippians passage, which emphasizes acting for the good of others. It also fits well the culmination of the passage, which says God enables creatures to follow Jesus' example by living lives of love. Enabling involves the self acting to empower others.

Kenōsis translated as "self-giving, others-empowering love" corresponds well with passages found throughout Scripture. Readers often find passages saying God's action is necessary for creaturely life and love, for instance. I could offer many examples, but John puts it plainly: "We love because he first loved us" (1 Jn 4:19). John also says, "apart from [God] you can do nothing" (Jn 15:5), which implies that we rely on God's gift of agency. Although in a flair of hyperbole, Paul illustrates this when he says, "I can do all things through [Christ] who strengthens me" (Phil 4:13). God's creating, life-giving and love-empowering presence is required for all creation, says Paul, for in God "we live and move and have our being" (Acts 17:28). This love is revealed most profoundly in the cross. As Victor Furnish puts it, "the saving power of God revealed in the cross is the power of God's self-giving love."[19] A major advantage of understanding kenosis as self-giving, others-empowering love, in fact, is that the theme appears in various forms throughout the Old and New Testaments, even if the word *kenōsis* is not used.

Kenosis as self-giving, others-empowering love must be clarified, however. Divine self-giving does not mean creatures actually become divine. When self-giving, God does not bestow divinity upon creatures thereby making them deities. While humans can become Christ-like and can bear the divine image (2 Pet 1:4), they remain

---

[19]Victor Paul Furnish, *The Theology of the First Letter to the Corinthians* (Cambridge: Cambridge University Press, 1999), p. 74.

creatures. God's self-giving does not convert creatures into gods.

Understanding God to possess self-giving, others-empowering love also does not mean God loses the divine self after loving others. Self-giving does not make God literally selfless. This point seems important to mention because when creatures become "imitators of God, as beloved children, and live in love" (Eph 5:1-2), they retain their selves in this loving. Buddhists, not Christians, seek the literal loss of self. God doesn't lose the divine self when giving.

Kenosis as self-giving, others-empowering love also supports healthy self-love. Self-giving love only sometimes involves self-sacrifice. Some Christians have unfortunately believed that self-giving love opposes acting for one's own well-being. By contrast, kenosis as self-giving love supports the truth that self-love has a legitimate place in Christian ethics. Love decenters self-interest, but it does not destroy it.

The context in which we find *kenosis* shows Paul's concern that his readers promote what many call "the common good." Self-giving kenosis promotes overall well-being. In addition, those who imitate Christ's actions to promote well-being ultimately glorify God. Jesus' kenotic life and death reveal that God engages in self-giving, others-empowering love. To put it differently, Jesus' kenosis reveals that God self-gives to promote overall well-being.[20] The Philippians passage concludes by indicating that God's kenotic love empowers us to promote good as we live out our salvation.[21]

ESSENTIAL KENOSIS AND THE PRIMACY OF LOVE

Having clarified what we might mean by *kenosis*, we need to explore the *essential* in essential kenosis. Essential kenosis considers the self-giving, others-empowering love of God revealed in Jesus Christ to be logically primary in God's eternal essence. In God, love comes first.

[20]Some distinguish between *kenosis* and *plērōsis*. The latter word expresses the fullness of giving, while some interpret *kenosis* in terms of withdrawing. My understanding of *kenosis* as self-giving, others-empowering love overcomes the need to complement *kenosis* with *plērōsis*.

[21]Jeffery F. Keuss explores some dimensions of this in *Freedom of the Self: Kenosis, Cultural Identity, and Mission at the Crossroads* (Eugene, OR: Pickwick, 2010).

Essential kenosis says God's love is a necessary and eternal attribute of God's nature. "[God's] steadfast love endures forever," as the psalmist puts it (throughout Ps 136), because God's loving nature is eternal.

To say kenosis is a necessary, eternal and logically primary attribute of the divine nature means that God expresses kenosis inevitably. Doing so is part of what it means to be God. John's three-word sentence, "God is love" (1 Jn 4:8, 16), can be easily interpreted as supporting this view. "God is love" means love is the necessary expression of God's timeless nature. God relentlessly expresses love in the quest to promote overall well-being (*shālôm*).

God must love. To put it as a double negative: God cannot not love. Kenotic love is an essential attribute of God's eternal nature.[22] God loves necessarily. The love creatures express is sporadic, occasional and contingent because creatures do not have eternally loving natures. But God's eternal nature is love, which means God could no more stop loving than stop existing. God's love is uncontrollable, not only in the sense that creatures cannot control divine love but also in the sense that God cannot stop loving. To use a phrase popular among some believers, love is the "heart of God."

Because God must act like God, God must love.

This brings up an important point about the relation between God's love and freedom. God is not free to choose *whether* to love because God's nature is love. Essential kenosis agrees with Jacob Arminius when he says, "God is not freely good; that is, he is not good by the mode of liberty, but by that of natural necessity." For "if God be freely good, he can be or can be made not good." In fact, Arminius considered blasphemous the idea that God is freely good.[23] Similarly, essential kenosis says God's loving goodness is a necessary aspect of God's unchanging nature. It is impossible for God to be unloving because being so would require God to be other than divine.

---

[22]Frank Macchia makes a similar point in *Baptized in the Spirit: A Global Pentecostal Theology* (Grand Rapids: Zondervan, 2006), p. 259.

[23]Jacob Arminius, "It is the Summit of Blasphemy to Say That God Is Freely Good," in *The Works of James Arminius*, trans. James Nichols (1828; repr., Grand Rapids: Baker Books, 1991), 2:33-34.

Essential kenosis says, however, that God freely chooses *how* to express love in each moment. God is free in this important sense. In each moment God freely chooses to love one way instead of another because multiple options are available. God is free when choosing among possible ways to promote *shālôm*.

A significant virtue of open and relational theology is that it says God loves necessarily. But because it affirms an open future the actual events of which God cannot know until they occur, it also says God freely chooses how to love among various possible loving actions.[24] A God who necessarily loved and foreknew a completed future could not act freely. Although "the steadfast love of the LORD never ceases," it is freely "new every morning" (Lam 3:22-23)!

God necessarily loves, but God freely chooses *how* to love in each emerging moment.

We creatures differ from God in many respects, and Christians have believed it important to stress these differences. Although created in God's image, we are not divine. We can avoid idolatry, in part, by emphasizing God's unique status as the One worthy of our worship. God is God, and creation is not.

Creation differs from God in that free creatures are free both in deciding whether to love and in deciding how to express love. They do not have eternal natures in which love is preeminent and necessary. Because of this, for instance, creatures can choose sin and do evil. God's nature is love, however. This means God can neither sin nor do evil. But God can both want to love us and love us necessarily because love is essential.[25]

Love is God's preeminent attribute. God's kenotic love logically precedes divine power in the divine nature. This logical priority qual-

---

[24]This argument is crucial for overcoming the legitimate criticism William L. Rowe makes against non-open and relational theologies in which a good God necessarily creates the best of all possible worlds. See Rowe's argument in *Can God Be Free?* (Oxford: Oxford University Press, 2004).

[25]I am grateful to Nicholas Carpenter for his discussion that led me to realize that God loving necessarily does not exclude God wanting to love others. Because God's nature is love, God can both want to love creatures and necessarily love them.

ifies how we should think God works in and with creation. As John Wesley puts it, love is God's "reigning attribute,"[26] because as his brother Charles sang, "God's name and nature is love."[27] We should agree with C. H. Dodd: "to say 'God is love' implies that *all* His activity is loving activity. If He creates, He creates in love; if He rules, He rules in love; if He judges, He judges in love. All that he does is the expression of his nature, which is—to love."[28]

God's attributes—especially power—are best understood in the light of love.

To say love is logically paramount in God does not mean that we disregard other divine attributes, such as sovereignty, omniscience, everlastingness or omnipresence. Nor should we consider the other attributes unimportant. But the way we talk about God reveals how we explicitly or implicitly prioritize these attributes. We saw evidence of this in the previous chapter when various statements from John Sanders reveal that he implicitly affirms God's sovereign choice as logically prior to love.

The vast majority of theologians fail to take uncontrolling love as God's logically preeminent attribute. We see the logical prioritizing of sovereign choice, for instance, when theologians say God is free to choose whether to love. Choosing whether to love implies that choice logically comes first for God. If divine love logically precedes divine choice, God necessarily loves because loves comes first. Essential kenosis is exceptional when it says uncontrolling love is logically preeminent in God's nature.

Essential kenosis says love comes first in God.

Essential kenosis stands between two related views of God's love and power. One view says God voluntarily self-limits. God could control others entirely but (usually) chooses not to do so. As we have seen, the voluntary-self-limitation view cannot answer well why God

---

[26]John Wesley, *Explanatory Notes upon the New Testament* (Salem, OH: Schmul, 1975), p. 637.
[27]Charles Wesley, "Wrestling Jacob," in *A Collection of Hymns for the Use of the People Called Methodists*, vol. 7 of *The Works of John Wesley* (Nashville: Abingdon, 1983), pp. 250-52.
[28]C. H. Dodd, *The Johannine Epistles* (London: Hodder & Stoughton, 1946), p. 112.

does not un-self-limit, in the name of love, to prevent genuine evil. But there are other problems with this view.

The voluntary-self-limitation view also implies that love is *not* the logically primary aspect of God's nature. Consequently, the view faces additional problems. If love is not the logically primary attribute, we have no reason to believe that God does not sometimes choose to hate us. If sovereign choice precedes self-giving love, we have no reason to think that God will not sin. If God's nature is not first and foremost love, nothing prevents deity from choosing to break bad. Numerous problems arise when we believe divine will logically comes prior to divine love. Most theologians appeal to mystery when faced with these problems.

We can only trust unreservedly the God in whose nature love is essential, eternal and logically primary.

The other view standing near essential kenosis says external forces or worlds essentially limit God. This view gives the impression that outside actors and powers not of God's making hinder divine power. Or it says God is subject to laws of nature, imposed upon God from without. God is caught in the clutches of exterior authorities and dominions, and these superpowers restrict sovereignty.

This view seems to describe God as a helpless victim to external realities. Some criticize this view as presenting a "finite God" because outside forces or imposed laws curb divine activity. Many wonder how this God can be worthy of worship. While I think we have good reasons to think God's power is limited in certain respects, this view places God under a foreign authority. This God is too small.[29]

Essential kenosis stands between these two views. It rejects both voluntary self-limitation of God and the view that external powers, gods, worlds or laws limit God. Essential kenosis says limitations to divine power derive from God's nature of love. The Creator does not volun-

---

[29]One of the better books on the quest to find a right-size God is John B. Cobb Jr. and Clark H. Pinnock, eds., *Searching for an Adequate God: A Dialogue Between Process and Free Will Theists* (Grand Rapids: Eerdmans, 2000). Essayists and respondents include David Ray Griffin, William Hasker, Nancy Howell, Richard Rice and David L. Wheeler.

tarily self-limit, nor does creation rule its Maker. Instead, God's self-giving, uncontrolling love is a necessary, eternal and logically primary aspect of the divine nature. And God's actions originate in love.

God's expression of love takes many forms.[30] Divine love is full-orbed, and Scripture tells us this in various ways. For instance, God expresses *agapē* by repaying evil with good and doing good even to those who act unjustly. *Agapē* promotes *shālôm* in response to that which promotes sin, evil and the demonic. God forgives and loves even those who disobey. As our "Father in heaven," God lovingly sends good gifts of sun and rain to all, even to the unjust (Mt 5:45). *Agapē* loves in spite of others who do not love. We should imitate God's *agapē* by turning the other cheek (Mt 5:39) and responding to curses with blessings (Lk 6:28).

God expresses *philia* by partnering with all creation, but especially the more complex creatures, to promote the common good. God is a friend who suffers with us and "daily bears us up" (Ps 68:19). *Philia* promotes well-being by coming alongside to establish collaborative friendships. We can be God's partners and co-conspirators by following the Spirit's lead. God's collaborative love seeks all who want to work for well-being, which is God's purpose (Rom 8:28). In love, God calls us to be "fellow workers" and "co-laborers" (1 Cor 3:9; 2 Cor 6:1).

God expresses *eros* by inspiring and appreciating the beauty of creation and calling creatures to enhance or increase it.[31] God creates the world and calls it "good" (Gen 1:4, 10), and this good creating continues. Despite the evil that sometimes occurs in that world, God continues to appreciate and create beautiful things from the dust. Divine *eros* creates and enhances good in others. We should express *eros* not only by thinking on what is true, honorable, pleasing and excellent; we should express *eros* by doing these things

---

[30]See argument for the diversity of forms of love in Daniel Day Williams, *The Spirit and the Forms of Love* (New York: Harper & Row, 1968); and Nicholas Wolterstorff, *Justice in Love* (Grand Rapids: Eerdmans, 2011), chap. 9.

[31]Elaine Padilla argues this forcefully in *Divine Enjoyment: A Theology of Passion and Exuberance* (New York: Fordham University Press, 2015).

(Phil 4:8-9). The Spirit works in wild and wonderful ways to love a world created good.

God promotes overall well-being through full-orbed love.

Divine love gives and receives, empowering creatures to live, live better and live well. God takes into account the context and relationships of each creature when acting for its good. This involves God offering forms of life, possibilities, opportunities and various other ways of existing. While God always loves to the utmost, the forms of divine love vary depending on the situation, entity or creature. God is intimately involved, and divine love is pluriform.

Loving diverse others requires diverse actions from deity. God is not a steady-state force or impersonal iceberg. Instead, essential kenosis affirms that divine action varies because God is personally involved in giving and receiving relations with all creatures. The heavenly vision for well-being prompts diverse divine actions of love. While God's love is unwavering and wholehearted, the way God loves varies from moment to moment, creature to creature.[32] Only a personal God loves in such reciprocal relationships.

Divine love is tailor-made for each creature in each instant.

In all of this, God seeks *shālôm*, also known as the kingdom of God. Because God loves the world (Jn 3:16) and desires to redeem all creation (Rom 8:19-22), all creatures are recipients of divine love. God acts variously to establish the reign of love throughout all creation as the Great Lover of us all. This work of love involves promoting overall well-being in its widely diverse and multiple dimensions.[33] The love of God is shed abroad because the Spirit cares about each creature and the common good (Rom 5:5). Abundant is the love God lavishes upon creation (1 Jn 3:1)!

---

[32]I explore this set of ideas in "Testing Creaturely Love and God's Causal Role," in *The Science and Theology of Godly Love*, ed. Matthew T. Lee and Amos Yong (DeKalb: Northern Illinois University Press, 2012), pp. 94-120.

[33]I address the dominant forms of love, including defining these forms, in *Defining Love: A Philosophical, Scientific, and Theological Engagement* (Grand Rapids: Brazos, 2010), chaps. 2, 6; and throughout *The Nature of Love: A Theology* (St. Louis: Chalice, 2010). These books also delve into issues of divine love and the meaning of well-being.

ESSENTIAL KENOSIS AND EVIL

The preceding sets the stage for explaining how essential kenosis answers the primary question thwarting efforts to make sense of life: why doesn't a loving and powerful God prevent genuine evil? The essential kenosis model of providence offers one principal answer, although it includes various dimensions. Let me state this answer simply:

God *cannot* unilaterally prevent genuine evil.

For some people, to say "God cannot" is to blaspheme. In their view, God's power has no limits whatsoever. Those who embrace the omni-cause model of providence, for instance, cringe when they hear the phrase "God cannot." They will not reconsider their belief that God controls all things, even in light of God's self-giving, others-empowering love. To them, God's sovereignty requires unlimited omnipotence.

Most theologians and theistic philosophers throughout history, however, have said we cannot understand God's power well if we believe it unconditionally unlimited. God cannot bring about all conceivable states of affairs.[34] There are limits to God's power.

Most scholars say, for instance, that God cannot do what is illogical. God cannot make a round square, cannot make $2 + 2 = 5$ and cannot simultaneously make a man both married and a bachelor. God cannot make us free and not free at the same time.[35] These activities would require God to do what is logically contradictory, and as Thomas Aquinas says, "whatever involves a contradiction is not within the scope of [God's] omnipotence."[36]

Most Christian scholars say God cannot do other things. God cannot change the past, for instance. God cannot now make Martha Washington the first president of the United States because George was actually first. God cannot now prevent the Nazi holocaust because

---

[34]For a concise summary of the issues of God's limitations in relation to omnipotence, see Joshua Hoffman and Gary Rosenkrantz, "Omnipotence," in *A Companion to Philosophy of Religion*, ed. Philip L. Quinn and Charles Taliaferro (Malden, MA: Blackwell, 1999), pp. 229-35.

[35]One of the more influential defenses in response to charges that theism is logically incompatible with evil is Alvin Plantinga's work in *God, Freedom, and Evil* (Grand Rapids: Eerdmans, 1977).

[36]Thomas Aquinas, *Summa Theologica* (New York: McGraw-Hill, 1963), 1.15.3, pp. 163-64.

those days are (thankfully!) over. God cannot change the outcome of Super Bowl XLII to give the New England Patriots a perfect season.

The belief that God cannot change the past arises from the commonsense view that backward causation is impossible. Aquinas is again helpful: "Some things . . . at one time were in the nature of possibility . . . [but] now fall short of the nature of possibility." Consequently, "God is not able to do them, because they themselves cannot be done."[37] Reverse causation is impossible even for God.

Many scholars also say God cannot act contrary to God's own nature. "[God] cannot deny himself," as Paul puts it (2 Tim 2:13), or change the divine essence, as James says (Jas 1:17). Scripture mentions other things God cannot do because of God's unchanging nature. For instance, God cannot lie (Heb 6:18; Tit 1:2), cannot be tempted by evil (Jas 1:13) and cannot become exhausted (Is 40:28). The Bible explicitly says God cannot do some things.

Most scholars also say God cannot do other things.[38] For instance, God cannot decide to be 467 parts instead of triune, cannot sin, cannot self-duplicate and cannot self-annihilate. These limitations derive from God's own nature, not from some outside force or factor. "When we make such assertions as these," says Jacob Arminius, "we do not inflict an injury on the capability of God." We must beware, says Arminius, "that things unworthy of Him not be attributed to his essence, his understanding, and his will."[39] As C. S. Lewis puts it, "not even Omnipotence can do what is self-contradictory."[40] God cannot do some things because they are inherently impossible for deity.

Absolute sovereignty is absolutely unbelievable.

---

[37]Thomas Aquinas, *Summa Theologica* (New York: Cosmo, 2007), 1.25.4, p. 139. Jonathan Edwards puts it this way: "In explaining the nature of necessity, that in things which are past, their past existence is now necessary" (*Freedom of the Will* [New York: Leavitt & Allen, 1857], p. 10, §12). See also Alvin Plantinga, "On Ockham's Way Out," *Faith and Philosophy* 3 (July 1986): 235-69. I am grateful to James Goetz and Frank Macchia for alerting me to some of this material.

[38]Jacob Arminius offers a long list of things God cannot do in "Twenty-Five Public Disputations," in *The Works of James Arminius*, trans. James Nichols (1828; repr., Grand Rapids: Baker Books, 1991), 1:135.

[39]Ibid.

[40]C. S. Lewis, *Miracles: A Preliminary Study* (New York: HarperCollins, 2001), p. 90.

Essential kenosis endorses these limitations on God's power. But it adds an important limitation to the list by identifying another set of actions not possible for God. This additional set of actions is not possible because uncontrolling love is the logically preeminent attribute of God's nature.

Essential kenosis says God's self-giving, others-empowering nature of love necessarily provides freedom, agency, self-organization and lawlike regularity to creation. Because love is the preeminent and necessary attribute in God's nature, God cannot withdraw, override or fail to provide the freedom, agency, self-organizing and lawlike regularity God gives. Divine love limits divine power.

God cannot deny God's own nature, which necessarily expresses self-giving, others-empowering love.

When giving freedom, agency, self-organization and lawlike regularity to creation, the gifts God gives are, to use the Paul's language, "irrevocable" (Rom 11:29). Out of love, God necessarily gifts others in their moment-by-moment existence, and God cannot rescind these endowments. To do so, says essential kenosis, would require God to deny the divine nature of love. And according to Scripture, that's not possible.

This aspect of divine limitation makes it possible to solve the problem of evil.[41] It also allows essential kenosis to answer other perplexing questions of existence.[42] Essential kenosis explains why God cannot prevent the genuine evil that creatures cause, including

---

[41]My full solution to the problem of evil involves five aspects. I am mainly addressing the theoretical aspect in this book, which revolves around reconceiving divine power. The other aspects pertain to divine empathy, pedagogy, healing and strategic activism. I sketch out those dimensions in my essay "An Essential Kenosis Solution to the Problem of Evil," in *God and the Problem of Evil*, ed. James K. Dew Jr. and Chad Meister (Downers Grove, IL: InterVarsity Press, forthcoming).

[42]For instance, essential kenosis explains why God cannot totally control creatures to provide crystal-clear, unambiguous and therefore inerrant revelation. It explains why God cannot entirely control situations so that just and equal distribution of goods and services is provided to all. And it can be part of an overall theory of initial creation that avoids the pitfalls of *creatio ex nihilo*. For my thoughts on this latter issue, see "God Always Creates out of Creation in Love: *Creatio ex Creatione a Natura Amoris*," in *Theologies of Creation: Creatio ex Nihilo and Its New Rivals*, ed. Thomas Jay Oord (New York: Routledge, 2014), pp. 109-22.

the genuine evils we encountered when reading the true stories in chapter one. Here are some reasons why.

First, this model of providence says God necessarily gives freedom to all creatures complex enough to receive and express it. Giving freedom is part of God's steadfast love. This means God cannot withdraw, override or fail to provide the freedom a perpetrator of evil expresses. God must give freedom, even to those who use it wrongly.

John Wesley describes this aspect of essential kenosis well. When explaining providence, Wesley says, "Were human liberty taken away, men would be as incapable of virtue as stones. Therefore (with reverence be it spoken) the Almighty himself *cannot* do this thing. He cannot thus contradict himself or undo what he has done."[43] God must give and cannot take away free will.

Essential kenosis applies this to all life. But it especially helps to make sense of intense suffering and atrocities caused by free choices. By acting alone, God cannot thwart evil freely done by those exercising divinely derived freedom. Consequently, this model of providence allows us to say God is not culpable for failing to prevent the dastardly deeds free creatures sometimes do.

Because of God's immutable nature of self-giving, others-empowering love, God cannot prevent genuine evil.

For instance, as God immediately became aware of the Tsarnaev brothers' plans, God could predict they would plant bombs alongside the route of the Boston Marathon. But because God necessarily gives freedom, God could not unilaterally prevent the bombing. To do so would require removing free will from the brothers, which a loving God who necessarily gives freedom cannot do. Therefore, God could not have prevented the Boston Marathon bombing by acting alone.

Because God necessarily gave freedom to those who raped Zamuda

---

[43]John Wesley, "On Divine Providence," sermon 67, in *The Works of John Wesley*, ed. Albert C. Outler (Nashville: Abingdon, 1985), pp. 534-50, § 15. Wesley also says that God does not "take away your liberty, your power of choosing good or evil." He argues that "[God] did not *force* you, but being *assisted* by [God's] grace you, like Mary, *chose* the better part." "The General Spread of the Gospel," sermon 63, in *The Works of John Wesley*, ed. Albert C. Outler (Nashville: Abingdon, 1985), 2:281, emphasis original.

and killed her family, God could not have prevented this tragedy by acting alone. God's love is uncontrolling, and in kenotic love God provides freedom to others, including Zamuda's torturers. Consequently, God is not culpable for failing to prevent Zamuda's pain and the death of her family.

It is important to distinguish between God being influential when giving freedom and God being morally culpable for failing to prevent evil. Essential kenosis affirms God's pervasive influence but denies that God can control others. Because God providentially gives freedom to creatures complex enough to express it, God gives freedom that creatures use for good or evil (or morally neutral) activities. God acts as a necessary, though partial, cause for all creaturely activity.

Because God *must* give freedom and cannot override the gift given, we should not blame God when creatures misuse freedom. An uncontrolling God is not culpable when creatures oppose what this loving God desires. Creatures are blameworthy.

Parenting illustrates this. The parents of a rapist are causally responsible for bringing him into the world. Their sexual union made possible his existence. Assuming these parents did an adequate job of teaching their son right and wrong, we would not consider them morally culpable when their son freely chooses rape. We blame the rapist and regard him as culpable, not his parents, although the parents are necessary causes for his existence.

Analogously, God creates and gives freedom to do good or ill in each moment. But God's self-giving, others-empowering love means God cannot withdraw, fail to provide or override the freedom God necessarily gives. Consequently, we are wrong to blame God when genuine evil occurs. God is not culpable.

God's love necessarily gives freedom.

Second, essential kenosis explains why God doesn't prevent evil that simple creatures with agency cause or even simpler entities with mere self-organizing capacities cause. God necessarily gives the gifts of agency and self-organization to entities capable of them because doing so is part of divine love. God's others-empowering love extends to the least and simplest of these.

God cannot withdraw, override or fail to provide agency and self-organization to any simple organism or entity that causes genuine evil. The kenotic love of God necessarily provides agency and self-organization. God's moment-by-moment gifts are irrevocable. Consequently, God is not culpable for failing to prevent the evil that basic entities, organisms and simple creatures may cause.

For instance, cellular or genetic mutations and the malfunction of simple structures in baby Eliana Tova apparently caused her debilitating condition. Because God necessarily gives agency and self-organization to the entities and organs of our bodies, God could not unilaterally prevent Eliana Tova's ailments. To prevent them would require God to withdraw, override or fail to provide agency and self-organization to her body's basic organisms, entities and structures. A loving God who necessarily self-gives and others-empowers cannot do this.

Realizing that God cannot unilaterally prevent suffering caused by simple entities helps us make sense of suffering caused by natural malfunctions or disasters. This means, for instance, we should not accuse God of causing or allowing birth defects, cancer, infections, disease, hurricanes, earthquakes, tsunamis, or other illnesses and catastrophes. The degradation brought by such calamities does not represent God's will. Instead, we can blame simple structures, various natural processes of the world, small organisms or creation gone awry. Because God's self-giving, others-empowering love makes agency and self-organization possible, God is not culpable for the evil that less-complex entities cause.

In the previous chapter, we looked briefly at the free-process response to evil. Although I criticized one form of the free-process response, essential kenosis affirms an alternative form. Because essential kenosis says God gives agency and self-organization to creation and this giving derives from God's loving essence, it overcomes problems that arise in versions of the free-process defense that imply God's gifting is entirely voluntary. According to essential kenosis, the dynamic, sometimes chaotic and partially random universe with its various systems and processes emerges from God's necessarily creative and kenotic love. The free process of life is an essential expression of divine grace.

God's love necessarily gives agency and self-organization.

Third, essential kenosis helps us make sense of the random mutations, chance events and accidents that cause evil. While some randomness is beneficial, other randomness is devastating and fails to make the world as good as it could have been. We should not blame anyone or anything for randomly generated misfortunes. They are indiscriminate, unplanned and unforeseen. But essential kenosis explains why God doesn't prevent them.

Preventing evils caused by random events would require God to foreknow and control these events occurring at whatever level of complexity we find them. Controlling randomness would require God to withhold the simple power to become and exist with stable regularity. To control randomness, God would need to foreknow random events were about to occur and then interrupt the lawlike regularities of existence that make them possible. But to do so, says essential kenosis, God would have to "deny himself," to use biblical language. God cannot do this, because the gifts of lawlike regularities are irrevocable, and God does not know which possibilities for randomness will become actual.

God's universal and steadfast self-giving love has the effect of establishing lawlike regularities throughout creation as God lovingly makes existence possible. The spontaneity present at all levels of existence derives from God's gift of existence. Kenotic love necessarily imparts lawlike regularities as God creates and interacts with creatures. The lawlike regularities of the universe derive from God's loving expressions, which themselves are grounded in God's nature of uncontrolling love.

In chapter two, we explored Euthyphro's dilemma in light of lawlike regularities or what many call the "laws of nature." We noted problems with saying that God created these laws. We also noted problems with saying that natural laws are external to God. I briefly offered a third way.

Essential kenosis says that lawlike regularities in creation derive from God's persistent and loving activity. These regularities are neither entirely voluntary nor do they transcend God from the outside. Rather, God's loving activities reflect the eternally unchanging divine essence of love. Consequently, God's loving nature is the ultimate source of creation's lawlike regularities, and the God who loves necessarily cannot interrupt the love expressed to all. Rather than being an external watchmaker, God's ongoing, ever-influential love conditions all creation as the One in whom all things live and move and have their being (Acts 17:28).

Lawlike regularities affect all creation. But they especially regulate the simplest entities and aggregate systems of existence. Simple entities have far less flexibility. Aggregates—like planets, pebbles and paper—are not self-organizing agents. Interrupting lawlike regularities would require God to fail to provide existence to portions of creation. But God cannot do this because of steadfast love.

Regularities of existence—so-called natural laws—emerged in evolutionary history as new kinds of organisms emerged in response to God's love. The consistency of divine love creates regularities as creatures respond, given the nature of their existence and the degree and range of agency they possess. God's eternal nature of love both sets limits and offers possibilities to each creature and context, depending on their complexity. In this, God's love orders the world. And because God's nature is love, God cannot override the order that emerges.

On this issue, I agree with John Polkinghorne when he says that "the regularities of the mechanical aspects of nature are to be understood theologically as signs of the faithfulness of the Creator."[44] Essential kenosis adds, however, that the Creator's faithfulness derives from that Creator's loving nature. In fact, it is in the context of the apostle Paul emphasizing divine faithfulness that we find the biblical

---

[44]In Thomas Jay Oord, ed., *The Polkinghorne Reader: Science, Faith and the Search for Meaning* (Philadelphia: Templeton Press, 2010), pp. 124-25.

claim about God's inherent limitations: "[God] remains faithful," because God "cannot deny himself" (2 Tim 2:13).

Polkinghorne also says that the regularities described by physics "are pale reflections of [God's] faithfulness towards his creation. . . . He will not interfere in their operation in a fitful or capricious way, for that would be for the Eternally Reliable to turn himself into an occasional conjurer."[45] I agree with Polkinghorne here as well. But I would say that God *cannot* interfere with these lawlike regularities, not just that God *will not* interfere.

The processes and regularities in life derive from God's nature of essentially kenotic love.

For instance, God could not have unilaterally prevented the rock that killed the Canadian woman whose story we encountered earlier. Because God necessarily gives existence to all creation—including rocks—and because existence is characterized by lawlike regularities, God alone could not have averted this tragedy. To prevent unilaterally the rock killing the woman, God would need to forgo loving interaction with some portion of creation. Contradicting God's nature and thereby failing to love creation—even failing to love rocks by not endowing them with existence—is something a necessarily loving God cannot do.[46]

Additionally, God could not have foreknown this specific accident. Although God would have known it was possible, various random factors and the free will of both drivers mitigate against God's foreknowing that an errant rock would cause this tragic death. God's ongoing presence in all moments of time is *time-full*. Essential kenosis takes the time-full reality of existence and God's time-full existing as crucial for understanding why God cannot foreknow or prevent genuine evils such as this. Divine love necessarily compels God to act in ways that generate lawlike regularity.

---

[45]John C. Polkinghorne, *Science and Providence: God's Interaction with the World* (West Conshohocken, PA: Templeton Press, 2005), p. 30.

[46]For one of the better explorations of God's love and power in relation to all of creation, especially nonhumans, see Christopher Southgate, *The Groaning of Creation: God, Evolution, and the Problem of Evil* (Louisville, KY: Westminster John Knox, 2008).

GOD IS AN OMNIPRESENT SPIRIT

While we should say God cannot prevent genuine evil because doing so requires nullifying the divine nature of uncontrolling love, another important set of issues remains. These issues are part of the fundamental claim of essential kenosis that God acting alone cannot prevent genuine evil. Let me begin to address these issues with this question: if we creatures sometimes thwart an act of evil, why can't a loving God?

For instance, if we can step between two combatants intent on throwing punches and thereby prevent evil, why can't God do the same? If parents can sometimes stop one child from injuring another, why can't God? If we can build a dam and thereby stop a flash flood from wreaking unnecessary havoc, why can't God prevent evil this way? And if creatures can marshal others to use tools or instruments to prevent genuine evil, why doesn't God do the same? We don't need foreknowledge to prevent such evils. Why can't a God without exhaustive foreknowledge do what we sometimes can?

To answer these questions, we need to look at a fourth way that essential kenosis says God is limited. This answer affirms the traditional Christian view that God is a loving, omnipresent spirit. Those who affirm this traditional view, however, often fail to think through its implications. Believing God is an omnipresent spirit has consequences for answering well why God cannot prevent evil in ways we sometimes might.

Being an omnipresent spirit affords God unique abilities and limitations.

To say God is a loving spirit is to say, in part, that God does not have a divine body. God's essential "being" or "constitution" is spiritual. The classic language is "incorporeal." Jesus says, "God is spirit" (Jn 4:24), and Scripture is replete with similar statements about God's being. Essential kenosis affirms the common Christian view that God is essentially an incorporeal and omnipresent agent.

Because God is spirit, we cannot perceive God directly with our five senses. We cannot literally taste, touch, see, hear or smell God.

Christians have proposed various theories, however, to explain how God's spiritual presence exerts causal force upon creation.[47] The details of these theories deserve a fuller explanation than possible here.[48] But I am attracted to theories that conceive of God as a spirit whom we *directly* perceive through nonsensory means.[49] I also believe we can infer God's actions indirectly by perceiving what God has made, including the created world in general, other creatures and ourselves.

The second divine attribute typically neglected in discussions of evil is God's universality. God is present to all creation and to each entity because God is omnipresent. Rather than being localized in a particular place in the way creatures are localized, the Creator is present to all.

To say that God is an omnipresent spirit does not need to mean that God has no physicality whatsoever. I believe there is always a physical dimension to the divine presence although we cannot perceive it with our five senses. Describing God's omnipresence and physicality in God has always been difficult for Christians because God is not locally situated and not perceptible by our five senses.

Attempts to describe the Creator using creaturely comparisons are partly helpful. There is a venerable tradition within Christian theology, for instance, that says God is like a mind. The Hebrew word *rûaḥ* sometimes refers to God and can be translated "mind." This analogy is helpful because although we cannot perceive minds with our five senses, we believe they have causal influence. Minds also have a subjective unity, which allows them to make decisions and act purposively. God's spiritual being is like a mind in these ways.

Saying God is like a mind, however, has several weaknesses. For instance, creaturely minds are not omnipresent whereas God is omni-

---

[47]See Thomas Jay Oord, "The Divine Spirit as Causal and Personal," *Zygon* 48, no. 2 (2013): 466-77.

[48]I propose one solution in Thomas Jay Oord, "A Postmodern Wesleyan Philosophy and David Ray Griffin's Postmodern Vision," *Wesleyan Theological Journal* 35, no. 1 (2000): 216-44.

[49]I have been influenced toward this view by theologians like John B. Cobb Jr., who speaks of "nonsensory perception of God" and "nonsensuous experience of the divine presence in our lives" (*Grace and Responsibility: A Wesleyan Theology for Today* [Nashville: Abingdon, 1995], p. 75). But other theologians propose theories to account for divine causation by the Spirit.

present. Creaturely minds, say most people, have a beginning. By contrast, God is everlasting. And depending on what mind-body theory one affirms, we may wonder if the mind has a physical dimension, although I think it does.

I particularly like the analogy that says God's spiritual being is like air or wind. This description appears many places in Scripture. In fact, the New Testament word for "spirit"—*pneuma*—is also the word for "wind" or "air." And the biblical word *rûaḥ* can be translated "breath." Wind has a physical dimension although we cannot see it. Wind also exerts causal force. We see the effects of the wind, sometimes by observing tiny particles as they are whisked about.

Just as we cannot see wind, we also cannot see God. Despite not being observed, we attribute at least some effects in our world to divine causation (Jn 3:8). Many of us believe ourselves influenced by this unseen Friend, for instance. And some biblical passages suggest that air—breath—is God's creating presence. As Job puts it,

> The spirit of God has made me,
>   and the breath of the Almighty gives me life. (Job 33:4)

The wind analogy also has limitations, of course. Wind is not omnipresent, which means it can flow, move from one place to another and be absent in some things. Air also has no will so it cannot make decisions or act purposively. Wind possesses no subjective experience.

All analogies between God's spiritual being and something creaturely fail in some way. My main point in exploring God's being as a loving omnipresent spirit, however, is to help us think about why God cannot by using a divine body prevent genuine evil.

As an omnipresent spirit with no localized divine body, God cannot exert divine bodily influence as a localized corpus. This means God cannot use a divine body to step between two parties engaged in a fight, for instance. God doesn't have a wholly divine hand to scoop a rock out of the air, cover a bomb before it explodes or block a bullet before it projects from a rifle. While we may sometimes be blameworthy for failing to use our bodies to prevent genuine evils, the God without a localized divine body is not culpable.

God cannot prevent evil with a localized divine body because God is an omnipresent spirit.[50]

God can, however, marshal through persuasion those with localized bodies. They can exert creaturely bodily impact in various ways. God can call a teacher to stand between a bully and the bully's victim. God can call the firefighter to reach through a burning window to grab a terrified toddler. God can even call lesser organisms and entities to use their bodily aspects, in whatever limited way, to promote good or prevent evil. In all this, says essential kenosis, God acts without having a localized divine body and without totally controlling others.

Of course, creatures and organisms may not respond well to God's call. God may want to prevent some evil and call a creature to use its body for that purpose. But creatures may fail to respond well, disobey and sin. Humans above all other creatures know well the reality of using their bodies for evil ends. Most believers call this sin.

The omnipresent Spirit is not culpable for the evil that results when creatures fail to love. God may want groups to intercede, but these groups may ignore God's commands. When we fail to respond well to God's calls, we are to blame. The loving and omnipresent Spirit without a localized divine body is not guilty.

Thankfully, creatures sometimes respond well to God's call. They "listen" to God's call to prevent some impending tragedy or stop an ongoing conflict. When creatures respond well, we might even say that God prevented that evil. This should not mean that God *alone* prevented it. Creatures cooperated, playing necessary roles by using their bodies to fulfill God's good purposes. Our saying God did it should be interpreted as expressing the belief that God played the primary causal role in the event or is the ultimate source of this positive activity.

---

[50]Depending on one's view of the incarnation, of course, one may think Jesus is an exception to the view that God does not have a localized divine body. That discussion requires another book. But I agree with many theologians who distinguish between God's essential and eternal being and God's temporary incarnation as a localized human, Jesus of Nazareth.

Creaturely cooperation inspired the statement "we are God's hands and feet." It also inspired the saying "the world is God's body" because we can act as members of the body of Christ (1 Cor 12:15-19). These statements only make sense, however, if we do not take them literally. We do not literally become divine appendages; the world is not literally a divine corpus. God remains divine, and we are God's creations.

When creatures respond well to God's leading, the overall result is that God's will is done "on earth as it is in heaven." When God's loving will is done, we might credit, praise and thank the Creator. "Thanks be to God!" This oft-spoken phrase is appropriate. But we can also rightly acknowledge creaturely cooperation required for establishing what is good. Creatures can be God's coworkers, ambassadors and viceroys.[51] God gets the lion's share of the credit for good, but it is also appropriate to thank creatures who cooperate with their Creator. A thankful pat on a neighbor's back does not rob God of glory.

A COERCIVE GOD OF LOVE IS FICTIONAL

In the previous chapter, I said the God whose preeminent attribute is uncontrolling love could not create controllable creatures. If God's love cooperates rather than controls, never forces its way on the be-loved and risks rather than imposes guarantees, love as the logically preeminent attribute prevents God from entirely determining others. An essentially loving God who *could* totally control others does not exist because God's love cannot control. To illustrate my argument, I said the idea that a loving God could control others is as fictional as the idea that mermaids could run marathons.

Essential kenosis explains why the God whose logically preem-inent attribute is love cannot control others. If God were to coerce others by withdrawing, overriding or failing to provide freedom, agency or self-organization, God would need to renounce the divine nature of self-giving, others-empowering love. If God were to

---

[51]For the biblical justification of this view, see 1 Cor 3:9; 2 Cor 5:20; 6:1; Eph 6:11-12; 2 Tim 2:3-4, 12; Rev 5:10; 20:6; 22:5.

prevent random events by interrupting the lawlike regularities of existence, God would need to renounce the divine nature of uncontrolling love. But God cannot contradict God's own nature, so divine coercion is impossible.

In light of essential kenosis, we might rephrase the mermaid illustration: the idea that God, whose logically preeminent attribute is self-giving, others-empowering love, could override, fail to provide or withdraw freedom, agency or self-organization or could interrupt the lawlike regularities of existence is as fictional as the idea that mermaids could run marathons. Mermaids cannot run marathons, and a kenotic God cannot coerce.

A controlling God of love is fictional.

A number of people take it as obvious that, as John Sanders put it, "love does not force its own way on the beloved."[52] They agree with Sanders when he says God's love "does not force [creatures] to comply."[53] In these statements, Sanders expresses the common view that love never coerces, in the sense of controlling others entirely or forcing its own way. To people with this view, it is a fundamental given—an a priori truth—that love does not withdraw, override or fail to support the freedom, agency or self-organization of others. Love does not control.

Let's call this common view "love by definition is noncoercive." This view arises from the deep intuition that love never controls others entirely. In relation to the God whose nature is love, this view entails that God *cannot* control others entirely. If love is inherently uncontrolling and God loves necessarily, God is incapable of coercion.

The claim that God cannot coerce, however, is especially vulnerable to misunderstanding. *Coerce* has multiple meanings. In everyday language, we often use the word in its psychological sense. In this sense, to coerce is to place intense psychological pressure on a creature or group to motivate it to act in a particular manner. To those being

[52]John Sanders, *The God Who Risks: A Theology of Providence*, rev. ed. (Downers Grove, IL: Inter-Varsity Press, 2007), p. 193.
[53]Ibid., p. 174.

pressured, this may feel like bullying, a serious threat or extreme force.

In the psychological sense of *coerce*, the person being coerced retains free will. Threats and emotional pressures do not deprive their subjects of freedom. The person may yield to the pressure and thereby avoid negative consequences or gain positive ones. The person may freely choose not to yield and thereby reap negative consequences. Coercion, in the psychological sense, doesn't entail total control of others because those involved retain some measure of free will.

Others equate the word *coerce* with violence. Those wanting to reduce violence in the world (which includes most people) may say they want to reduce coercion. Actions that these people label as coercive include violent acts of war, domestic altercations, interpersonal conflict and acts of terror. For them, to act violently is to coerce. In such cases, violence involves bodies or other localized physical objects wreaking destruction.

A growing literature explores whether it makes sense to say God is violent or ever calls us to use our bodies or other objects violently.[54] Some in this discussion also use *coerce* to mean "act violently." Often at the center of this debate is how to interpret particular scriptural passages suggesting divine violence and the apparently violent actions of Jesus. Sometimes the question is whether we ought to use violent force when acting in relation to others.

A third way some use *coerce* pertains to the use of bodies to impact other bodies. The parent who picks up a screaming two-year-old and puts the child in a crib may be said to coerce or control the two-year-old. The child may not want to be in the crib. But the stronger and bigger body prevails. We might call this the bodily impact sense of *coerce*, because it involves bodies exerting force upon other bodies and things in the world.

I am not using *coerce* in the psychological, violence or bodily impact senses. I am using it in the metaphysical sense. In the meta-

---

[54]The number of important books on this subject is large. One of the better contributions is Eric A. Seibert, *The Violence of Scripture: Overcoming the Old Testament's Troubling Legacy* (Philadelphia: Fortress, 2012).

physical sense, to coerce is to control entirely. This involves unilateral determination, in which the one coerced loses all capacity for causation, self-organization, agency or free will. To coerce in this metaphysical sense is to act as a sufficient cause, thereby wholly controlling the other or the situation. To coerce is to control.

Love does not coerce in the metaphysical sense because it never controls others. Applied to God, the inability to coerce in the metaphysical sense means God cannot control others or situations. God's love is uncontrolling.[55] Essential kenosis says God cannot coerce, in the sense of acting as a sufficient cause or unilaterally determining others. In addition, God is not a bully and God does not act violently. Because God does not have a localized physical body with which to exert direct bodily impact, God does not use divine bodily impact.[56]

Divine love is uncontrolling, which means God cannot coerce.

Some people, however, are not convinced that love *never* forces its way or controls others. They admit love usually invites cooperation or contribution. They may think love typically does not overrule or overpower. But they think love might at times require coercion in the metaphysical sense. Therefore, they think God sometimes coerces.

These people can imagine instances in which, if it were possible, a loving person ought to control another person or situation to guarantee a positive outcome or avoid an evil one. For them, love is *not* by definition uncontrolling. When it comes to God, these people believe divine love sometimes involves coercion, in the metaphysical sense of completely controlling others or situations.

To those unconvinced that love, a priori, never forces its way, a robust a posteriori argument exists for why God's love never coerces. In other words, there is compelling evidence for why we should think

---

[55]Catherine Keller endorses this view in *God and Power: Counter-Apocalyptic Journeys* (Minneapolis: Fortress, 2005).

[56]Essential kenosis is neutral on whether God ever calls creatures to act violently. There are good reasons, however, to interpret biblical texts, broadly speaking, as advocating nonviolence. On this, see C. S. Cowles, *Show Them No Mercy: Four Views on God and Canaanite Genocide* (Grand Rapids: Zondervan, 2003); Gregory Love, *Love, Violence, and the Cross: How the Nonviolent God Saves Us Through the Cross of Christ* (Eugene, OR: Cascade, 2010); and Seibert, *Violence of Scripture*.

God cannot control others entirely. Using abductive argument, it makes sense to say God cannot coerce based on this evidence. In short, the evidence suggests God cannot coerce.

Few explore this view adequately. Perhaps those who know it are reticent to rethink their assumptions about God's power. Many may not feel comfortable thinking God has limitations, even if those limitations originate from God's nature. Some may believe reconceiving God's power opposes traditional theological views. Some may worry about political or social implications should they rethink their view of God's power.

The idea that the evidence suggests God cannot coerce begins with a common view of divine love. It says the God who loves perfectly would want to prevent all genuine evil. God's care would entail thwarting horrors and tragedies if doing so were possible. Many believers affirm this way of thinking about divine benevolence. To many, in fact, "perfect love" (1 Jn 4:18) seems to require it. God would want to prevent every event that, all things considered, makes the world worse than it might have been had another possible event occurred instead.

The argument from evidence affirms that God seeks to establish the kingdom of love, to use biblical language. Among other things, this means promoting overall well-being, flourishing or *shālôm*. Our loving Heavenly Parent, like loving earthly parents, wants to promote good and prevent genuine evil because God abhors evil and desires the common good. God cares for all.

Jesus Christ is primary evidence for most Christians that God seeks well-being through noncoercive means. Although Jesus can be angry or even exert strong force on occasion (e.g., clearing the temple), Jesus never acted coercively in the sense of controlling others entirely. The a posteriori evidence of the life of Jesus, whom Christians believe reveals God better than any other person, suggests that God does not coerce.

The argument from evidence also affirms that genuinely evil events occur. Evil is real. Our fundamental intuitions tell us that some events make the world worse overall, and at least some such events could have been avoided. Genuine evils need not have occurred. We encountered examples of genuine evils in chapter one. But we could point to countless others.

We not only find evidence for genuine evil in what we encounter; we also act as if genuine evil occurs. As we saw in earlier discussions, this is one of life's experiential nonnegotiables. Our natural reactions demonstrate that we know evil happens, even if some people deny it in what they say or write. The way we live our lives reflects our fundamental intuition that genuinely evil events occur.

Upon affirming that a loving God wants to prevent genuine evil though genuine evils occur, the argument from evidence concludes that a loving God must not prevent genuine evil because God cannot control others or situations. In other words, the evidence indicates or suggests that God cannot coerce. To put it differently: because genuine evils occur and God always loves, we are right to infer that God must not be able to coerce to prevent genuine evil. This abductive argument is straightforward. But preconceived notions of God's power often prevent many from taking it seriously.

The argument from evidence, of course, is susceptible to counterarguments. Reasoning from evidence is never airtight, and abduction involves interpretation. In previous chapters, we explored some of those counterarguments, but none proved convincing.[57]

There is one counterargument to the claim that the evidence of life suggests God cannot coerce, however, that I find more robust. Rather than appealing to mystery, this argument says we *do* have evidence that God sometimes coerces, in the metaphysical sense of the word. Sometimes God *does* control others or situations. In other words, this argument also appeals to evidence.

---

[57]The main counterargument given for why a God of love would not prevent genuine evil is not really an argument at all. It's an appeal to mystery. Implicitly or explicitly, many say we cannot know whether the events we consider genuinely evil actually are so. Many people say God has some immediate reason or future plan that requires suffering. In some mysterious way, God preventing suffering would be worse than allowing it. Mystery appeals cannot provide satisfying answers to our most fundamental questions, especially those related to God's providence in light of good and evil, randomness and regularity. The mystery card spoils the deck.

Those who say God sometimes controls entirely point to unusual, astonishing or baffling events that are good. They claim God entirely controlled the situation or individuals required to make these events possible. In fact, this is how some people define a miracle: a supernatural act in which God totally controls an individual or situation or interrupts natural causes to bring about an unusual but positive outcome.

Those who make this argument often point to miracles in the Bible or their own lives. Such miracles may involve healings, serendipities, exorcisms, transformed lives or even resurrections. They claim these unusual events provide evidence that God sometimes controls others or situations. In their view, God would have to coerce for these events to occur.

I think this argument is worth exploring. After all, I also believe in miracles. I think an adequate model of divine providence needs to account for miracles—miracles in Scripture and those we encounter today—if it can make sense of life. Miracles matter.

I believe we can affirm miracles we consider authentic, however, without also claiming God controls others entirely or interrupts natural laws. To explain my view, I explore miracles in the final chapter. My exploration accounts for miracles in light of essential kenosis. I believe that an all-loving and almighty God acts providentially and sometimes miraculously through self-giving, others-empowering love. But this never involves control because God's love is uncontrolling.

8

Miracles and God's Providence

*I*n the previous chapter, I described the essential kenosis model of providence. This model says self-giving love is logically preeminent in God's nature. God's moment-by-moment gifts of love necessarily empower creatures in various ways. God cannot withdraw, override or fail to provide the freedom, agency or self-organization God lovingly gives. Essential kenosis says these gifts are irrevocable (Rom 11:29) because God "cannot deny himself" (2 Tim 2:13).

Lawlike regularities arise as the natural effects of the love an omnipresent God expresses throughout all creation. Because God's nature is self-giving love, God cannot interrupt the lawlike regularities derived from divine giving. The prophet Jeremiah, for instance, identifies the natural regularities of day and night and the consistency in the solar system as derived from God's steadfast love (Jer 33:25). The regularity of the seasons and the provisions God offers creatures are additional examples of God's lovingly faithful covenant (Gen 8:22; Ps 104).[1] God's steadfast love faithfully supports and necessarily maintains a measure of order in the universe while also empowering the freedom, self-organization and spontaneity necessary for novelty.

Chance and random events in the universe are possible because God provides free will, agency, self-organization, spontaneity and the generative power to be. Complex and simple creatures—even the

---

[1] David Fergusson expresses this well in "The Theology of Providence," *Theology Today* 67 (2010): 274.

smallest units of existence—use these God-given capabilities in various ways. Sometimes the spontaneity God gives creation results in chaotic evil. But God can sometimes use the randomness generated by spontaneity and freedom to bring about good. In fact, God uses random and chance events when creating.[2] With relentless love, God continually creates (*creatio continua*) through being-giving activity that Scripture writers verbally express as "let there be" (Gen 1).

Essential kenosis explains why a loving God does not prevent genuine evil. Out of love, God necessarily provides creation and all creatures what they need to exist and act. Although intrinsically good because divinely created, creatures sometimes act in ways that cause evil. God cannot prevent the horrors and holocausts caused by free will, agency, self-organizing entities and random events because God's self-giving love necessarily creates, sustains, inspires and operates in the universe. The time-full and living God of love cannot foreknow and thereby prevent the evil that free creatures do or random events cause. As an omnipresent and incorporeal spirit, God does not have a localized divine body with which to thwart evils through divine bodily impact. God calls upon creatures to use their bodies to cooperate with God to do good and prevent evil.

In all God's activities, love presides over and preconditions God's sovereignty.

THE ALMIGHTY GOD

But is the God described by essential kenosis weak?

Upon discovering that God cannot control others or situations, some may think this model of providence depicts an inept deity. I will show that this is not true. Some may think the God who always engages creatures through self-giving, others-empowering love must be ineffective. Wrong again. Some may think the God unable to coerce is not the One described in Scripture as creator, sustainer and source of miracles. Incorrect! Although essential kenosis insists that God

---

[2]See Paul Ewart, "The Necessity of Chance: Randomness, Purpose and the Sovereignty of God," *Science and Christian Belief* 21 (2009): 111-31.

cannot coerce, it accounts for God as the almighty creator, sustainer and source of miracles who always acts through uncontrolling love.

The God described by essential kenosis is consistent with the God described in the broad biblical witness. Unfortunately, some believers think they must choose between believing that God sovereignly controls all or that God is a feeble bystander in the affairs of life. Like the broad biblical witness, essential kenosis rejects both views. It does so by insisting that divine sovereignty always expresses the power of self-giving and uncontrolling love.

There is no consensus among believers on how best to understand God's power. The Christian tradition's greatest thinkers describe divine sovereignty in different ways. Biblical translators typically use *almighty* when rendering in English those Greek and Hebrew words describing God's power. But Scripture is not clear on what it means for God to be almighty. Many philosophically oriented theologians use *omnipotent* to portray God's power although the word is not found in the Bible. It also carries connotations some believe at odds with creaturely free will, resistance and randomness.

I follow the word choice of most biblical translators and use *almighty* when describing divine power. As I see it, God is almighty in at least three senses. God is . . .

1. mightier *than all* others.

2. the only One who exerts might *upon all* that exists.

3. the ultimate source of might *for all* others.

God is mightier than all others. The first sense of *almighty* simply says God has neither superiors nor equals in might. God is without peer in power. Although creatures can do some things God cannot do (e.g., sin, exist only in one location, forget an appointment), God is overall the mightiest being that exists. Writers of Scripture often say this, especially in comparison to idols or foreign gods. God has no match, and no other being is greater (Ps 40:5).

God exerts might upon all. The second sense of *almighty* says God exerts might upon all creatures and all creation. Although in an interrelated universe each creature exerts power upon some others, only God exerts might upon all. God is the only one with influence and causal force upon all that exists. God's active power creates and sustains the universe and its inhabitants, and nothing could exist without God's gift of existence. To put it philosophically, God is a necessary cause in the being and becoming of all actual entities. Loving grace creatively makes possible the existence of all creatures, and divine power upholds all creation (Heb 1:3).

God is the ultimate source of might for all others. The third sense in which God is almighty says God is the ultimate source of might. God supplies power for all others, thereby empowering them to be or act. Without divine enabling, no entity, creature or universe could exert causal influence. God acts first in each moment to provide the fundamental energy creatures need to act or be. Some theologians, especially those in the Wesleyan tradition, call this "prevenient grace" because God's loving power precedes and makes possible creaturely responses.[3] In this grace-shaped enabling, creaturely abilities have their wellspring in God (2 Cor 3:5).

God's almighty power in these three senses does not involve coercion. God can be the mightiest without controlling others. God can exert power upon all creation without unilaterally determining any. God can be the ultimate source of power—empowering and enabling others—without dominating any creature or situation entirely. *Almighty* is not coercive.

God does not arbitrarily give power. Instead, God's empowering gifts derive from the divine nature of love. This means God necessarily rather than arbitrarily shares power with creation. Kenotic love palliates sovereign power. As the Almighty One, God always exerts might through the self-giving kenosis of uncontrolling love.

Divine love preconditions God's almightiness.

---

[3]See Kenneth J. Collins, *The Theology of John Wesley: Holy Love and the Shape of Grace* (Nashville: Abingdon, 2007); Randy L. Maddox, *Responsible Grace: John Wesley's Practical Theology* (Nashville: Kingswood, 1994); and Thomas Jay Oord and Michael Lodahl, *Relational Holiness: Responding to the Call of Love* (Kansas City, MO: Beacon Hill, 2005).

In addition, we rightly describe God as almighty despite God not having a wholly divine body, not doing the illogical or impossible, and not being able to deny the divine nature. The almighty God I am describing is, as Anselm might say, the greatest conceivable being.[4] Given the divine nature, divine incorporeality and the logically possible, God's power is maximal. In sum, the God of essential kenosis is almighty.

But can the almighty God described by essential kenosis act miraculously? If God's loving nature gives freedom, agency, self-organization and lawlike regularities and if God cannot coerce, do miracles ever occur? How does essential kenosis account for miracles?

Do Miracles Occur?

At the conclusion of the previous chapter, I noted that some people think miracles require that God coerce. Divine coercion is the metaphysical view that God entirely controls creatures, entities and situations by failing to give, taking away or overriding freedom or agency. Divine coercion would also occur if God suspended the lawlike regularities in nature unilaterally. If God can control creatures or interrupt creation's consistencies by absolute fiat, God can coerce. Because I believe miracles occur through God's uncontrolling love, I will explain how miracles occur when God acts miraculously through kenosis.

There are good reasons why many people—including some Christians—reject miracles altogether. After all, some purported miracles turn out to be hoaxes, hysteria or misunderstandings. Other miracles are not objectively verified by qualified experts (e.g., physicians) but seem merely to represent the wishful hopes of devotees.[5] Suggestibility can incline some to believe themselves or others to be healed, for instance, especially when captivating authorities do the suggesting.

Other people reject the idea that miracles occur because most

---

[4]Anselm, "Proslogion," in *St. Anselm: Basic Writings*, ed. and trans. Sidney D. Deane (Chicago: Open Court, 1962).

[5]Candy Gunther Brown explores this issue, documenting healing in *Testing Prayer: Science and Healing* (Cambridge, MA: Harvard University Press, 2012), chap. 3.

people wanting miracles do not experience them.[6] The vast majority of prayers for miracles go unanswered, in the sense that those praying do not get the results they request. Those who do experience a miracle—healing, for instance—are often healed only temporarily. This prompts skeptics to wonder if the miracle was genuine.[7] The disproportionate number of unanswered prayers leads some to think the few miracles that do occur are actually fortunate coincidences.

These are all understandable reasons that some reject the idea that authentic miracles occur. But the most powerful reason to reject miracles relates to the problem of evil.[8] If God can enact miracles to do good or prevent evil, why doesn't God enact miracles more often? Why doesn't a miracle-working God heal, resurrect, control nature and act in other ways to prevent evil and make our lives better?

If God sometimes voluntarily acts miraculously but not at other times, the problem of selective miracles arises. Christine Overall states the problem well: "In choosing to favor just a few individuals, God shows himself to be arbitrary in his beneficence to some and cruel and unfair in his neglect of others."[9] Consequently, it's natural to wonder why an alleged consistently loving God enacts miracles so inconsistently.

In what follows, I will not argue that all claims for miracles are legitimate. But I do think Christians can and should believe God sometimes acts miraculously. I agree with those scholars who say we must take miracles seriously in light of the sheer number of miracle reports today and throughout history.[10] The miracle claims of vast

[6]Even some of the greatest saints mentioned in the Bible were not healed although they requested healing (see Gal 4:13-14; Phil 2:27; 1 Tim 5:23).

[7]See Brown, *Testing Prayer*, chap. 6.

[8]David and Randall Basinger explore this in *Philosophy and Miracle: The Contemporary Debate* (Lewiston, NY: Mellen, 1986).

[9]Christine Overall, "Miracles and Larmer," *Dialogue* 42 (2003): 131.

[10]This is a main argument in Craig S. Keener's work *Miracles: The Credibility of the New Testament Accounts*, 2 vols. (Grand Rapids: Baker Books, 2011). See also Paul Alexander, *Signs and Wonders: Why Pentecostalism Is the World's Fastest Growing Faith* (San Francisco: Jossey-Bass, 2009); Candy Gunther Brown, *Global Pentecostal and Charismatic Healing* (Oxford: Oxford University Press, 2011); and Harold Koenig, *The Healing Power of Faith: How Belief and Prayer Can Help You Triumph over Disease* (New York: Touchstone, 1999).

numbers of people are not easily dismissed, even if we think some are misguided, involve wishful thinking, are hoaxes or are not genuine for some other reason.

If we want to make sense of reality, we must account for miracles.

Just as theologians do not agree with each other on how best to define God's power, they also do not agree on how best to define miracles.[11] Defining miracles is especially difficult given that people in various religious traditions report having witnessed them.[12] Theologians offering definitions embrace particular views of how God acts in relation to freewill creatures, creaturely agents, basic entities and the lawlike regularities of creation. A theologian's view of God's providence understandably influences his or her understanding of miracles.

The way some theologians define miracles makes it difficult to think any event involves special action on God's part. In these definitions, *miracle* is an entirely subjective assessment. Friedrich Schleiermacher, for instance, says a miracle "is simply the religious name of an event" that "refers purely to the mental condition of the observer."[13] On this view, a miracle has nothing to do with an unusual objective occurrence or unique divine action.

Claiming that *all* miracles are *entirely* explained by the mental conditions or presuppositions of the observers requires us to dismiss countless miracles that make an objective difference in the world. Sometimes blind people really can begin to see, for instance. Sometimes those pronounced dead are revived. Sometimes cancer does disappear. Sometimes the lame begin to walk. Consequently, those who have witnessed miracles and those who believe the miracle reports in the Bible need an adequate account for the objective nature of the miraculous.

---

[11]For one of the better concise attempts to define miracles, see David Basinger, "What Is a Miracle?," in *The Cambridge Companion to Miracles*, ed. Graham H. Twelftree (Cambridge: Cambridge University Press, 2011), pp. 19-35.

[12]For discussions of miracles in Christianity, Judaism and other religious traditions, see *Cambridge Companion to Miracles*.

[13]Friedrich Schleiermacher, *On Religion: Speeches to Its Cultured Despisers* (New York: Harper & Brothers, 1958), p. 88.

Since the rise of modern science, some theologians have defined miracles as violations of the laws of nature. Many scholars point to philosopher David Hume as the origin of this definition,[14] and versions of it dominate academic discussions of miracles today.[15] Defining miracles as violations of natural laws, however, is problematic for various reasons. I list four.[16]

First, it is difficult if not impossible to identify what laws a purported miracle violates. A person must understand the laws of nature well (which no one seems to do) before knowing if an event violated these laws. Second, although nearly everyone affirms that nature exhibits regularities, many scholars question on scientific grounds the notion of "laws of nature."[17] Because of this and other reasons, I have been using the phrase "lawlike regularities" to describe consistent occurrences in creation. Third, those who embrace this definition of miracles typically think either that the laws of nature transcend God or that God voluntarily inserted laws that can be violated at any time. Describing the regularities of existence in these ways presents insurmountable obstacles to the problem of evil. Saying as I have that God's incessant love generates the regularities of existence avoids these problems. Fourth, defining miracles as violations of the laws of nature does not fit the vast majority of claims about miracles in Scripture, in history or today. Upon witnessing a miracle, few if any observers say, "Amazing! The laws of nature have just been violated!"

Rather than defining miracles as violations of the laws of nature, some theologians offer a related definition. They say miracles are God's intervention in the natural processes of life. This way of defining miracles shifts the focus from laws of nature to supernatural causation in relation to the causal workings of a particular situation

---

[14]David Hume, "An Enquiry Concerning Human Understanding," in *On Human Nature and the Understanding*, ed. Antony Flew (1748; repr., New York: Collier, 1962), p. 119.

[15]Robert A. Larmer offers one of the stronger criticisms of David Hume's understanding of miracles in *The Legitimacy of Miracle* (Plymouth, UK: Lexington, 2014).

[16]Amos Yong, in *The Spirit of Creation: Modern Science and Divine Action in the Pentecostal-Charismatic Imagination* (Grand Rapids: Eerdmans, 2011), chap. 4, also identifies problems that come from thinking that miracles amount to violations of the laws of nature.

[17]See, for instance, Rom Harré, *Laws of Nature* (London: Duckworth, 1993).

or person. Associated with this way of thinking is the idea that God intervenes among natural causes or processes to enact a miracle.

The problem with this definition of miracles is the central assumption built into it. The word *intervene* unfortunately implies that God resides outside nature and its causality. God must enter into a closed system of natural causes. Interventionist language undermines central Christian convictions about God's continual and necessary causation in creation. It implicitly denies divine omnipresence.

The God always present to and active in creation never needs to intervene.

If God is a necessary cause in every entity or occurrence, no entity or event—whether spectacular or mundane—is fully explicable by natural causes or processes alone. Believers should affirm God's omnipresence with its continual causal activity in the universe. Theologians should say that no event—whether that event is miraculous or mundane—is fully explainable by natural causes or processes. For believers, full explanations require metaphysical claims. Creaturely causes alone never sufficiently explain an occurrence.

Sometimes theologians talk about divine intervention for miracle as "supernatural action." The word *supernatural* can have various meanings. It can simply mean that God acts, or it can refer to action by spiritual beings of various kinds. Some simply use the word to admit not having an explanation for an occurrence. It is a substitute for *mystery*.

Saying a miracle occurs through God's supernatural action, however, may tempt us to think God completely controlled a thing or outcome, setting aside, working around or overpowering all natural causes. In other words, believers might easily interpret *super* and *natural* to mean that God overrides entirely—coerces—the natural course of events or creation causes. *Intervene* is also sometimes used to claim God controlled persons or situations entirely to enact a miracle. Miracles, in these senses, involve God's unilateral determination. This seems to be what Phillip Johnson has in mind, for instance, when he defines miracles as "arbitrary breaks in the chain of material causes and effects."[18] In this sense, miracles require divine control.[19]

I have often mentioned the problem with thinking God can completely control others or situations. A God who supernaturally intervenes to coerce entities or interrupts natural processes when enacting miracles would be culpable for failing to use coercion or interruption to prevent genuine evil in other circumstances. The problem of selective miracles becomes acute. The God who could control in this way, for instance, should have miraculously prevented all the genuine evils we encountered in chapter one.

DEFINING MIRACLES

For various reasons, none of the definitions of miracles I have mentioned thus far is satisfying. Instead of thinking miracles are entirely in the mind of the observer, I think they are objective events in the world. Instead of defining miracles as violations of natural laws or divine interventions, I think God is already present to and active in all creation. Instead of believing miracles require supernatural control, I believe miracles occur by means of God's uncontrolling love in relation to the universe and its creatures.

In contrast to the definitions we have addressed, I offer this definition of a miracle: a miracle is an unusual and good event that occurs through God's special action in relation to creation. This definition has three essential elements. Miracles

1. are unusual events;

2. are good events; and

3. involve God's special action in relation to creation.

To provide clarity, I explore the first two elements in this section and special divine action in the next.

---

[18]Phillip E. Johnson, *Reason in the Balance: The Case Against Naturalism in Science, Law & Education* (Downers Grove, IL: InterVarsity Press, 1998), p. 46.

[19]One of the better arguments against the notion that miracles require divine coercion is found in David Ray Griffin, *Religion and Scientific Naturalism: Overcoming the Conflicts* (Albany: State University of New York Press, 2000).

Some people consider all life and every occurrence to be miraculous. For various reasons, however, this is not the way believers typically refer to miracles. It is not how biblical writers and most Christians throughout history have described miracles, signs and wonders. While Christians typically believe God is lovingly present throughout all creation and is the source of its existence, they reserve *miracles* for particular events instead of them all.

The signs and wonders we read about in the Bible or in history or those we encounter today are noteworthy, in part, because they are surprising.[20] They are uncommon or extraordinary. As Augustine put it, a miracle is an "unusual" event "beyond the expectation or ability of the one who marvels at it."[21] While all life is a sacred gift, believers reserve *miracle* for events that exceed usual expectations.

Beyond-the-ordinary events capture our attention in ways the usual and mundane do not. Miracles may fill us with awe or astonishment. We may tremble in worship or shout ecstatically with joy. We may bow in silent reverence. Whatever our response, miracles indicate that something unusual occurred.

Of course, some believers identify God's work in an event but do not think it unusual. They expected this wonderful occurrence. Because they are not surprised, these believers typically do not claim to have witnessed a miracle. Others will encounter the same event but *not* expect it. Believers who do not expect the occurrence are more likely to call it miraculous.

For instance, I often thank God for helping physicians administer medicines or perform medical procedures that bring healing. "Thanks be to God!" I say. But I rarely call these healings miracles because I've come to expect God to work through trained physicians and tested medicines. These healings are not unusual in my part of the world. As I see it, healthcare workers often cooperate with God's love in the world.

---

[20]One of the better sources documenting contemporary miracles is Keener, *Miracles*.

[21]Augustine, "The Advantage of Believing," in *The Fathers of the Church*, vol. 4, trans. Ludwig Schopp (Washington, DC: The Catholic University of America Press, 2002), p. 437.

A person not familiar with the benefits of modern medicine, however, may call these same events miraculous. They are unusual. An Amazon jungle native, for instance, may not expect a speedy recovery when first encountering modern medicine and trained physicians. Her surprise over the healing fills her with wonder, and she may claim to have witnessed a miracle. The difference between the Amazon believer and me on this is primarily what we think is unusual.

Miracles are unusual events.

Some unusual events leave us awestruck and impressed by the power they display, but they are not positive, loving or good. These occurrences cause harm, destruction or evil. Plagues and holocausts come to mind. The shock and awe of military firepower can be breathtaking and unusual but nasty and brutal. Powerful is not the same as miraculous. In fact, biblical writers say that not all powerful signs and wonders derive from a loving God (see Mt 24:24; 2 Thess 2:9).

Unless we are among those who claim God is the sole cause of all events, we are not likely to call every awesome, powerful or surprising event a miracle. Sheer power is not miraculous, and some awe-filled events are awful. Goodness and not sheer power, says Jesus, the greatest of miracle workers, should be prized above all (see Lk 10:20). Consequently, we should reserve *miracle* to describe unusual events, whether powerful or not, that we believe promote well-being in some way. Miracles are beneficial.[22]

We sometimes disagree, of course, about whether an unusual or unexpected event is truly good. The surprising summer rain may help a wilting crop, and the farmer may call it a miracle. Those swimming at the nearby pool may regard the unexpected rain a nuisance and *miracle* never crosses their minds. The difference pertains to their value judgments of this surprising event. These scenarios emphasize

---

[22]Scholarly research exploring the link between love, prayer and miracles, especially in the pentecostal and charismatic traditions, is particularly fascinating. See results of the Flame of Love project, including Matthew T. Lee, Margaret M. Poloma and Stephen G. Post, *The Heart of Religion* (New York: Oxford University Press, 2013); and essays in Matthew T. Lee and Amos Yong, eds., *The Science and Theology of Godly Love* (DeKalb: Northern Illinois University Press, 2012). See also Brown, *Testing Prayer*.

that value claims partially determine what we consider miraculous. We need not all agree on the value of an event, however, to believe that some events in life promote well-being and others do not.[23]

Miracles are events we deem good.

DIVINE ACTION IN RELATION TO CREATION

In addition to being unusual and good, miracles involve special divine action. Essential kenosis claims, however, that special action never involves total divine control. It does not require God withdrawing, overriding or failing to provide freedom, agency or self-organization to creation. Special divine action does not entail interrupting the lawlike regularities of existence or interfering with processes that arise from God's consistent, existence-giving love for all creation. As I use the phrase "special divine action," it does not mean supernatural intervention in the sense of God superseding nature.

The special divine action that makes miracles possible occurs when God provides new possibilities, forms, structures or ways of being to creatures.[24] These gifts for the miraculous may reflect dramatic or remarkable ways of existing should they be embodied or incorporated. The possible ways that creatures act and possible situations that might emerge are prospects God gives for new and sometimes awe-inspiring ways of being in the world. Special divine action involves God giving new forms of existence to which creatures or creation might conform.

Miracles are possible when God provides good and unusual forms of existence.

---

[23]Unbelievers rarely if ever identify unusual and good events as miraculous. Atheists' denials of miracles come from their prior commitment to atheism. Occasionally, however, self-proclaimed atheists affirm miracles in the way believers affirm them. When atheists do so, they unconsciously or intuitively affirm God's existence despite their verbal claims otherwise. I suspect stories describing how a miracle prompted an atheist to become a theist are accounts in which self-identified unbelievers were already unconsciously inclined toward belief.

[24]This can be argued philosophically in many ways, from appealing to Aristotelian formal causation to Whiteheadian notions of eternal objects. But in my view such causation coincides with God's efficient causation upon the creatures or context in question. Formal causation relies upon efficient causation, although the two differ.

The novel opportunities and new ways of existing that God provides are context and creature appropriate. God takes into account the relevant ways creatures have acted in the past and might act in the future. God takes into account the past actions of other creatures and entities pertinent to the person or place. In light of the past and present, God lovingly invites creatures and creation to cooperate to enact a future in which well-being is established in surprising and positive ways. When creatures respond well to this special divine activity, miracles occur.

God's self-giving love takes a variety of forms. These forms make available redemption, release from oppression, fresh beginnings, healings, transformation, resurrections, exorcisms, rescues and more. Because the context warrants them, new forms of existing, new possibilities for acting or new avenues for transformation become the basis for a new event in relation to creation. God sometimes desires well-being through diverse forms and multifarious dimensions.

Because God steadfastly loves all creation, God is not able to present forms of existence that would be unloving. God's steadfast love cannot coerce some elements of creation when offering ways of existing or dramatic changes to others. Despite this limitation, the possibilities God can present to creation may surprise us and inspire joy. They may be unusual and good in ways that exceed our expectations.

Because miracles occur through God's special but uncontrolling love, creation plays a necessary part in miraculous events. This is an essential element of the third phrase in my definition of a miracle: miracles always occur in relation to creation. God's self-giving love invites creaturely cooperation for radically surprising actions that promote overall well-being. For this reason, miracles are neither coercive interventions nor the result of natural causes alone. Miracles occur when creatures, organisms or entities of various size and complexity cooperate with God's initiating and empowering love.

When creatures cooperate with their Creator, shālôm may unfurl in extraordinary ways.

With this view of special divine action and the necessary role of creaturely cooperation in mind, we turn to examine the miracles reported in the Bible and history more generally. Unfortunately, many believers try to account for miracles by assuming God acts in controlling ways.[25] Instead of regarding uncontrolling love as the preeminent divine attribute, many think God completely controls others or violates the laws of nature to enact miracles.

Given the prominence believers typically give controlling power, many may be surprised at how biblical writers actually describe divine action when reporting miracles. Unfortunately, interpretive assumptions often override scriptural evidence. In fact, many believers will find the following statement shocking, although I think it is true: the Bible gives no explicit support to the view that miracles require divine control.

I know of no miracles described in the Bible or that believers have witnessed in history that require God to coerce. As I have argued elsewhere, no biblical text explicitly supports divine coercion, including those texts addressing the initial creation of the world,[26] the incarnation of Jesus,[27] God's resurrecting Jesus from the dead,[28] the ultimate destiny of creation (eschaton)[29] and all events in between.[30]

---

[25]For a general discussion of biblical reasons for denying that God controls, see Terence E. Fretheim, *About the Bible: Short Answers to Big Questions*, rev. ed. (Minneapolis: Augsburg, 2009), pp. 93-98.

[26]A large number of biblical scholars argue that Genesis 1 and other biblical creation narratives always describe God's creating in relation to something (chaos, water, deep, etc.). No biblical passage says God creates from literally nothing. Those who do affirm *creatio ex nihilo*, however, should acknowledge that God would not have coerced when creating from nothing. If *creatio ex nihilo* is true, nothing would have initially existed for God to coerce when first creating the universe. I explore these issues in my essay "God Always Creates out of Creation in Love: *Creatio ex Creatione a Natura Amoris*," in *Theologies of Creation: Creatio ex Nihilo and Its New Rivals*, ed. Thomas Jay Oord (New York: Routledge, 2014), pp. 109-22.

[27]The Holy Spirit conception of Jesus was done in relation to Mary. And Scripture says that Mary cooperated with God's incarnation plans ("be it unto me," Lk 1:38 KJV).

[28]I argue for a noncoercive resurrection, as Jesus' body and spirit cooperate with God's raising activity. Find my arguments in *The Nature of Love: A Theology* (St. Louis: Chalice, 2010), pp. 147-52.

[29]Although some biblical depictions of the eschaton are dramatic, violent and spectacular, none involve divine coercion in the sense of God totally controlling creatures or creation. And if God's action in the eschaton is also loving, there are good reasons to believe the redemption of all things will not involve divine coercion. See ibid., pp. 152-57.

[30]The closest thing to divine coercion we find in the Bible is a reference to God hardening Pharaoh's heart. Not only do other verses in the story say Pharaoh hardened his own heart, but the

The God of the Bible is active, influential and powerful. But there are robust biblical reasons to believe God always acts through self-giving, others-empowering, uncontrolling love.

Biblical writers describe God as the ultimate source of miracles, of course. The signs and wonders recorded in holy writ describe unusual and good events, and Scripture's authors often explicitly identify God as the origin of these events. Miracles are thought to be special against the backdrop of God's faithful and ordinary actions to create and sustain creatures. Unlike magic,[31] miracles typically confirm a message, validate a person's ministry or teach a lesson, all the while enhancing well-being in some surprising way.[32]

Biblical writers frequently say in an explicit way that creatures or creation plays a role in the occurrence (or not) of miracles. These accounts strongly support the essential kenosis view that miracles happen without divine coercion. In fact, most miracle stories in Scripture explicitly say that creatures played an essential role. Miracles involve creaturely cooperation as God acts in special but uncontrolling ways when relating to creation.

Healings are the most obvious examples of miracles involving creaturely contribution, and healings are the most common miracles mentioned in the Bible.[33] Biblical authors frequently say creaturely

---

more important point is that most translators have simply assumed divine coercion when choosing words like *hardened* to describe God's activity in relation to Pharaoh. Biblical scholar Terence Fretheim affirms the hardening, but he says that "an act of hardening does not make one totally or permanently impervious to outside influence; it does not turn the heart off and on like a faucet" (*Exodus: Interpretation* [Philadelphia: Westminster John Knox, 2004], p. 97). And, says Fretheim, "divine hardening did not override Pharaoh's decision-making powers" (*Exodus*, p. 99). Additionally, we find both the J(Y)ahwist and Priestly strands in the text. Both strands portray the hardness of Pharaoh's heart as his own negative reaction to signs from God. Both emphasize God triumphing over Egyptian deities. Brevard Childs concludes that the hardness-of-heart motif in Exodus "has been consistently over-interpreted by supposing that it arose from a profoundly theological reflection and seeing it as a problem of free will and predestination" (*The Book of Exodus: A Critical, Theological Commentary* [Louisville, KY: Westminster John Knox, 2004], p. 174).

[31]Magic does not promote well-being and is not associated with special divine action. See Is 47:12-14; Acts 8:9-13; 19:19.

[32]See Graham H. Twelftree, *Jesus the Miracle Worker: A Historical and Theological Study* (Downers Grove, IL: InterVarsity Press, 1999).

[33]For instance, see Mt 8:1-13; 9:1-7; Mk 2:1-12; 5:30-36; 9:14-26; 10:46-52; Lk 5:17-25; 7:1-10; 8:26-39, 40-56; 17:11-19; 18:35-43; Jn 4:43-53; 11:32-44.

faith is necessary for miraculous healings. For instance, Jesus tells a hemorrhaging woman who reached out to touch him, "Daughter, your faith has made you well; go in peace, and be healed of your disease" (Mk 5:34). To the blind beggar who asks for healing, Jesus says, "Go; your faith has made you well" (Mk 10:52). Ten lepers cooperate with Jesus' instructions to show themselves to the priests. Jesus explains to the one who returns to express thanks that "faith has made you well" (Lk 17:19).

In these and many other examples, the one healed or helped contributes in some way to the miraculous event. In fact, many miracles seem to involve psychosomatic and even psychosocial elements, and this supports the claim that cooperative faith acts as a significant catalyst for healing. Emotions, expectations, meditation or general state of mind can affect bodily members. Mind influences matter; the mental and physical are mutually causal.

Sometimes miraculous healing occurs because of the faith of people other than the one healed. For instance, Jesus healed a paralyzed man because of his friends' faith. When Jesus saw the faith of the friends who lowered the paralytic through a roof, Jesus healed the man and credited the faith of his friends for the miracle (Mk 2:1-12). To the Roman centurion who asks Jesus to heal the centurion's servant, Jesus says, "Let it be done for you according to your faith" (Mt 8:5-13). Thanks in part to Ananias's cooperative faith, the apostle Paul miraculously regained sight (Acts 9:10-19).

These parables indicate that a variety of creaturely factors and actors play roles in miracles.

Strong evidence supporting the essential kenosis view of miracles comes from biblical stories in which healings do not occur because creatures did not cooperate. Some stories say that disbelief—an obvious form of noncooperation with God—prevents miraculous healings.[34] When Jesus returns to his hometown, for instance, the people do not respect and honor him. Mark reports that Jesus "could do no

---

[34]See, for instance, Mt 13:58; 17:20-21; Mk 6:5-6; 9:29; Lk 9:41.

deed of power there" because of "their unbelief." Notice that Mark says miracles *could not* be done; he does not say Jesus voluntarily decided not to perform miracles (Mk 6:5-6). This also seems to be the meaning of Jesus' warnings about a wicked generation and its desire for signs. Their uncooperative wickedness does not allow them to perceive God's miraculous work in the world (Mt 12:39; 16:4; Lk 11:29).

One of the more spectacular miracles of the New Testament involves both inanimate objects and the faith of individuals. Jesus miraculously walks on water when joining disciples in a boat. Peter asks to join Jesus on this walk. When Jesus invites him, Peter takes a step of faith. For a moment, he walks on water. But Peter's faith decreases, his fear increases and he sinks (Mt 14:22-33).

This story suggests that Jesus' activity did not cause the water molecules to amass to hold up Peter. If this miracle concerned Jesus' ability to solidify water molecules, the molecules should have kept Peter afloat despite his lack of faith. But Peter's initial faith and the subsequent lack of faith were the deciding factors in this miracle. This supports the essential kenosis argument that creaturely cooperation plays a necessary role in miraculous action although it does not explain entirely how such nature miracles occur. I will address nature miracles shortly.

I have been identifying Jesus' miracles recorded in the New Testament because he is the most prominent miracle worker mentioned in the Bible. But writers of Scripture report the occurrence of other miracles not done by Jesus. We find reports in Acts and occasionally in the New Testament letters. Peter and Paul perform miracles, for instance.

Surprising and unexpected events attributed to God's action are mentioned in the earliest biblical texts most Christians call the Old Testament. According to Scripture, Elijah, Elisha and Moses performed miracles. These special divinely initiated actions often play a part in authenticating the good news of message or messenger.

By far the most common miracles mentioned in the Bible involve transformed lives, healings and exorcisms of various types. These are also by far the most common miracles witnessed today and throughout history. Accounting for these miracles is of utmost importance in any explanation of how God acts miraculously but noncoercively. Essential kenosis accounts for them, in part, by pointing out the creaturely cooperation involved in each. And it says that God's special action always involves uncontrolling love.

The salvation God provides when delivering creatures from sin is the greatest miracle of all. God acts first when offering salvation, and creatures enjoy salvation when they respond appropriately to God's initiative. Given the ingrained habits of sin, such miraculous salvation is unusual and good; it also requires God's initiating special action. The essential kenosis model of providence strongly supports the causal activity in the miracle of salvation. The uncontrolling love of God provides the possibility of abundant life.

ACCOUNTING FOR NATURE MIRACLES

Person-oriented or organism-related miracles easily fit the essential kenosis claim that miracles do not require divine control. These miracles include both loving divine action and intentional creaturely cooperation. They can occur without violating the lawlike consistencies of creation because God has given creatures of various complexities free will, self-organization, the capacity to act or all of these.

Much less common but still important are miracles mentioned in the Bible involving inanimate objects and systems of nature. These less-common events are often called nature miracles.[35] They do not involve persons, spirits, bodily organs or less-complex organisms capable of response. Nature miracles involve unusual but good events that occur in relation to aggregates of entities and the lawlike regularities that characterize the systems and processes of creation.

Many biblical scholars do not think Jesus actually performed the

---

[35]The label "nature miracles" is problematic for several reasons, not least because it implicitly separates humans and other creatures from the processes, structures and inanimate objects of the world. But I employ the label in my discussion because of its widespread use in literature discussing miracles.

nature miracles mentioned in the Gospels.[36] They are skeptical because Jesus accompanies every nature miracle with a lesson, whereas person-oriented miracles, such as healings, are often portrayed as ends in themselves. Contemporary scholars of both the Old and New Testaments typically say nature-miracle stories have an educational function not dependent upon their objective verifiability. Nature miracles have a pedagogical purpose.

For instance, one well-known miracle in the New Testament is Jesus feeding the multitudes with a few fish and a little bread. In the various versions of this story, Jesus "breaks" fish and bread. His disciples then distribute fish and bread to thousands of people. According to different versions of the story, Jesus uses this miracle to teach lessons to the disciples. Most lessons say God is a generous provider (see Mt 14:13-21; 15:29-39; Mk 6:30-44; 8:1-21; Lk 9:10-17; Jn 6:1-15).

If this nature miracle actually occurred, it is important to note that it occurred in relation to creation: bread, fish and people. The agency of the disciples played a part in the miracle as they distributed the food. The receptivity of the crowds played a role too. Scripture does not reveal how the fish, bread or other creaturely forces may have participated in enacting the miracle. We are left to speculate about the various causes involved in the feeding of multitudes with few initial resources.

In another New Testament story, Jesus performs a nature miracle despite a lack of faith in the disciples. In this miracle, Jesus calms wind and waves while chiding the disciples for having "little faith" (Mt 8:26; Mk 4:40; Lk 8:25). This miracle involved aggregations of entities without the capacity for faith—amassed water molecules—not personal agents with free will. More importantly, the point Jesus makes about having little faith is not primarily about Jesus' capacity to calm storms. The point of the miracle is that the disciples should not worry.

---

[36]Barry L. Blackburn, "The Miracles of Jesus," in *The Cambridge Companion to Miracles*, ed. Graham H. Twelftree (Cambridge: Cambridge University Press, 2011), p. 119.

If nature miracles do occur, it is safe to assume that creaturely forces and factors played some role in them. After all, nature miracles, like all miracles, involve God's special action in relation to creation. We have no evidence on which to argue that God ever acts miraculously in a vacuum. Essential kenosis presumes that creaturely causation of some kind is present in all miracles, even when biblical narratives do not identify the creaturely causes.

Essential kenosis can make sense of genuine nature miracles. When doing so, this model of divine providence does not appeal to intentional creaturely cooperation. After all, it makes little sense to say that the inanimate objects involved in natural miracles respond to God, at least in the way persons, agents or organisms can respond. Even though biblical writers sometimes personify inanimate objects or systems of nature (e.g., "the stone would shout out" [Lk 19:40]; "the heavens declare" [Ps 50:6]), most people will find it odd to say inanimate objects and systems intentionally cooperate with God. An essential kenosis explanation of nature miracles requires speculating about how God acts noncoercively without relying entirely upon intentional creaturely cooperation.

For instance, it seems odd to say that the Red Sea intentionally cooperated with God when the Israelites walked through it fleeing Pharaoh's armies. Because aggregates such as water likely have no intentions or free will, many think they must choose between either an entirely naturalistic explanation of the Red Sea crossing or an explanation that relies upon supernatural coercion.

The naturalistic explanation typically given says violent winds dried sections of the Red Sea temporarily, allowing the Israelites to pass unscathed. The winds then diminished to drown Pharaoh's army. These winds have dried sections of the Red Sea at other times in history so this explanation is plausible and should be taken seriously.[37]

---

[37]"In flat marshy districts large areas are often intermittently covered by shallow water or laid dry by the action of the wind; e.g., almost annually in the spring high winds off the Persian Gulf blow in waters at high tide to cover all the area lying south of Zobeir in Iraq, a distance of about twenty-five miles." *The New Interpreter's Bible* (Nashville: Abingdon, 1994), 1:938.

The supernatural explanation of the Red Sea crossing says God must have overridden the laws of nature or totally controlled the waters to make a way for the escaping Israelites and then drown the Egyptians. Those who think divine sovereignty includes coercion typically give this explanation. For them, supernatural intervention to control creation is required to explain the parting of the waters and their subsequent return to normalcy.

The problem with a naturalistic explanation is not the claim that nature plays a causal role in the miracle. The problem is the assumption that God is not always already active, exerting causal influence in all aspects and levels of nature. So-called naturalistic explanations presuppose that nature is a closed system consisting entirely of natural causes. These explanations fail to begin with the view that a loving and omnipresent God continually creates and sustains all creation as a necessary cause.

Explanations of the Red Sea miracle relying upon divine control arise from the implicit view that God's power logically precedes divine love. This view raises the problem of selective miracles. For instance, if God used supernatural control at the Red Sea, why didn't God use supernatural control to stop the rock from killing the Canadian woman whose story we encountered in chapter one? Why didn't the God capable of the supernatural control of inanimate objects prevent the detonation of the bombs at the Boston Marathon? Why didn't God enact a nature miracle through supernatural control to prevent Zamuda's brutal rape and the death of her family? Why doesn't God use supernatural control to prevent a host of genuine evils that occur when inanimate objects and regularities in nature are the primary causes of genuine evil or could be used to prevent evil?

Because essential kenosis claims that God cannot override the lawlike regularities we see in the world, it employs various strategies to account for nature miracles. It explains nature miracles without appealing to intentional cooperation from creation's aggregates and systems. And it does so without claiming that God temporarily interrupts nature's lawlike regularities or completely controls aggregates.

One strategy available to the essential kenosis model of providence says God uses spontaneous or random events at various levels of existence, from the quantum level to those much more complex, when acting miraculously. When doing this, God responds to spontaneity and randomness at various levels of creaturely complexity by calling upon creatures to respond in good and surprising ways. God uses creaturely randomness and spontaneity when acting specially to provide novel forms and ways of existing.

In this miraculous activity, God's steadfast love does not supersede the lawlike regularities of nature, and God does not control. But God coordinates creaturely elements in ways that bring about unexpected and good results. This coordination is possible because of God's omnipresence and complete knowledge of what has occurred and is occurring.

This strategy does not afford God the capacity to do just anything, of course. There are limits to what a necessarily loving God can do even when offering forms of being and possibilities for action and when coordinating spontaneous events. These limits derive from God's self-giving, others-empowering love for all creation. Divine love necessarily grants being to other entities, and God cannot usurp the gift necessarily given. But when random or spontaneous events occur and the conditions provide for it, God can act in special ways to offer forms and possibilities in relation to creation that result in miracles.

Another strategy available to essential kenosis says that God offers novel possibilities to intentional agents and calls them to respond in ways that subsequently affect inanimate objects and natural systems. We encountered the framework for this strategy in chapter two when we explored chaos theory and the butterfly effect. Action by one creature in one location can be the first domino in a chain of cause-and-effect sequences that influence much larger systems, aggregates or creation elsewhere.

The actions by Moses, the wandering children of Israel, Pharaoh's army or others may have triggered a chain of sequences that affected inanimate objects, entities and systems of nature. Just as intentional human actions affect weather patterns today (e.g., climate change research, consequences of creaturely migration, the effects farming can have on ecosystems), actions by agents long ago could also be catalysts of nature miracles through chain reactions. Discovering the specifics of how such miracles occur may be possible as the intelligibility of chaos theory improves.

A third strategy for accounting for natural miracles while denying divine coercion focuses on God's calling upon free agents to act in ways that fit well with what God foreknows with high probability will occur among systems of nature or inanimate objects. In the case of Moses and the Red Sea, for instance, God may foreknow with high probability that winds would push back the water leaving ground dry enough for passage. We can predict weather patterns with some success; God's predictions are better. Moses may intuit God's "still small voice" that calls him to lead the Israelites to the water at the opportune time. In this strategy, the miracle that occurs involves God's call for special creaturely cooperation and God being aware of the developing conditions and processes of the natural world. Both divine and creaturely causes are at play.

God loves all creation. Because lawlike regularities arise from this relentless love, however, God must offer forms of existence and opportunities for action consistent with steadfast love for all creatures in a given context. Creatures that do not cooperate with God's intentions to enact good and surprising events can sometimes thwart divine attempts to enact miracles. And God's steadfast love for entities embedded in natural processes and subject to the regularities of existence at the aggregate level means God cannot control them entirely.

There are likely other ways God enacts nature miracles despite not being capable of complete control.[38] The advocate of essential kenosis

---

[38]I have not mentioned the possibility that the smallest entities of existence may have a very small measure of free will that God might influence in nature miracles. While I am not, in principle, opposed to this idea, I have a difficult time imagining it making a difference in miraculous events. Either the freedom is so limited in aggregates as to make it inconsequential, or the law of large numbers averages out the freedom of entities in aggregates such as to make this freedom ineffectual at the higher level. So while I'm open to freedom occurring at the micro level, I can-

has numerous reasons for affirming that God's self-giving love acts powerfully but in uncontrolling ways. Biblical passages with no mention of intentional creaturely causes should prompt us to speculate about the causal activities involved.

This speculation, which I have been doing in previous paragraphs, should be based on our view of God's power. While some may interpret miracles as involving divine coercion, this interpretation comes from their prior belief that God has the power to control and uses coercion when enacting miracles. Those who believe that the self-giving, others-empowering and uncontrolling love revealed in Jesus Christ is the preeminent attribute of the divine nature will interpret the same passages in ways that say God never controls when acting miracles.

A hermeneutics of uncontrolling love matters.

In sum, essential kenosis offers a robust model for how the almighty and loving God does miracles without coercing agents, entities or situations. No miracle story in the Bible explicitly mentions total divine control, and most specifically mention creaturely cooperation. All miracles involve special divine action that offers unusual and beneficial ways of existing, and miracles occur as creation cooperates. In agent- or organism-related miracles, creatures respond well to God's loving activity. In miracles among simple entities, aggregates of entities and systems of nature, God sometimes enacts miracles without transgressing the lawlike regularities that derive from God's love for all creation.

ADVANTAGES OF AN ESSENTIAL KENOSIS UNDERSTANDING OF MIRACLES

To conclude, I want briefly to identify advantages an essential kenosis understanding of miracles provides. Concluding in this way seems appropriate given my overall intent to make sense of a world that includes goodness and evil, randomness and regularities,

---

not at present fathom how it could be a resource in nature miracles.

freedom and agency, God, and even miracles.

The essential kenosis model of providence explains legitimate miracles in a way that accepts them as objective events that are good, are unusual and involve special divine action in relation to creation. This explanation denies that God controls others or situations when enacting miracles. God can act specially without entirely controlling creatures or creation more generally.

One advantage of this model comes from the definition of miracle that I offer. This definition overcomes obstacles that rightly keep some from believing that miracles occur at all. My definition supposes that miracles are objective events in the world. It denies that miracles violate the laws of nature. It rejects the problematic category of divine intervention because it does not identify miracles with the notion that God enters a closed system of natural causes from the outside. My definition presupposes that God is always already present to and active in the world.

This definition of miracles evades legitimate criticisms of other definitions.

Another advantage of the essential kenosis account of miracles is that it fits well with the biblical reports of miracles, which almost always mention a role for creaturely causation. Because none of the biblical miracles explicitly supports the idea that God uses coercion, essential kenosis is consonant with the biblical witness. In addition, I know of no extrabiblical miracle reports in human history that require affirming divine control to explain them. If, as I have argued, Scripture as a whole supports the view that God always expresses self-giving love, an essential kenosis account of miracles enjoys broad biblical support.

The biblical witness supports an essential kenosis understanding of miracles.

This understanding of miracles solves what I have argued is the most important reason some people deny miracles altogether: the problem of selective miracles. In typical understandings of miracles, it is proper to ask why God enacts miracles in some cases but not others. The God capable of coercion should control people or situations to enact miracles far more often to do good and prevent evil. The God who can violate the lawlike regularities of the universe ought to violate those regularities more often to make our lives better.

Essential kenosis removes the "selective miracles" reason for rejecting special divine action. God never has and never can control others entirely when acting miraculously. God does not selectively coerce to enact miracles for some people but not for others because control-based selectivity is not possible for the God whose nature is kenotic love. The essential kenosis notion of miracles overcomes the problem of evil in general and the problem of selective miracles in particular.

The God who cannot control others is not culpable for failing to coerce to enact miracles.

Another advantage of the essential kenosis understanding of miracles is that it explains why some people do not receive miracles when they ask in faith. For instance, many pray in faith asking for healing for themselves or others, but the ailments continue. Some die because their infirmity prevails. In light of the usual view of miracles, it is natural for victims of suffering to question God's love for them, become guilt ridden or believe their faith must be too small.

The creaturely cooperation aspect of miracles explains why many miracles do not occur despite the adequate faith of the petitioner. The organisms, body parts, organs and cells of our bodies can resist God's offer of new forms of life that involve healing. These creaturely elements and organisms have agency too, and this agency can sometimes thwart miracles. Even when we consciously say yes in faith to the divine desire for our well-being, our bodies may not cooperate with God's healing plans.

This means, in part, most people not healed should not feel guilty, believing they lack faith. After all, even the most faith-filled people in history, such as the apostle Paul, did not always experience miraculous healings when they wanted them (see Gal 4:13-14; Phil 2:27; 1 Tim 5:23; 2 Tim 4:20). Instead, we can believe that the God who gifts all entities with existence cannot entirely control elements or organs of our bodies that, contrary to our conscious wishes, may malfunction, deteriorate or become diseased.

This advantage is so important that I want to emphasize it. Essential kenosis says we should rarely if ever blame victims for their suffering and disease. We need not assume that the lack of healing is the fault of the unhealthy, nor should the faithful feel guilty for allegedly not having enough faith. Instead, we can blame those aspects of their bodies that cause misery. Rarely are cancerous cells and genetic malfunctions not healed because victims did not believe strongly enough. The God who loves all creation also loves those who pray for healing, even when their bodies do not or cannot cooperate with God's healing gifts.

Essential kenosis shifts blame from the faith-filled victim to bodily agents, organisms, organs or entities that do not or cannot cooperate with God.

The essential kenosis model of miracles also overcomes the either/or choice many presuppose when they fail to acknowledge God's healing derived from health-care procedures. Because God works through mental and physical health-care providers, we need not choose between saying that God heals through miracles and crediting natural means for healing. Whether the healing comes as a miracle or through the typical procedures of health-care providers, we can thank God for initiating restored health and also thank physicians, nurses, counselors and others who cooperate with God. God initiates all healing, but all healing also involves creaturely cooperation of some sort.

Essential kenosis affirms that God's activity makes possible the healing that comes through health-care providers.

This brings me to the advantage essential kenosis provides to ongoing theoretical discussions about the relation between science and theology. Some scholars in these discussions have thought we can entirely explain events in the world—even purported miracles—by referring to natural causes alone. This approach obviously presents problems to those who believe God is a necessary cause in miracles and all other events. But it also has not proven a successful explanation of reality overall.[39]

Others scholars in the science-and-theology discussion assume we can only explain some events—especially miracles—by referring to supernatural causes. By using the phrase "supernatural causes," they seem to claim that divine action alone explains some events. This approach obviously presents problems to scientists who believe they have good grounds to think natural causation contributes to the events in question. It is difficult to believe science offers any significant explanations of reality if we only consider accurate those explanations that appeal to supernatural causes.

Because essential kenosis says all events—even miracles—involve both creaturely and divine causation, neither scientific nor theological accounts of existence should be dismissed. But neither in itself is satisfying. In fact, a full explanation of an event, including a purported miracle, will include reference to both divine and creaturely causes.[40]

This means believers should welcome scientific explanations of what they consider miraculous events, so long as those scientific explanations do not pretend to give a full and sufficient explanation of what occurred. And scientists, especially scientists who believe in God, should allow for theological explanations of events in the world, so long as those explanations do not pretend to give a full and sufficient explanation of the event in question. A theocosmocentric approach to reality overcomes the temptation to ignore either the world or God when trying to make sense of things.

An essential kenosis view of miracles powerfully illustrates why we need both theology and science when trying to understand reality.

---

[39]A large number of scholars in the contemporary science-and-theology dialogue argue that we cannot make sense of reality by looking only at science or only at religion. One of the most eloquent voices for the argument is John Polkinghorne, whose many books on the topic include *Science and Theology* (Philadelphia: Fortress, 1998) and *The Polkinghorne Reader: Science, Faith, and the Search for Meaning*, ed. Thomas Jay Oord (West Conshohocken, PA: Templeton Press, 2010).

[40]Amos Yong comes to a similar conclusion in *Spirit of Creation*, chap. 3.

All these advantages to an essential kenosis view of miracles cumulatively present a final advantage: this way of understanding miracles may incline some to be more open to acknowledging miracles when they encounter them.[41] Some who believe in God—whether consciously or unconsciously—claim to witness miracles. But other believers are reticent to accept even the possibility of the miraculous, and, as I have noted, they often have legitimate reasons for their reticence.

Perhaps the definition of a miracle I have offered, which denies coercion and acknowledges creaturely cooperation, can give believers more confidence to claim that an unusual and good event involved special divine action. While realizing that some claims for miracles are hoaxes, misunderstandings, theological confusion or false in some other way, more believers may nonetheless become confident enough to acknowledge that some events in our world represent genuine miracles.

Essential kenosis may help us recognize objective miracles in the world.

I conclude this chapter's discussion by returning to what sparked my exploration of miracles in the first place. I argued that God's self-giving love never entirely controls others or situations in the world. The evidence of miracles does not require us to believe God coerces. Although God is almighty, uncontrolling love logically precedes sovereign choice in God's nature. God does not coerce when enacting miracles. Essential kenosis explains how God can act miraculously without controlling others.

---

[41]I am grateful to Bryan Overbaugh for sparking this general insight.

Postscript

We all want to make sense of life. But tragedies and evils—whether caused by free will, agency or random events—make it difficult to do so. The Boston Marathon bombing, a rock that accidentally killed a woman, a baby's acute debilitations, Zamuda's rape and her family's murder all need satisfying explanations. The answers most people give to God's role in these evils are unsatisfying. Believers in God want helpful answers to the biggest questions of life. In this book, I have offered answers that I find helpful.

In my work to provide satisfying answers, I have affirmed the reality of randomness and chance at various levels of existence. Scientists and philosophers rightly describe at least some events in the universe as random, in the sense of their not being entirely determined by anyone or anything. These events are not done on purpose, and no one intends them. No creaturely agent, factor or law controls these events, and neither does God. Randomness is real.

Lawlike regularities are also present in the cosmos. These lawlike regularities are the natural expressions or entailments of the all-embracing, all-sustaining and uncontrolling love of God. In fact, God's self-giving, others-empowering activity makes possible both regularity and randomness. God provides free will, agency, self-organization and spontaneity because God's love makes life possible. God's gifts and the ongoing flow of time mean that neither the creatures nor the Creator can foreknow with absolute certainty which possible events will someday become actual.

Most attempts to describe God's providence in the universe are not compelling. Some models present God as controlling; they at least say God could or occasionally does control. Some models deny genuine randomness. Some offer little explanatory consistency, which does not help us make sense of life. Some models of providence portray God as unaffected, impersonal and uninvolved, making it difficult to imagine how God lovingly relates to creatures. Some models deny that we can comprehend God in any way, which results in absolute mystery.

Open and relational theology is well suited to account for the randomness and regularities of our world. This approach to reality helps us make sense of our intuitions about free will, agency, self-organization, spontaneity and other causation. Open and relational theology supports the view that both genuinely good and genuinely evil events occur. And it argues that love resides at the center of the most satisfying answers to life's vexing questions.

Although many people intuitively believe love is uncontrolling, most theologians—even some open and relational theologians—have not considered kenotic love the logically preeminent attribute of God's nature. Instead, some think divine power precedes divine love. But placing sovereign choice before self-giving, others-empowering love prompts us to wonder why God doesn't occasionally control creatures to prevent genuine evils. When power logically precedes love, God could control others or situations if God wanted. We rightly wonder why the God capable of control does not, in the name of love, do so more often to prevent genuine evil.

I propose a model of providence I call essential kenosis. When describing this model, I draw from the broad themes of Christian Scripture, especially those pertaining to divine love, creaturely agency and the God-creation relationship. God's almighty love graces all creation all the time. Uncontrolling love is the mode by which divine providence operates because love logically comes first in God.

The distinguishing feature of essential kenosis is its claim that God cannot deny God's own nature of self-giving love. God necessarily gives freedom, agency, self-organization or spontaneity to creatures. Because the divine nature is self-giving, others-empowering love and God "cannot deny himself" (2 Tim 2:13), God cannot withhold, override or fail to provide these gifts to creation. The Creator necessarily gives, and these gifts are irrevocable.

Essential kenosis solves both questions raised at the outset of this book. To the question of why a loving and almighty God does not prevent genuine evil, essential kenosis says God necessarily loves and consequently cannot prevent such evil. For God to prevent such evils unilaterally, God would have to deny himself, which cannot be done.

To the question of how God can be providential despite randomness, chance and luck in the world—especially those events with negative consequences—essential kenosis says God gives existence, including spontaneity, to all things. Random events are possible because of God's existence-giving love. God cannot foreknow with certainty or prevent random events from generating negative consequences.

God's gifts provide being to creatures in each moment, and God is ever active in giving and receiving relationship with each creature. Kenotic love empowers creatures to be and to act, and this love enables complex creatures to act freely. When creatures and creation respond well to God's uncontrolling love, well-being is established. The kingdom of God is present. Love reigns in heaven and on earth. All that is good derives from God's essential kenosis, which comes before and makes possible creaturely response.

The God that essential kenosis describes has plans and purposes. God invites, commands and empowers creatures to respond well to them, but God never controls creatures or situations. God does not operate from a foreordained or foreknown blueprint. Instead, God enables others. Creatures who cooperate work toward God's good purposes.

The uncontrolling God of essential kenosis is faithful both to provide the regularities of existence and to enact miracles. Miracles are good and unusual events that involve God's special action to provide beneficial forms of existence to the world. God does not su-

pernaturally intervene in, control or violate creation. But through
God's persuasive love, both lawlike regularities and the special action
in miracles express divine providence.

Essential kenosis offers an adventure model of reality. This model
may strike some as a precarious paradigm of providence. Adventures
aren't safe, after all, because they have general goals, not predetermined designs. Adventures involve calculated risks, free decisions
and sometimes random occurrences. Love is an adventure without
guaranteed results.

The adventure model of providence that essential kenosis offers,
however, fits the world in which we live. Our world has genuine good
and evil, randomness and regularity, freedom, agency, disappoint-
ments, and even miracles. It also fits a vision of a God who does not
and cannot control others. If we read the Bible through the lens of
God's self-giving, others-empowering, kenotic love, we will find that
the essential kenosis model makes better sense of the broad biblical
witness than do other alternatives. Essential kenosis helps us make
sense of both the Bible and the world in which we live.

God's uncontrolling providence is an adventure of open and relational living. And in the logic of love, that makes sense.

Index

Finding the Textbook You Need

The IVP Academic Textbook Selector
is an online tool for instantly finding the IVP books
suitable for over 250 courses across 24 disciplines.

ivpacademic.com